THE FUNCTIONS OF THE EXECUTIVE

THE FUNCTIONS
OF THE EXECUTIVE

BY

CHESTER I. BARNARD

Formerly President of the New Jersey Bell Telephone Company

THIRTIETH ANNIVERSARY EDITION

with an Introduction by
KENNETH R. ANDREWS

*Donald K. David Professor of Business Administration
Harvard University*

CAMBRIDGE, MASSACHUSETTS
HARVARD UNIVERSITY PRESS

INTRODUCTION TO THE 30TH ANNIVERSARY EDITION

INTRODUCTION

NOW reprinted for the eighteenth time, *The Functions of the Executive* has steadily increased in influence and circulation since its first appearance. Almost four times as many copies were distributed by the publisher in 1967 as in 1939; each of the last five years and most of the others show an equally interesting increase over its predecessor. Barnard appears in virtually every bibliography on organization and is cited in such popular works as J. K. Galbraith's *The New Industrial State* (1967), which credits him with the "most famous definition of an organization." The respect won in all quarters by so austere and difficult a book is remarkable enough to deserve explanation. The intent of this introduction will be to relate this study of organization to the simple rationalistic theory that preceded it and to the baroque variety that came after. It may then be easier to understand why Barnard's voice remains audible and authoritative above the excitement generated by behavioral scientists, mathematical and statistical decision theorists, and other clinical and experimental students of organization behavior, to say nothing of the books of generals, prime ministers, presidents, and other practitioners.

Barnard's aim is ambitious. As he tells us in his own preface, his purpose is first to provide a comprehensive theory of cooperative behavior in formal organizations. Cooperation originates in the need of an individual to accomplish purposes to which he is by himself biologically unequal. With the enlistment of other individuals cooperation speedily becomes a constantly changing *system* made up of interrelated biological, psychological, and social elements. To survive, it must be "effective" in the sense of achieving organization purpose and "efficient" in the sense of satisfying individual motives. The executive must preside over and adapt to each other the processes which relate the cooperative system to its environment and which provide satisfaction to individuals.

The initial concept of cooperation leads to the definition of organization as a "system of consciously coordinated activities or forces of two or more persons." Essential to the *survival* of organization is the willingness to cooperate, the ability to communicate, the existence and acceptance of purpose. The executive functions are thus to provide a system of communication, to maintain the willingness to cooperate, and to ensure the continuing integrity of organization purpose. Barnard's elaboration of the executive functions ends in a consideration of leadership as the personal capacity for affirming decisions that lend quality and morality to the coordination of organized activity and to the formulation of purpose.

It would be gratuitous to recapitulate in his own book the whole of Barnard's theory. Its development in his hands, when considered against the background of his career, appears as a remarkable tour de force. Since *Organization and Management*, which came along ten years after *The Functions of the Executive*, is a set of papers either elaborating aspects of the original theory or marking miscellaneous occasions, the earlier book is the single major work of a man who was not really a writer. Most of Barnard's career was spent in executive practice. A Mount Hermon and Harvard education, cut off short of the bachelor's degree, was followed by nearly forty years in the American Telephone & Telegraph Company. His career began in the Statistical Department, took him to technical expertness in the economics of rates and administrative experience in the management of commercial operations, and culminated in the presidency of the New Jersey Bell Telephone

Company. He was not directly involved in the Western Electric experiments conducted chiefly at the Hawthorne plant in Cicero, but his association with Elton Mayo [1] and the latter's colleagues at the Harvard Business School had an important bearing on his most original ideas.

Barnard's executive experience at AT&T was paralleled and followed by a career in public service unusual in his own time and hardly routine today. He was at various times president of the United Services Organization (the USO of World War II), head of the General Education Board and later president of the Rockefeller Foundation (after Raymond Fosdick and before Dean Rusk), chairman of the National Science Foundation, an assistant to the Secretary of the Treasury, a consultant to the American representative in the United Nations Atomic Energy Committee, to name only some of his public interests. He was a director of a number of companies, a fellow of the American Association for the Advancement of Science and of the American Academy of Arts and Sciences. He was a lover of music and a founder of the Bach Society of New Jersey.

Barnard as a man, in the absence of gossip about him, stands somewhat apart, even from the organizations he headed — reserved, dignified, and somewhat awesome. He was not a teacher with disciples to cloak his memory with sentiment or to elaborate his ideas. His associates and successors in the Bell System have not made him a corporate or folk hero; those I have known do not find occasion to speak of him at all. No evidence is available to demonstrate or to call into question his personal ability to make organizations effective and efficient. His book has made its steady way on its own, in short, without benefit of publicly expressed affection by supporters.

If we look now at the strengths and the weaknesses of his

[1] A representative work is listed on pp. xxii–xxiii for each of the writers on organization mentioned in the course of this introduction.

work and its place in the literature of organization, we must note first that Barnard brought his ideas into form at the time when reports from the Western Electric experiments were coming into conflict with the theories of scientific management originating in the work of F. W. Taylor and in the rationalistic theory of organization formulated by Henri Fayol. *The Functions* is a direct outcome of Barnard's failure to find an adequate explanation of his own executive experience in classic organization or economic theory. His own extensive, unsystematic, and multi-disciplinary reading offered him few clues until his encounter with Pareto and with L. J. Henderson, a biochemist of interdisciplinary bent who studied and wrote about Pareto. Barnard was thus stimulated by what sociology could explain that classical economic and organization theory could not. His acquaintance with Henderson, Donham, Mayo and the other members of the coalition of social scientists and clinicians who were rediscovering human motivation in the Hawthorne Works was indispensable to the development of his central thesis. Barnard obtained access to the data and ideas which in effect made obsolete the concept of economic man and gave proof that the scientific and rationalist models of organization required revision.

The Mayo–Roethlisberger–Dickson–Whitehead reports on the Western Electric researches were clinically oriented to worker satisfactions and to the first level of supervision. Although they were animated by the excitement of discovery and illuminated by the usefulness of a new mode of interpreting social data, they did not offer a comprehensive model of organization. More like Fayol, Barnard was oriented by his experience to the executive levels and more interested in the firm in relation to its environment. The first great contribution of his book was therefore the construction of a total theory of organization which provided an alternative to the Fayol model and took into account the dramatic discoveries in the Bank Wiring observation and Relay Assembly Test rooms.

It is not easy to distinguish between concepts which Barnard invented and those which he reshaped, developed, and extended in his ambition to construct a complete theory. He seized upon the concept of an organization as a social system, elaborated it in original definitions of formal and informal organization, worked out the awkwardly designated but vital difference between *effectiveness* and *efficiency*, incorporated noneconomic motivation into a theory of incentives, and developed a controversial concept of authority. This last symbolizes neatly his revolt against the classical idea that command is the essential condition of obedience. "Authority is the character of a communication (order)," he wrote in a labored sentence, "in a formal organization by virtue of which it is accepted by a contributor to or 'member' of the organization as governing the action he contributes; that is, as governing or determining what he does or is not to do so far as the organization is concerned." It became necessary to invent the "zone of indifference" to support this definition. By postulating that there exists for each individual an area in which orders are acceptable without being questioned, he explains the everyday achievement of cooperation under the complication implicit in the idea that authority lies with the subordinate individual.

The strength of Barnard's concept of cooperative systems and of his explanation of the essential conditions for rarely attained effectiveness and efficiency seems to me to lie in the idea that purpose is central. He believes the definition of organization purpose to be peculiarly an executive function, made necessary to give meaning to the rest of the environment, to serve as unifying principle. Toward the end of the book, in passages where his personal convictions become visible, he couples purpose with responsibility — "the quality which gives dependability and determination to human conduct, and foresight and ideality to purpose." He was willing to rest his theory of cooperation upon an ethical ideal. I will try to establish later the enduring importance of this idea in the literature of organization.

In all this Barnard was importantly original. He summarized his own contributions after publication in terms of principal "structural" and "dynamic" concepts.[2] The important structural concepts he considered to be the *individual*, the *cooperative system*, the *formal organization*, the *complex formal organization*, and the *informal organization*. The dynamic concepts he identified as *free will, cooperation, communication, authority*, the *decisive process*, and *dynamic equilibrium*. The first two parts of his book he viewed as the anatomy or structure of cooperation; the last two parts were its physiology or economy.

The full originality of Barnard's work, sparsely and carefully recorded, can only be fully appreciated by reading and rereading his text. The most conspicuous weaknesses of the book, widely noted by critics and readers easily put off, are the abstractness of the presentation, the paucity and pedestrian quality of example, and the difficulty of style. He acknowledges this defect in the text itself and elsewhere. "The doctrine is difficult," he said in the *Harvard Business Review*, "labored, abstract, and abstruse." But he was little inclined to revise his approach, for he thought this level of discourse appropriate to scientific discussion. In rebuttal to a very loose use of commonplace terms by Professor Melvin T. Copeland, he invokes the familiar defense of all scholars accused of obfuscation:

He does not think it necessary to say what he means. I do, for the purpose

[2] "Comments on the Job of the Executive," *Harvard Business Review*, Spring 1940, p. 307n. In this article (pp. 295–308) Barnard answers Melvin T. Copeland's "The Job of an Executive," *Harvard Business Review*, Winter 1940, pp. 148–160.

which I attempted to pursue, but not necessarily for all other purposes. But whoever attempts to answer these questions or define such concepts will find it laborious, and will come out, I think, with abstract, "sociological," colorless propositions, rather unaesthetic and difficult, requiring hard study. Should we be afraid of that?

Barnard himself, it should be added, did not hesitate to reread something he valued. "I have read [Ross Ashby's *Design for a Brain*] five times and I am certainly going to read it five more," he said in a talk to students at Johns Hopkins University.[3] At any rate no one has ever said that one reading of *The Functions* was enough or that more than one was not worthwhile.

The ponderousness of Barnard's style is the mark, perhaps, of the amateur scholar. It is more surely an indication of how seriously he took his work and how much he wanted it to be a definitive theory, adequate not only for his own extraordinary mind and experience but for the rest of us as well. He tries too hard to conclude his inquiry and does not indicate how it might be extended into areas he chooses not to enter. Many of the other shortcomings of this work are really omissions which have been or still remain to be filled in by researchers and writers in his debt, or are aspects of his system of personal values. He says little, for example, about the institutions of top management — the executive group, the board of directors, or the offices of president and chairman. His treatment of purpose acknowledges its centrality, to be sure, but does not include attention to the *choice* of purpose in a changing world or to the processes of formulating goals and objectives for the organization. Although he must be credited with readmitting man to organization theory, he seems much less interested in a

[3] In "The Elementary Conditions of Formal Organization," an unpublished seminar paper of November 3, 1953, included in H. C. Sanders, Jr., "Management Theories in the Writings of Chester Irving Barnard," unpublished master's thesis, Southern Methodist University, June 1955.

living, growing person than in the abstract "Individual." He is not much concerned about personal involvement. His analysis of motivation suggests responsive behavior rather than full participation in the administrative process; it makes no room for the development of individuals, for the maturing of their needs, and for the dilution or strengthening of their commitment. The definition of authority understates the role of objective authority and appears to assign individuals the choice of acceptance or rejection rather than participation in the active integration of conflicting alternatives and interpretations. Leadership is effectively but abstractly examined; its problems are not analyzed. But no catalogue of faults can erode the conclusion that despite its turgidity and omissions, Barnard's book has remained important to its old readers and continues to attract new ones.

What is its continuing role in the literature of its field? In the first place it still performs a useful function in tempering the classical approach to organization. This approach is by no means dead. Its apostles — Taylor, Fayol, Urwick, Gulick, Mooney, Reiley — are still read. Books like those of Holden, Fish, and Smith, of Koontz and O'Donnell, give extensive classroom circulation to principles of management derived from Fayol. Their influence pervades less directly the folklore of management. One can still hear that to administer is to plan, organize, integrate, and measure, or to plan, organize, staff, and control, that a man should have only one superior, that the span of control should not exceed six or seven persons, and that responsibility should be commensurate with authority. Barnard's work is related to the more positive contributions of this school, for he believes in hierarchical organizations, in formal lines of authority and communication, and shares Urwick's admiration of Mary Parker Follett, the flexible classicist who was born before her time and with her "Law of the Situation" instructed Barnard in the nature of authority. We still need *The Functions of the Executive* to mark the great transition between the rational traditionalists and more recent schools and to temper the application to real situations of the still usable partial insights of his predecessors.

Of somewhat greater importance to us today are several other groups of students of organization and management — an organizational behavior or human relations group which has multiplied and subdivided prolifically since the Hawthorne studies, a systems or decision-theory group with mathematical and model building subgroups, a practitioner-oriented group studying the processes of formulating and implementing organization purpose, and a less homogeneous group of individual empiricists, consultants, teachers, historians, and general observers. These clusters of approaches have many differences as well as affinities within themselves. But Barnard remains universal enough to be of interest to virtually all the members of all sects of organization study. He is in many instances claimed by their membership. He continues, in any case, to be influential in tempering their doctrinal excesses and in complementing their particular strengths.

The insight into worker motivation developed by the Western Electric experiments has produced a varied body of literature dominated by behavioral scientists like Argyris, Bennis, Likert, McGregor, Roethlisberger, Whyte, and Zaleznik, as well as more specialized representatives of the individual disciplines of the social sciences. At its best the work of the kind suggested by these illustrative names has increased general awareness of the psychological and social determinants of human behavior. At its weakest it has led to the oversimplifications of McGregor's "Theory X" and "Theory Y," the Likert group's passionate preference for participative management, the exaggerations attending the growth of the National Training Laboratory's sensitivity training and the Blake-Mouton managerial grid. Barnard's book, reread after most of the works of this later group of investigators, reveals the classic qualities of integrity, economy, and equanimity. His contributions to these scholars have by no means dissipated his originality, for their biases and special preoccupations with such phenomena as emergent behavior limit their use of Barnard's concepts of purpose, leadership, and responsibility. There are, of course, distinguished exceptions to this implied criticism, as illustrated by Abraham Zaleznik's *Human Dilemmas of Leadership*. In my judgment this book reflects in its concern for individual development, its understanding of the organization setting of human behavior, and its acceptance of leadership as a critical function a creative extension of Barnard's breadth of view.

The systems or decision-theory group of writers has two subsections. The management and computer scientists have not yet addressed policy and organization problems to an important degree. The extension of sophisticated quantification to organization behavior may someday reach the complex processes involved in the management of cooperative systems. In the meantime a less mathematical approach, the principal figure in which is Herbert Simon, has built directly upon Barnard's elaboration of the social-system concept of organization. Barnard wrote an introduction to Simon's *Administrative Behavior*, which, together with Simon's subsequent text and comments, suggests an uneasy affinity originating more perhaps in Simon's harsh criticism of scientific management than in his loyalty to Barnard's own thesis. At any rate Simon and such Carnegie–Mellon colleagues as J. G. March and R. M. Cyert focus principally upon cognitive limits on rationality and come almost to equate management with decision making limited by the range of perception. Their study of decision processes carries forward Barnard's definition of executive processes as systems-determined activities but narrows it away from policy-formulating decisions. March and Simon's descriptive and analytical work derives the basic features of organization structure and function from the characteristics of human problem-solving processes and rational human choice. Rereading Barnard after becoming acquainted with this later important work reveals a relatively small role occupied by purpose and normative prescription in the Carnegie–Mellon work, its lack of concern for the processes by which organization purpose is formulated and with the criteria by which one set of purposes can be perceived as different in quality from another. The distance between Barnard and these direct but independent descendants reminds us of how uninspiring to the practitioner can be the findings and hypotheses of science and of how much imagination and sympathy with scientific and management responsibilities and points of view are required to bridge the gap.

Barnard's influence has of course extended to the many empirical and historical studies of organization by both students and practitioners. Here names like Copeland, Learned, Smith, Christensen, Sloan, Chandler, Drucker, and the case studies of the schools of business and public administration come to mind. Melvin T. Copeland and Barnard's exchange of articles in the *Harvard Business Review* (already referred to) began the contribution that Barnard offers to this group. Copeland, the influential pioneer of the long established studies of business policy, demurred at Barnard's theoretical terminology and structure and proffered his own "conceptual scheme" which he felt was more responsive to a changing world and more adequate for practitioners. Beginning with the primacy of policies, he describes an analytical process called "sizing up the situation," "deciding upon a plan of action," "organizing for the job," "instruction," "sequence and timing of moves," and "following through." The effectiveness of this attention to the company situation and what should be done about it in the classroom training of practitioners was considerable, but the terminology used did not begin to articulate the policy skills involved or make room for the new research in human behavior going on at the time.

Barnard in effect has demonstrated that it is possible to articulate a practitioner's theory of management which is coherent and capable of development and which can make use of research discoveries as well as of the equally important, if more intuitive, findings of experience. From the perspective of the thousands of studies of actual organizations recorded for the purpose of analysis and prescription and of the commentaries by men of experience, Barnard's book is revealed as the nearly unique example of a systematic examination and interpretation of a class of phenomena occurring everywhere but little understood. Copeland's successors, among whom I find myself, owe to Barnard the realization that in the interests of purpose and results research and practice can be reconciled, that disciplined interpretation can be applied to successive clinical studies of organization, and that a conceptual scheme can be simple enough to be used and yet exact and complex enough to accommodate continuing insights into the workings of complicated organization processes.

Limitations of space and knowledge make me necessarily cavalier in relating *The Functions of the Executive* to the diffuse and uneven literature on organization of the last thirty years. The continuing importance of Barnard's book and the deeper understanding of its permanent quality made possible by subsequent research and insight are nonetheless unmistakable. Its future influence is likely to manifest itself still as corrective of the parochial inhibitions of the academic disciplines or the discursiveness of reminiscence. More positively, I believe this book calls for the development of some of its own pioneering but incomplete conceptualization. The management of complex organizations appears to many of us concerned with it to require in particular more advanced concepts of purpose, more clearly defined ideas of professional responsibility, and a more usable understanding of the functions of leadership.

With the attention Barnard gives to purpose and responsibility in his later chapters, it is clear that he recognizes, as indicated earlier, the importance of purpose and commitment to purpose in organized activity. Perhaps because the goals of his own organization were relatively constant, he does not give full descriptive or prescriptive attention to the processes of formulation: how it is, how it may be, and how it should be formulated, and how it may be and should be — given an explicit set of values — evaluated for quality, relevance, and durability. Work is being done on the organization processes involved in the formulation of corporate strategy and the adaptation to the achievement of conscious purposes of what is known about organization. It will carry forward Barnard's conviction that purpose is the unifying principle of cooperative systems and that the efficiency of organization (in the sense of the satisfactions it provides its members) arises most importantly from the sense that the organization's purpose is proper and important. Those of us who are grateful for the work of behavioral scientists but impatient with the antiseptic assumption that our true concern is how organizations do work (rather than how they might work under more effective leadership) will continue to be guided by Barnard in the direction we follow.

Developing researchable and teachable concepts of purpose is indeed currently one of the principal concerns of business education. The study of business policy, concerned principally with the choice and implementation of long-term purposes affecting the whole organization and governing its changing relation with its environment, is now normally the integrative course of the professional business curriculum. Its concepts are consistent with Barnard's theory of cooperative systems and directly extend (without so deliberate an intent) his experience-based knowledge and analysis of environmental opportunities and constraints, the identification of organization resources and capabilities, the discovery and development of the aspirations and desires of the influential members of the organization — all processes which together constitute the determination of purposes.

Professional education for the management of business organizations has been concerned, all during the period since Barnard's book appeared, with concepts of responsibility. Barnard's view of responsibility as the quality giving dependability and determination to human behavior and "foresight and ideality" to purpose and his belief that organizations endure in accordance with the breadth of morality by which they are governed take on even greater relevance as professors in schools of professional management try to prepare students for what will be expected of private business in an era of worsening social problems and rising expectations. A concern for responsibility flows naturally from Barnard's total view of organization as both effective and efficient in senses which go far beyond classic economic theory.

The nature of leadership, viewed now as originality in the conception, institutionalization, and achievement of organization purposes of commanding quality, is once again of concern to students of management. Barnard knew as we almost all now know, that leadership is not a function of the individual only, though not unimportant on that account. He knew what more of us will find out for sure, that leadership in organizations means taking the initiative in the adaptation of organization resources and processes to clearly understood and attractive objectives — the formulation of which is not wholly an organization rather than an individual process. As progress is made in further identifying and articulating the nature of leadership in organizations, Barnard's stature will again not diminish, but appear more clear.

My argument then is that this book endures not only because it has been influential in the literature of organization following it, but more importantly because it continues to offer insight recognized to be important though not easily come by. It should remain important because Barnard's unfinished business has not yet been completed or his conceptual approach rendered obsolete. His voice is still authoritative because his wisdom came from a combination of intellect and experience, of an inclination for systematic thought and a generous exposure to responsibility and the necessity to achieve results through cooperation. His reading, as revealed by his references, was scattered and uneven, but his mind ordered the miscellany. His acquaintance with Henderson, Mayo, and the others illuminated the subject he had identified and the executive responsibility he knew intimately. His stature derives from his stamina in abstract thought, his capacity to apply reason to professional experiences, and his probable sensitivity and expertness in practice. I can think of no one who excels him in the simultaneous exercise of the twin capabilities of reason and competence or in the exploitation of their combined power. For these reasons *The Functions of the Executive* remains today, as it has been since its publication, the most thought-provoking book on organization and management ever written by a practicing executive.

Kenneth R. Andrews

Boston, 1968

REPRESENTATIVE WORKS OF WRITERS MENTIONED

Mayo, Elton. *The Human Problems of an Industrial Civilization.* New York: Macmillan, 1933.

Taylor, F. W. *The Principles of Scientific Management.* New York: Harper, 1911.

Fayol, Henri. *General and Industrial Administration.* London: Sir Isaac Pitman & Sons, 1949.

Henderson, L. J. *Pareto's General Sociology.* Cambridge: Harvard University Press, 1935.

Pareto, V. *The Mind and Society.* New York: Harcourt, Brace, 1935.

Donham, W. B. *Education for Responsible Living.* Cambridge: Harvard University Press, 1944.

Roethlisberger, F. J. and Dickson, W. J. *Management and the Worker.* Cambridge: Harvard University Press, 1939.

Whitehead, T. N. *Leadership in a Free Society.* Cambridge: Harvard University Press, 1936.

Copeland, M. T. *The Executive at Work.* Cambridge: Harvard University Press, 1951.

Urwick, L. F. *The Elements of Administration.* New York: Harper, 1943.

Gulick, Luther and Urwick, L. F. *Papers on the Science of Administration.* New York: Institute of Public Administration, 1937.

Mooney, J. D. and Reiley, A. C. *The Principles of Organization.* New York: Harper, 1939.

Holden, Paul; Fish, L. S.; and Smith, H. L. *Top-Management Organization and Control.* New York: McGraw-Hill, 1951.

Koontz, Harold and O'Donnell, Cyril. *Principles of Management.* New York: McGraw-Hill, 1955.

Follett, Mary Parker. *Dynamic Administration* (Metcalf, H. C. and Urwick, L. F., editors). New York: Harper, 1940.

Argyris, Chris. *Personality and Organization.* New York: Harper, 1957.

Bennis, W. G.; Benne, K. D.; and Chin, Robert. *The Planning of Change*. New York: Holt, Rinehart & Winston, 1961.

Likert, Rensis. *New Patterns of Management*. New York: McGraw-Hill, 1961.

McGregor, Douglas. *The Human Side of Enterprise*. New York: McGraw-Hill, 1960.

Whyte, William F. *Money and Motivation*. New York: Harper, 1955.

Zaleznik, Abraham. *The Human Dilemmas of Leadership*. New York: Harcourt, Brace, 1966.

Blake, R. R. and Mouton, J. S. *The Managerial Grid*. Houston: Gulf Publishing Co., 1964.

Simon, H. A. *Administrative Behavior*. New York: Macmillan, 1959.

March, J. G. and Simon, H. A. *Organization*. New York: Wiley, 1950.

Cyert, Richard M. and March, J. G. *A Behavioral Theory of the Firm*. Englewood Cliffs, N.J.: Prentice-Hall, 1963.

Learned, E. P.; Christensen, C. R.; Andrews, K. R.; and Guth, W. D. *Business Policy: Text and Cases*. Homewood, Ill.: Richard D. Irwin, 1965.

Smith, G. A. and Christensen, C. R. *Policy Formulation and Administration* (fourth edition). Homewood, Ill.: Richard D. Irwin, 1962.

Sloan, A. P. *My Years with General Motors*. Garden City, N.Y.: Doubleday, 1964.

Chandler, A. D. *Strategy and Structure*. Cambridge: The M.I.T. Press, 1962.

Drucker, Peter. *The Practice of Management*. New York: Harper, 1954.

THE FUNCTIONS OF THE EXECUTIVE

AUTHOR'S PREFACE

THIS book is a revision and expansion of the manuscript prepared for eight lectures at Lowell Institute in Boston in November and December 1937, under the same title.

A knowledge of the point of view from which an effort of this kind developed is sometimes helpful to the reader; so that it may be of interest if I relate briefly the circumstances which have led me to write the book. The honor of Dr. A. Lawrence Lowell's invitation came at a time when belatedly I was reading Justice Cardozo's Yale Lectures, "The Nature of the Judicial Process." This conjunction incited an attempt to arrange for orderly presentation hypotheses which I had gradually constructed through several years concerning the executive processes, which are specialized functions in what we know as "organizations." If these functions are to be adequately described, the description must be in terms of the nature of organization itself. I had attempted in the previous year to sketch a portion of a theory of organization in an effort to stimulate others to take it up. Except for the interest and encouragement given me at that time by Dean Wallace B. Donham of the Harvard Graduate School of Business Administration and his associates — Professors Cabot, Henderson, Mayo, and Whitehead — I should probably not have attempted an essay of the scope of this.

Many times I have noted that executives are able to understand each other with very few words when discussing essential problems of organization, provided that the questions are stated without dependence upon the technologies of their respective fields. This is strikingly true, in fact chiefly observable, when men of radically different fields discuss such questions. It is not due to any common nomenclature or general study of organization systems. Until quite recently there has been little literature that could at all serve as a common basis of understanding, and it is unknown and not of much interest to most major executives. Moreover, if the questions are considered not as practical but as theoretical problems, the common understanding seems invariably to disappear as quickly as it does if the discussion relapses into illustrations from their respective technologies. Yet clergymen, military men, government officials, university officials, and men of widely diversified businesses, when not conscious of an attempt to discuss organization as such, have seemed to show an understanding — or better, a sense — that is quite similar. To me it has long seemed probable that there are universal characteristics of organization that are active understandings, evaluations, concepts, of men skilled in organizing not only in the present but in past generations, which have also been perceived by careful and astute observers and students.

But nothing of which I knew treated of organization in a way which seemed to me to correspond either to my experience or to the understanding implicit in the conduct of those recognized to be adept in executive practice or in the leadership of organizations. Some excellent work has been done in describing and analyzing the superficial characteristics of organizations. It is important, but like descriptive geography with physics, chemistry, geology, and biology missing. More than the topography and cartography of organization would be necessary to understand the executive functions; a knowledge of the kinds and qualities of the forces at work and the manner of their operation would also be needed.

Furthermore, the sociologists, social psychologists, economists, the scholars in political science and historians, as I viewed their work, had described many of the phenomena resulting from these forces, and had given some explanation of them, but I had found little agreement among them. Always, it seemed to me, the social scientists — from whatever side they approached — just reached the edge of organization as I experienced it, and retreated. Rarely did they seem to me to sense the processes of coördination and decision that underlie a large part at least of the phenomena they described. More important, there was lacking much recognition of formal organization as a most important characteristic of social life, and as being the principal structural aspect of society itself. Mores, folkways, political structures, institutions, attitudes, motives, propensities, instincts, were discussed *in extenso*; but the bridge between the generalizations of social study on the one hand and the action of masses to which they related on the other was not included, I thought.

The search for the universals of organization has been obstructed, I suspect, by the long history of thought concerning the nature of the state and of the church. The center of this thought relates to the origin and nature of authority. Its consequence appears to be a legalism that prevents the acceptance of essential facts of social organizations. No theory of organization that conflicts with the doctrines of the law can be acceptable unless it also explains these doctrines. The doctrine of states as sources and bases of formal organizations in society — the doctrine relevant in legal theory to all corporate organizations, such as those of municipalities, universities, business institutions, armies — is inconsistent with the theory that all states are based upon organizations. But the latter hypothesis cannot be accepted unless it is able to explain both the facts of states and their obvious dominance in some respects over the organizations from which they arise. Thus I found myself in an impasse. On one hand, theories which accounted for important aspects of organized society were unsatisfactory when confronted with theories of the state. On the other hand, the latter utterly failed, even when spun out into their endless applications in judicial decisions, to explain the most elemental experience of organized effort.

The confusion resulting from these considerations was first partly overcome by the chance reading of Ehrlich's *Fundamental Principles of the Sociology of Law*. The thesis of this study is that all law arises from the formal and especially the informal understandings of the people as socially organized, and that so far as these practices and understandings are formulated in substantive law and promulgated by lawmaking authorities the "law" is merely the formulation. Its source is not rulers, legislatures, or courts, however constituted, but the people as *organized* in families and communities of various kinds. Even though his treatment be overdrawn, as Vinogradoff thinks, or his scheme be but an alternative to other juristic theories, as Pound says in his introduction to the English translation of Ehrlich, the fact remains that at least this student recognized as competent in his field gives an approach that is broadly consistent with the facts as I have experienced them.

Next to the question of authority as a cause for confusion concerning organization, I would place the course of the development of economic thought in the last century and a half and the exaggeration of the economic phases of human behavior which the early formulation of economic theory made far too convenient. Granting the utility of abstracting from social action that aspect which we call "economic," the relatively developed theories so effectively constructed by Adam Smith and his successors depressed the interest in the specific social processes within which economic factors are merely one phase, and greatly overemphasized economic interests. This was conjoined with an exclusion of adequate consideration of motives in pure economic theory, a materialistic philosophy rooted in utilitarianism, and a prevalence of highly erroneous conceptions of the place of the intellectual, as distinguished from the emotional and physiological, processes in social behavior. All of this meant, and still means in the current thought of many, that man is an "economic man" carrying a few non-economic appendages.

Such a view, it seems to me, forced — perhaps might be expected to force — the neglect of concrete specific local organization and the individual in relation to it as the locus of action in society whether economic or not. At least this I can assert: though I early found out how to behave effectively in organizations, not until I had much later relegated economic theory and economic interests to a secondary — though indispensable — place did I begin to understand organizations or human behavior in them. I do not mean merely that non-economic organizations — such as the political, the educational, the religious — are also to be found, and are of primary importance; I mean specifically with reference to business organizations that non-economic motives, interests, and processes, as well as the economic, are fundamental in behavior from the boards of directors to the last man. The contrary view is almost always implicit and frequently explicit in the statements not only of business men but of labor men, politicians, statesmen, professional men, educators, and even of church ministers. As one result, effective leadership has to be based on intuitions that are correct, notwithstanding doctrines that deny their correctness. Very often, I think, we attempt social integration by methods imposed by a false logic to the very limit that common sense and hard experience will permit.

The tangible result of this experience and these beliefs is this book. The need for it lies in the confusion and uncertainty which now attend the subject, and the extent to which especially the purposeful and constructive activities of men in present society are governed by formal organizations. It also lies in the relations of such organizations to society in general, and in the degrees to which the activities of formal organizations, as contrasted with institutions and other abstract generalities of social life, provide the structure and processes of social systems.

Formally this work is divided into four parts, but in a sense it consists of two short treatises. One is an exposition of a theory of coöperation and organization and constitutes the first half of the book. The second is a study of the functions and of the methods of operation of executives in formal organizations. These two subjects, which may be conveniently distinguished for some purposes, are in concrete action and experience inseparable. It is possible that I have not adequately taken into account that this is not obvious to many and that for this reason I have not made sufficiently clear the unity of the whole book. Indeed the quite different characters of the two halves of the book may contribute to a false sense of the separateness of the two subjects.

In the first half I have attempted to compress so far as pertinent all of the knowledge which has come to my mind from the sciences concerning the conditions of social behavior. It will occur to the reader, as it has to me, that this field might well be left to those who have the requisite scientific experience supported by adequate knowledge and appropriate techniques of scholarship. The important justification for my effort is that this knowledge, for the present purposes, must be stated in terms of organization. It is in this field that for thirty years I have had intimate and continuous experience. Those who possess the general knowledge and the scientific training required usually do not have such experience.

Many of the difficulties the reader may encounter in the first half of the book are not, however, entirely due to the pioneer character of the effort. They are inherent in the complexity of concrete coöperative systems. P. W. Bridgman notes that "the totality of situations with which we are confronted, including society in its economic, political, esthetic, and religious aspects, is enormously more complex than the situations presented by any well defined scientific activity such as physics or chemistry." [1] It seems to me quite in order to cease encouraging the

---

[1] P. W. Bridgman, *The Intelligent Individual and Society* (New York: The Macmillan Co., 1938), p. 10.

expectation that human behavior in society can be anything less than the most complex study to which our minds may be applied. However desirable clarity and simplicity of statement, it is not desirable to underestimate either the difficulties of observation and experiment or those of constructing hypotheses that may prove helpful. Nor should we be misled, as I think nearly all of us are, by the relative ease with which most of us manage to adjust ourselves to our worlds. We have less understanding of what we do, how we do it and why we do it, than does the pitcher of a baseball — and for his case in the whole world there is not as yet the anatomical, physiological, neurological, and psychological knowledge — and perhaps not the mathematical technique — necessary to explain what he does in seconds without ever having heard these names.

However, some of those whose present interest in fundamental theory is limited may find it desirable to begin with the second half of the book at Chapter X. This is the exposition in very general terms of the functions, processes, essential problems, of the executive or of leadership of organizations and of the management of coöperative systems. It is based chiefly upon personal experience and observation, although in formulating the material the theory of the first half of the book and the aid of other books have been indispensable.

I am aware of some of the faults in this presentation of the subject which I have been unable to correct. Considering the fact that I suppose it to be in some respects new, it is deficient in clarity and illustrations, especially since it is addressed to so many groups of widely different attitudes and experience. Unfortunately, most illustrations from modern experience involve technologies that require extensive explanation. The switchboard example given in Chapter V will make this evident. Moreover, this treatment is incomplete and unfinished in many respects; many years and many men would be required, I think, to complete or finish such a study.

Still more do I regret the failure to convey the *sense* of organization, the dramatic and aesthetic feeling that surpasses the possibilities of exposition, which derives chiefly from the intimate habitual interested experience. It is evident that many lack an interest in the science of organization because they are oblivious to the arts of organizing, not perceiving the significant elements. They miss the structure of the symphony, the art of its composition, and the skill of its execution, because they cannot hear the tones.

Copies of my Cyrus Fogg Brackett Lecture given at Princeton University on March 10, 1936 were distributed to the audience at the Lowell Institute primarily as an aid to understanding the present Chapters XIII and XIV. It is reprinted here as an Appendix for the same purpose, and because in general it explains some aspects of the behavior of executives, especially their mental processes, not sufficiently treated in the main text.

For patient and effective assistance, I am greatly indebted to Major Edward S. Johnston, U.S.A., who carefully read the earlier manuscripts and gave me both useful criticism and much illustrative material. I am especially grateful to Lawrence J. Henderson, Abbott and James Lawrence Professor of Chemistry in Harvard University, who at great expense of time has given me invaluable advice concerning many questions of method, and indispensable aid and encouragement regarding the exposition as a whole.

It is also a pleasure to record my appreciation of the indefatigable assistance of my secretary, Miss Lillian Whitney, who not only effectively produced the successive editions of the manuscript, but so efficiently organized the numerous details of my affairs that this study was feasible.

C. I. B.

South Orange, New Jersey
July 15, 1938.

CONTENTS

PART I

PRELIMINARY CONSIDERATIONS CONCERNING COOPERATIVE SYSTEMS

PART II

THE THEORY AND STRUCTURE OF FORMAL ORGANIZATIONS

PART III

THE ELEMENTS OF FORMAL ORGANIZATIONS

CONTENTS

PART IV

THE FUNCTIONS OF ORGANIZATIONS IN COOPERATIVE SYSTEMS

APPENDIX

PART I

PRELIMINARY CONSIDERATIONS CONCERNING
COOPERATIVE SYSTEMS

For the efficiency of an army consists partly in the order and partly in the general; but chiefly in the latter, because he does not depend upon the order, but the order depends upon him. All things, both fishes and birds and plants, are ordered together in some way, but not in the same way; and the system is not such that there is no relation between one thing and another. There is a definite connexion. Everything is ordered together to one end; but the arrangement is like that in a household, where the free persons have the least liberty to act at random, and have all or most of their actions preordained for them, whereas the slaves and animals have little common responsibility and act for the most part at random. — ARISTOTLE, *Metaphysics*

CHAPTER I

INTRODUCTION

WITH all the thought that has been turned upon the unrest of the present day in the literature of social reform one finds practically no reference to formal organization as the concrete social process by which social action is largely accomplished. This concrete process is ignored almost completely, even as a factor in any social condition or situation. For example, in the current literature on labor conditions, policies, organizations, etc., almost nothing is said, by any of the various groups discussing the subject, about the necessities of the organization of work, or about the executive functions and their organization as related to it. If one examines Sir Josiah Stamp's recent book, *The Science of Social Adjustment*, a stimulating and penetrating inquiry into the causes of the disturbance of social equilibrium, one will find scarcely a line to indicate the existence of formal organizations, despite the author's active connection with them; nor a single suggestion regarding the study of them as one of the important fields of scientific exploration looking toward the more apt adjustment of society to changing conditions.

To me, this failure of attention is like leaving a vital organ out of anatomy or its functions out of physiology. Careful inspection of the observable actions of human beings in our society — their movements, their speech, and the thought and emotions evident from their action and speech — shows that many and sometimes most of them are determined or directed by their connection with formal organizations. This is most obviously true of the actions of persons as employees and housewives, which occupy perhaps one quarter of their time, but most persons in their "non-working" hours are members or participants in other organizations. Including families, businesses of more than one person, various municipal corporations, autonomous or semi-autonomous governments and branches of government, associations, clubs, societies, fraternities, educational institutions, religious groups, etc., the number of formal organizations in the United States is many millions, and it is possible that the number is greater than that of the total population.[1] Probably few persons belong to less than five or ten such organizations, and many belong to fifty or more. Their individual conduct is dominated or qualified or conditioned by these relationships directly. Moreover, there are in a short period of a day or a week many millions of formal organizations of short duration, a few hours at most, which are not named and are seldom thought of as organizations.

For the present, formal organizations may be described rather than carefully defined. The more important of them are associations of coöperative efforts to which it is possible and customary to give definite names, that have officers or recognized leaders, that have reasons for existence that may be approximately stated — such as governments, government departments, churches, universities, labor units, industrial corporations, symphony orchestras, football teams.

Formal organization is that kind of coöperation among men that is conscious, deliberate, purposeful. Such coöperation is omnipresent and inescapable nowadays, so that it is usually contrasted only with "individualism," as if there were no other process of coöperation. Moreover, much of what we regard as reliable, foreseeable, and stable is so obviously a result of formally organized effort that it is readily believed that organized

---

[1] The calculation of the possibilities is merely a complex exercise in permutations and combinations, and would produce quantities of astronomical magnitude. A faint indication is given on page 108 when only very small groups are under consideration.

effort is normally successful, that failure of organization is abnormal. This illusion from some points of view is even useful, with considerable caution, in many of our important affairs, at least under what we call "normal" conditions.

But in fact, successful coöperation in or by formal organizations is the abnormal, not the normal, condition. What are observed from day to day are the successful survivors among innumerable failures. The organizations commanding sustained attention, almost all of which are short-lived at best, are the exceptions, not the rule. It may be said correctly that modern civilization is one characterized by the large residue of organizations that are in existence at any given time; but this does not imply that the particular organizations of that time have been or will continue to be in existence long. Similarly, it is recognized that the existence of a population does not necessarily imply longevity, but merely the balancing of constantly recurring deaths by births.

Thus most coöperation fails in the attempt, or dies in infancy, or is short-lived. In our western civilization only one formal organization, the Roman Catholic Church, claims a substantial age. A few universities, a very few national governments or formally organized nations, are more than two hundred years old. Many municipalities are somewhat older, but few other corporate organizations have existed more than one hundred years. Failure to coöperate, failure of coöperation, failure of organization, disorganization, disintegration, destruction of organization — and reorganization — are characteristic facts of human history.

This is hardly disputable. Explanations of the fact usually make reference to the perversity of human nature, to egoism, to the combative instinct, to "false" economic systems, or to the struggle for food and the limits of its supply. More specific explanations refer to faults of structure — "defective constitutions" — or to bad functioning, lack of solidarity or spirit, poor leadership or management. Any of these weaknesses may be present, but at root the cause of the instability and limited duration of formal organizations lies in the forces outside. These forces both furnish the material which are used by organizations and limit their action. The survival of an organization depends upon the maintenance of an equilibrium of complex character in a continuously fluctuating environment of physical, biological, and social materials, elements, and forces, which calls for readjustment of processes internal to the organization. We shall be concerned with the nature of the external conditions to which adjustment must be made, but the center of our interest is the processes by which it is accomplished.

The functions of the executive with which the last part of this treatise is concerned are those of control, management, supervision, administration, in formal organizations. These functions are exercised not merely by high officials in such organizations but by all those who are in positions of control of whatever degree. In the large-scale and complex organizations, the assistants of executives, though not themselves executives, are occupied in the work of these functions. Also in many instances the responsibility for authoritative decisions is formally lodged in organized groups, such as legislative bodies, boards, committees, and then these groups may be said to have executive functions. On the other hand it not infrequently occurs that high officials in organizations, though known as executives and occupying important positions, exercise few or unimportant and incidental executive functions; and at least some work of all executives is not executive in the sense which concerns us. It will be noted, then, that the functions to which this study relates are only roughly suggested by the predominant occupation of most persons who are called executives, and that we are not to be restricted by conventional titles or by special definitions of the word "executive."

Neither are we to be restricted to the executive functions in industrial or commercial organizations. On the contrary, all classes or types of formal organizations are within the scope of observation for our purposes. The nature and processes of such organizations determine what the executive functions are and how they are to be performed. Although we shall have most in mind major or important organizations, there are also many other formal organizations of little importance or duration which also require consideration.

Before these processes are discussed, however, some time must be given to analyzing and defining the terms involved. Accordingly, beginning with a section of preliminary considerations concerning coöperative systems, the first half of this book will be devoted to the development of a theory of formal organization in the attempt to frame a conceptual scheme which may be a useful tool in the study or discussion of the problems of concrete organizations. With this fundamental scheme clearly set forth, the second half of the book will take up in greater detail the elements of formal organization, the relation to them of the executive functions, and finally the place of the executive functions in the survival of coöperation.

CHAPTER II

THE INDIVIDUAL AND ORGANIZATION

I HAVE found it impossible to go far in the study of organizations or of the behavior of people in relation to them without being confronted with a few questions which can be simply stated. For example: "What is an individual?" "What do we mean by a person?" "To what extent do people have a power of choice or free will?" The temptation is to avoid such difficult questions, leaving them to the philosophers and scientists who still debate them after centuries. It quickly appears, however, that even if we avoid answering such questions definitely, we cannot evade them. We answer them implicitly in whatever we say about human behavior; and, what is more important, all sorts of people, and especially leaders and executives, act on the basis of fundamental assumptions or attitudes regarding them, although these people are rarely conscious that they are doing so. For example, when we undertake to persuade others to do what we wish, we assume that they are able to decide whether they will or not. When we provide for education or training we assume that without them people cannot do certain things, that is, that their power of choice will be more limited. When we make rules, regulations, laws — which we deliberately do in great quantities — we assume generally that as respects their subject matter those affected by them are governed by forces outside themselves.

The significance of these observations may be made clearer by noting the extreme differences of conception regarding the "individual" — to take one word — in discussions of coöperation and of organizations and their functions. On the one hand, the discrete, particular, unique, singular individual person with a name, an address, a history, a reputation, has the attention.

On the other hand, when the attention transfers to the organization as a whole, or to remote parts of it, or to the integration of efforts accomplished by coördination, or to persons regarded in groups, then the individual loses his preëminence in the situation and something else, non-personal in character, is treated as dominant. If in such situations we ask "What is an individual?" "What is his nature?" "What is the character of his participation in this situation?" we find wide disagreement and uncertainty. Much of the conflict of dogmas and of stated interests to be observed in the political field — the catchwords are "individualism," "collectivism," "centralization," "laissez-faire," "socialism," "statism," "fascism," "liberty," "freedom," "regimentation," "discipline" — and some of the disorder in the industrial field, I think, result from inability either intuitively or by other processes to reconcile conceptions of the social and the personal positions of individuals in concrete situations.

These considerations suggest that in a broad inquiry into the nature of organizations and their functions, or in an effort to state the elements of the executive processes in organizations, a first step should be to set forth the position or understanding or postulates especially concerning the man, the "individual," and the "person," and related matters. Without such a preliminary survey it is quite certain that there will be unnecessary obscurity and unsuspected misunderstanding. This does not mean that I shall attempt either a philosophic or a scientific inquiry. It does mean that I must present a construction — a description or definite scheme — to which consistent reference is implied throughout this book.

Accordingly, in this chapter, I shall briefly discuss the following subjects: I, The status of individuals and the properties of persons generally; II, the method of treating individuals and persons in this book; III, certain characteristics of personal behavior outside coöperative systems; and IV, the meaning of "effectiveness" and "efficiency" in personal behavior.

I. Concerning, 1, The Status of Individuals and 11, The Properties of Persons

1

(*a*) First of all, we say that an individual human being is a discrete, separate, physical thing. It is evident that every one believes, or usually acts as if he did, in this individual physical entity. For other and broader purposes, however, it seems clear that no thing, including a human body, has individual independent existence. It is impossible to describe it, use it, locate it, except in terms of the rest of the physical universe or some larger isolation of it. For example, if the temperature of the environment changes, that of the thing or of the body must change (except within limits of adjustment biologically determined). Its weight is a function of gravitational attraction; its structure depends upon gravity both directly and indirectly. Thus at the outset we note that the human being, physically regarded, may be treated either as an individual thing or as a mere phase or functional presentation of universal physical factors. Which is "correct" depends upon the purpose. When the architect calculates the live-load capacities of his floor structures he is thinking of men not as individual human beings but as functions of gravitational attraction; other aspects of them he disregards.

(*b*) The mere body, however, whether for limited and practical purposes regarded as a physical object or regarded as a phase or function of general physical factors, is not a human being. As a living thing it possesses a power of adjustment, an ability to maintain an internal balance, and a continuity, despite incessant changes within and wide variations without itself. Moreover, it possesses a capacity of experience, that is, an ability to change the character of its adjustment as a result of its history. This means that the human body, viewed by itself, is an organism, something whose components are both physical and biological. Although the physical factors are distinguished from the biological they are not separable in specific organisms. In other words, living things are known by behavior, and all living behavior is a synthesis of both physical and biological factors. If either class of factors are removed, the specific behavior ceases to be manifest, and the physical form also undergoes changes that would otherwise not occur. But if a single organism is so composed, this means that it not only presents universal physical factors but also a long race history, so that the organism is an individual when we forget all these facts, and if we remember them becomes a whole conglomeration of things that we cannot even see.

(c) Human organisms do not function except in conjunction with other human organisms. This is true first because they are bisexual. It is also true because in infancy they require nurture. Moreover, the mere presence of organisms without reference to sexuality, parenthood, or infancy, compels interrelations or interactions between them; as physical objects they cannot occupy the same space, there is an interchange of radiant energy between them, they reflect light to each other. Biologically they compete for food — which is both a physical and a biological requirement.

The interactions between human organisms differ from those between mere physical objects or between a physical object and an organism in that experience and adaptability are *mutually* involved. The adaptation required and the experience relate not merely to things or functions determined by factors inherent in each of the organisms separately, but to the mutuality of reaction or adjustment itself. In other words, the mutual reaction between two human organisms is a series of responses to the *intention* and *meaning* of adaptable behavior. To the factors peculiar to this interaction we give the name "social factors," and we call the relationship "social relationship."

On first consideration, a physical thing endowed with life

that has interacted with other similar organisms becomes more and more unique, separate, distinct, just as a point where many lines cross seems to the mind more definitely a point than one where only two lines cross. But when we stop to think of the history of its physical components, of its long line of ancestors, and the extent to which it embodies the effects of actions of others, it becomes less and less distinct, less and less an individual, more and more a mere point where the crossing lines are more important than the place where they cross. The individual is then a symbol for one or more factors, depending on the breadth of our interest.

Sometimes in everyday work an individual is something absolutely unique, with a special history in every respect. This is usually the sense in which we regard ourselves, and so also our nearest relations, then our friends and associates, then those we occasionally meet, then those we know about, then those we hear about, then those that are in crowds, those represented by statistics, etc. And the farther we push away from ourselves the less the word "individual" means what it means when applied to you and me, and the more it means a spot showing some aspect of the world that commands our attention. Then an individual becomes not a particular man but only a worker, a citizen, an underprivileged man, a soldier, an official, a scientist, a doctor, a politician, an economic man, an executive, a member of an organization.

In this book we mean by the individual a single, unique, independent, isolated, whole thing, embodying innumerable forces and materials past and present which are physical, biological, and social factors. We shall usually not be concerned with how he came to be or why, except as this is directly involved in his relations to organization. When we wish to refer, as we frequently must, to aspects, phases, or functions of individuals, we shall use other words, such as "employee," "member," "contributor," "executive," or otherwise limit our reference.

II

The individual possesses certain properties which are comprehended in the word "person." Usually it will be most convenient if we use the noun "individual" to mean "*one* person" and reserve the adjectival form "personal" to indicate the emphasis on the properties. These are (*a*) activities or behavior, arising from (*b*) psychological factors, to which are added (*c*) the limited power of choice, which results in (*d*) purpose.

(*a*) An important characteristic of individuals is activity; and this in its gross and readily observed aspects is called behavior. Without it there is no individual person.

(*b*) The behavior of individuals we shall say are the result of psychological factors. The phrase "psychological factors" means the combination, resultants, or residues of the physical, biological, and social factors which have determined the history and the present state of the individual in relation to his present environment.

(*c*) Almost universally in practical affairs, and also for most scientific purposes, we grant to persons the power of choice, the capacity of determination, the possession of free will. By our ordinary behavior it is evident that nearly all of us believe in the power of choice as necessary to normal, sane conduct. Hence the idea of free will is inculcated in doctrines of personal responsibility, of moral responsibility, and of legal responsibility. This seems necessary to preserve a sense of personal integrity. It is an induction from experience that the destruction of the sense of personal integrity is the destruction of the power of adaptation, especially to the social aspects of living. We observe that persons who have no sense of ego, who are lacking in self-respect, who believe that what they do or think is unimportant, who have no initiative whatever, are problems, pathological cases, insane, not of this world, *unfitted for coöperation*.

This power of choice, however, is limited. This is necessarily true if what has already been stated is true, namely, that the individual is a region of activities which are the combined effect of physical, biological, and social factors. Free will is limited also, it appears, because the power of choice is paralyzed in human beings if the number of equal opportunities is large. This is an induction from experience. For example, a man set adrift while sleeping in a boat, awaking in a fog in the open sea, free to go in any direction, would be unable at once to choose a direction. Limitation of possibilities is necessary to choice. Finding a reason why something should *not* be done is a common method of deciding what should be done. The processes of decision as we shall see [1] are largely techniques for narrowing choice.

(*d*) The attempt to limit the conditions of choice, so that it is practicable to exercise the capacity of will, is called making or arriving at a "purpose." It is implied usually in the verbs "to try," "to attempt." In this book we are greatly concerned with purposes in relation to organized activities.

It is necessary to impress upon the reader the importance of this statement of the properties of persons. They are fundamental postulates of this book. It will be evident as we proceed, I think, that no construction of the theory of coöperative systems or of organizations, nor any significant interpretation of the behavior of organizations, executives, or others whose efforts are organized, can be made that is not based on *some* position as to the psychological forces of human behavior. There is scarcely a chapter in which those given are not exemplified.

An explicit statement on the question of free will, and certainly an avowed discussion of it, is usually to be found only in philosophic or scientific treatises. I must state my position because it determines the subsequent treatment in many ways.

[1] In Chapter XIV, "The Theory of Opportunism."

For this reason I should also add at this time that the exaggeration in some connections of the power and of the meaning of personal choice are vicious roots not merely of misunderstanding but of false and abortive effort. Often, as I see it, action is based on an assumption that individuals have a power of choice which is not, I think, present. Hence, the failure of individuals to conform is erroneously ascribed to deliberate opposition when they *cannot* conform. When the understanding is more nearly in accordance with the conception of the free will stated above, a part of the effort to determine individual behavior takes the form of altering the conditions of behavior, including a conditioning of the individual by training, by the inculcation of attitudes, by the construction of incentives. This constitutes a large part of the executive process, and is for the most part carried out on the basis of experience and intuition. Failure to recognize this position is among the important sources of error in executive work; it also results in disorganization and in abortive measures of reform, especially in the political field.

The narrow limitations within which choice is a possibility are those which are imposed jointly by physical, biological, and social factors. This is a conclusion from personal experience and direct observation of the behavior of others. It will be well illustrated in what follows. Hence, it may be true to say at the same time that a power of choice is always present and that the person is largely or chiefly a resultant of present and previous physical, biological, and social forces. Nor does this deny that the power of choice is of great importance. Though choice may be limited very narrowly at a given moment, the persistence of repeated choices in a given direction may ultimately greatly change the physical, biological, and social factors of human life. To me it is obvious it has done so.

II. The Treatment of Individuals and Persons in this Study

Conformably to what has been written above, persons are treated in two ways in this book. In this matter we also conform to the ordinary practice of men as seen in their behavior. It is evident that we often regard men from the more nearly universal point of view, as phases, aspects, functions, which are greater spatially or durationally than individuals can be. For example, when we speak of managers, of employees, of voters, of politicians, of customers, etc., we have in mind certain *aspects* of individuals, certain kinds of activities of persons, not the whole individual. At other times we regard them as specific objective entities in discriminating their functional relationship to us or to other larger systems. We take into account the whole of the individual so far as we can. In practice we shift from one point of view to the other, or through rather vague intermediate positions, depending upon the circumstances and our purposes, with amazing skill in some cases; but we become much confused in talking about which point of view applies to our statement. In the latter respect only am I now trying to differ from usual practice.

In this book persons *as participants in specific coöperative systems* are regarded in their purely functional aspects, as phases of coöperation. Their efforts are de-personalized, or, conversely, are socialized, so far as these efforts are coöperative. This will be more specifically justified as a method of procedure in Chapter VI. Second, as *outside* any specific organization, a person is regarded as a unique individualization of physical, biological, and social factors, possessing in limited degree a power of choice. These two aspects are not alternative in time; that is, an individual is not regarded as a function at one time, as a person at another. Rather they are alternative aspects which may simultaneously be present. *Both are always present in coöperative systems.* The selection of one or the other of these aspects is determined by the field of inquiry. When we are considering coöperation as a functioning system of activities of two or more persons, the functional or processive aspect of the person is relevant. When we are considering the person as the *object* of the coöperative functions or process, the second aspect, that of individualization, is most convenient.

As to any given specific coöperative system at a given time, most individuals in a society have no functional relationship in any direct sense.[2] Individuals connected with any given coöperative system have a dual relationship with it — the functional or internal relationship which may be more or less intermittent; and the individual or external relationship which is continuous, not intermittent. In the first aspect, some of the activities of the person are merely a part of a non-personal system of activities; in the second aspect the individual is outside, isolated from, or opposed to the coöperative system. It will be made evident as we proceed that in practical operation as well as in our analysis this dual-aspectual treatment of the individual is recognized and required.

III. The Behavior of Individuals

It will be useful at this place further to consider persons in their individual aspect, as external to any coöperative systems. In this aspect persons choose whether or not they will enter into a specific coöperative system. This choice will be made on the basis of (1) purposes, desires, impulses of the moment, and (2) the alternatives external to the individual recognized by him as available. *Organization results from the modification of the action of the individual through control of or influence upon one of these categories.* Deliberate conscious and specialized control of them is the essence of the executive functions.

We shall call desires, impulses, wants, by the name "motives." They are chiefly resultants of forces in the physical, biological,

[2] See p. 84.

and social environments present and past. In other words, "motives" are constructions for the psychological factors of individuals in the sense previously discussed in this chapter, inferred from action, that is, after the fact. No doubt sometimes what we mean by "imagination" is a factor in the present situation. No doubt also, persons can occasionally be aware of their "motives." But usually what a man wants can be known even to himself only from what he does or tries to do, given an opportunity for selective action.[3]

Motives are usually described in terms of the end sought. If the action of a man is to obtain an apple, we say the motive of the action is to obtain an apple. This is misleading. The motive is rather the satisfaction of a "tension" resulting from various forces; and often we recognize this. We say that "the motive is to satisfy hunger." This is often surmise. The motive may be purely social — to give the apple away; or it may be a means of social action to buy something else. In most cases the end sought or the action taken represents motives of composite origin — social and physiological. This cannot be determined, and is usually unknown to the person whose action is involved. That the motive is of complex origin, however, is often clearly indicated by the importance of the conditions or circumstances which surround the end consciously sought. For example, a boy wants an apple, but it is evident that he wants an apple on the farmer's tree — not one at home or in the store. It is common experience that specific objects sought are often only sought under certain conditions or by certain processes. Of this we may not be aware unless the objects are offered or are available under other conditions or other processes which we reject.

---

[3] I do not necessarily mean by this that in any *specific* situation the motives of men may usually be determined by what they do or say at that time. On the contrary there are many situations in which the motives of men are to be only inferred by (1) what they do and say in this situation; (2) what they have said and done in the past in similar and in dissimilar situations; (3) what they do and say after the situation.

The activities incited by desires, impulses, wants — motives — sometimes result in the attainment of the end sought and satisfaction of the tension. Sometimes they do not so result. But they always have other effects which are not sought. Usually these unsought effects are regarded as incidental, inconsequential and trivial. For example, a man running to catch an animal for food gives off heat energy to the atmosphere, pulverizes a small amount of gravel, tears off a bit of skin, and somewhat increases his need of food while attempting to secure it. At other times consequences not sought for are not regarded as trivial. For example, the man running may move a stone which starts an avalanche which destroys his family, or his dwelling, or his stock of stored food.

IV. Effectiveness and Efficiency in Personal Behavior

The statement in the preceding paragraph is one of facts so obvious that they are neglected. They are among those of first importance in this study. They lead to distinctions in the meanings of the words "effective" and "efficient" both in relation to personal action and to organization action. We shall at this time consider their significance only as respects personal action.

When a specific desired end is attained we shall say that the action is "effective." When the unsought consequences of the action are more important than the attainment of the desired end and are dissatisfactory, effective action, we shall say, is "inefficient." When the unsought consequences are unimportant or trivial, the action is "efficient." Moreover, it sometimes happens that the end sought is not attained, but the unsought consequences satisfy desires or motives not the "cause" of the action. We shall then regard such action as efficient but not effective. In retrospect the action in this case is justified not by the results sought but by those not sought. These observations are matters of common personal experience.

Accordingly we shall say that an action is effective if it accomplishes its specific objective aim. We shall also say it is efficient if it satisfies the motives of that aim, whether it is effective or not, and the process does not create offsetting dissatisfactions. We shall say that an action is inefficient if the motives are not satisfied, or offsetting dissatisfactions are incurred, even if it is effective. This often occurs; we find we do not want what we thought we wanted.

The specific ends sought by men are of two kinds, physical and social. Physical ends are material objects and physical conditions,[4] such as warm air, light, shade, etc. They are found in a "purely" physical environment. They are often found also in conjunction with a social environment. Social ends are contact, interrelations, communication, with other men. Such ends usually must be sought in a general social environment and always in some specific physical environment. Hence, whatever the specific ends, they serve to satisfy complex motives of persons. Usually a specific end of a physical class involves social consequences not sought. Always a social end involves physical consequences not sought.

The actions through which ends are sought are always physical (or physiological); they may also be social. In either case they involve unsought consequences that may give satisfaction or dissatisfaction. Social processes are those in which the action is a part of the system of actions of two or more men. Its most common form is verbal communication.

In accordance with the above we may say that the motives of men who enter into coöperation are almost invariably composite physiological and social motives in the sense that they are at least socially and physiologically conditioned. They may

[4] Including living things. Usually in this book we do not discriminate between biological and physical factors except with reference to the human being.

be predominantly physiological or predominantly social, but usually neither influence may be safely regarded as predominant.

In this chapter I have attempted to state the position essential to the conceptual scheme developed in this book as the means of presenting a theory of organization and a significant description of the executive processes. On the one side, those philosophies that explain human conduct as a presentation of universal forces, that regard the individual as merely responsive, that deny freedom of choice or of will, that make of organization and socialism the basic position, are found to rest upon facts that are widely observed and that govern men's behavior and thought in social situations. On the other side, those philosophies that grant freedom of choice and of will, that make of the individual an independent entity, that depress the physical and social environment to a secondary and accessory condition, are also consistent with other facts of behavior and thought. I undertake no reconciliation of the opposition in these philosophies or whatever scientific theories they may rest upon. For the present, at least, the development of a convenient and useful theory of coöperative systems and of organization, and an effective understanding of the executive processes, require the acceptance of both positions as describing aspects of social phenomena. What, then, is needed for our purposes is to state under what conditions, in what connections, or for what purposes one or the other of these positions may be adopted usefully, and to show how they may be regarded as simultaneously applicable. Coöperation and organization as they are observed and experienced are concrete syntheses of opposed facts, and of opposed thought and emotions of human beings. It is precisely the function of the executive to facilitate the synthesis in concrete action of contradictory forces, to reconcile conflicting forces, instincts, interests, conditions, positions, and ideals.

CHAPTER III

PHYSICAL AND BIOLOGICAL LIMITATIONS
IN COOPERATIVE SYSTEMS

THE most common implication of the philosophy of individualism, of choice and free will, lies in the word "purpose." The most common expression of the opposite philosophy of determination, behaviorism, socialism, is "limitations." Out of the existence, or belief in the existence, of purposes of individuals and the experience of limitations arises coöperation to accomplish purposes and overcome limitations. The concrete processes involved are in industries called "technologies," in the professions "techniques," in organizations "practices" and "institutions," in religions "rituals," and in private conduct "adaptable behavior," "*savoir faire*," "selection of appropriate means to ends."

All of us understand some of these processes, and are interested in a few of them. None of us understand or are interested in many of them. Whole careers are spent in the mastery of a few special techniques, and in some aspects these are frequently matters of elaborate exposition. The general significance of these processes, however, especially in relation to individual and organization behavior, appears not to have been developed. It is now necessary to reduce these processes to a few principal considerations which are essential to understanding the reasons for coöperation, the instability of organization, and the function of decision in executive work. This will be undertaken here as a convenience in reading the whole book, notwithstanding that to do so may initially appear in some respects to state merely the obvious and in other respects to become unnecessarily didactic.

The questions which we ask ourselves are straightforward, simple, direct, easy to ask — but difficult to answer. They are: I, Why or when is coöperation effective? II, What are the objects of coöperative processes? III, What are the limitations of coöperation? IV, What are the causes of instability in coöperative systems? V, What effect has coöperation upon the ends sought?

The answers to these questions in this chapter are developed, for purposes of simplicity, on the assumption that only biological and physical factors are present, reserving for later consideration social factors. This requires the treating of human beings somewhat as automatons which we manipulate. We assign them their purposes, and grant them no sentiments of satisfaction.

I

If we eliminate from consideration personal satisfactions, and assign to individuals purposes that represent essentially biological needs, their coöperation has no reason for being except as it can do what the individual cannot do. Coöperation justifies itself, then, as a means of overcoming the limitations restricting what individuals can do. Therefore, we should first consider what in general are their limitations.

At once we note that the limitations of the accomplishment of a purpose are the joint effect of two classes of factors: (1) the biological faculties or capacities of individuals; and (2) the physical factors of the environment. We should carefully observe the emphasis upon "joint." A limitation is a function of the *total* situation viewed from the standpoint of a purpose. Without the purpose given there is no significance to the word "limitation" in this context; and a limitation stated as applicable to a factor can only be described in terms of the other factors. For example, take the simple case of a stone too large for a man to move. This may be stated as "stone too large for man" or as "man too small for stone." In the first expression we say that the limitation lies in the physical environment of the man; in the other we state that the limitation lies in the biological powers of the man; but clearly the limitation is in the total situation. It can only be conveniently expressed, however, as a limitation of one factor in conjunction with the other. The alternative expressions are equally good. The choice will generally fall in concrete situations on that 'factor, described as "limiting," which appears to our minds to be alterable; but it is apparent that in general a change in any factor may be sufficient so to change the total situation that the limitation disappears.

Now it is apparent that what an isolated man would recognize as limitations lie generally in the physical environment, since his powers are not greatly variable. He will therefore operate on the environment if it limits the attainment of purpose. Biological powers are set to work to overcome the limitation by changing a physical factor of the situation. The reasons that they apparently lie in the environment are that only in the cases where a purpose is seen to be *possible* of accomplishment are limitations recognized, and that in those cases where a change of biological powers would be effective, the possibilities are intuitively. rejected. Overcoming a limitation is a means to an end; when the limitation cannot be overcome the end must be dropped.

As compared with many animals the power of a man to attain ends by the alteration of physical factors of the environment is considerable, though not greater than that of some animals. For the most part, however, individual adaptation consists of restricting major purposes to the elemental and detailed purposes, to the choice of easily available alternatives. If we regard the physical factors of the environment generally as fixed, this may then be regarded as due to the biological characteristics of men. Their powers are restricted.

It is an obvious fact of general observation that the biological powers of two or more men working together exceed in some respects and under some conditions those of individuals. This *to the extent it is believed to be true* may at once transfer the limiting factor from the physical to the biological field. Something cannot be done either because of physical limitations or biological limitations. What may be impossible without aid may be possible with aid. Hence, when biological powers are regarded as the limiting factor, and it is believed that by coöperation these limitations can be overcome, *then* the limiting factor becomes coöperation itself. If it proves not possible to secure coöperation (which happens on innumerable occasions in one's personal experience) then a physical condition reverts to its original position as to the limiting factor; and if it cannot be overcome a purpose is abandoned.

Thus, at what we may call the primary stage, purposes, regarded as within the possibility of accomplishment (as a matter of intuition, common sense, experience), encounter physical limitations. Accomplishment is then possible by two routes involving simple series of successive limitations, as follows:

SERIES 1	SERIES 2
When possibility of coöperation is not recognized	*When coöperation is recognized as possible*
a. Discrimination of a physical limitation to be overcome by personal action.	a. Discrimination of a physical limitation.
	b. Alternative discrimination of a biological limitation.
	c. Recognition of a coöperative limitation.
	d. Physical limitation to be overcome by coöperative action.

It will be well to repeat that in this chapter we are leaving out of account social factors, and therefore any purpose which is social in character (except coöperation, which is treated for the present somewhat as a mechanical combination). Then the purposes will depend upon the recognition of the availability of means. Coöperation as a means will be contemplated on the basis of experience; but experience shows that while coöperation often succeeds, it also and perhaps more often fails.

Since coöperation, in its primary state, is effective when it overcomes or circumvents a biological limitation of individuals, the first step in the answer to our question as to why or when coöperation is effective requires consideration of the powers of individuals, and the conditions under which coöperative combination of them is effective. It will be convenient to approach the matter from the negative side, that is, to answer the question "why or when is coöperation ineffective?" The reasons for ineffectiveness may be summarized as follows: (1) The possible degree of effectiveness of combination of any human powers is under most favorable circumstances small. (2) The individual operates as a whole, using all his faculties or abilities in combination. Circumstances favorable to combination in respect of one power are unfavorable as respects others. Accordingly, combination always involves disadvantages which may offset advantages, if any. (3) Items 1 and 2 imply, as experience and observation easily confirm, that in all except the most favorable circumstances effectiveness, if possible, depends upon an ordered combination of personal efforts. The ordering required is a matter of discovery or of invention.[1] Ordinary experience and the history of science, invention, and discovery suggest that discoveries and inventions are to be expected rarely except in an elaborate society. In general, this ordering is a matter of devising the scheme of specializations of effort and function. It will be presented in Chapter X, "The Bases and Kinds of Specialization."

---

[1] I have left out of account here learning, which implies teaching and imitation, because they involve both social factors and more complex situations than those with which we are now concerned.

The following is now desirable to support and illustrate items 1 and 2.

The biological limitations of human beings as respects adaptation to the physical environment may be grouped into the following three classes: (*a*) those relating to the application of human energy to the environment in pushing, pulling, lifting, lowering, grasping, resisting objects and forces; (*b*) those relating to perception; and (*c*) those relating to the understanding of, or response to, the environment — continuously effective conduct depends upon adopting purposes or making decisions that *can* be effected.

Translating these limitations into terms of "faculties" or "abilities" of individuals, we may list for attention the following: mechanical power, mechanical adaptation, sensory ability, perceptive capacity, memory, imagination, capacity of choosing. The inquiry is then narrowed to the question, "Under what conditions and why is coöperative effort effective in overcoming individual limitations in respect to these faculties?"

(*a*) Let us take first the common case of applying energy mechanically. Effective coöperation in this respect means that the ability of the group exceeds the ability of an individual.[2] There are several quite different types of cases. The most numerous cases are those in which coöperation is effective by reason of the *power factor*. The simplest are those where a higher concentration of power than the individual possesses is required against one object; for example, moving a stone too

---

[2] It is to be noted that the comparison is not between group effectiveness and the aggregate of the effectiveness of individuals operating singly. When the question is one of group accomplishments compared with the aggregate of individual accomplishments of the same persons, efficiency, not effectiveness, is the point under determination. But when merely the overcoming of limitations is concerned, the thing done effectively by coöperation cannot be done by the individual at all. The point involves the meaning of "economical" and is discussed in Chapter XVI, "The Executive Process," and also in Chapter V.

large for one man to move. More complex cases are those where work must be done at different points simultaneously. Much work depends upon its being done quickly, because forces in the environment are tending to undo what has been accomplished even while the work is in process. Hence the *speed of work* must be more than sufficient to offset these opposing forces.

Again there are conditions where the effort of individuals is sufficient, but their *endurance* is not, and work once started must be completed; for example, when hay is cut and must be stacked before nightfall because of impending rain, or where artillery or supplies must be moved within time limits.

Cases in which the power and speed factors are predominant are obviously those where the coöperative principle is that of simultaneity of effort. There are other cases, however, where work may be described as contemporary or simultaneous, where the power required is small — perhaps less than that of one man — and speed is not involved. In these cases the superiority of *mechanical adaptation* is in point, arising from the mechanical limitations of the human being; for example, his height or length of arm or number of fingers is strictly limited, even though his power is sufficient.

Thus contemporaneous coöperation may be effective where the power factor, the endurance factor, speed of performance, or mechanical adaptation in the group is superior to the corresponding factor in the individual. However, *continuity* rather than simultaneity of effort is required under many conditions. A man alone may not be able to move a ball up an inclined plane or the side of a hill because he is unable to exert continuously the energy necessary — without rest or without shift of position, neither effectively possible because the ball will roll backwards in the interval of rest or shift. In such a case two or more men are necessary.

Even in "pure" cases, without any regard to efficiency, it must be evident that it requires considerable ingenuity to make such coöperation successful. Conflicts of principles are constantly present. Thus bringing together enough men to give adequate power often introduces difficulties of mechanical adaptation — enough men do not have sufficient room to work, making necessary the selection of strong men as against weak. Or simultaneity of operations at once raises questions of dependability and control. But in fact "pure" cases are probably infrequent. The work to be done is complex in practice, power being requisite at one time, speed at another, mechanical adaptation at another, continuity of effort at another, and so on. Entirely aside from the question of economy, it is usually not easily possible to secure precisely the coöperative group adapted to a particular task, so that in practice a working group will be well adapted for one part of the task, less so for another part, not at all for the next, positively ill-adapted for the next, and so on. Hence, the very process which produces effectiveness in one respect is usually also a cause of ineffectiveness in another.

(b) Coöperation in the application of physical energy, by individuals, of course, is not possible without coöperation of sense organs and in perception. Not only do virtually all other aspects of coöperation depend upon it, but in a wide range of circumstances it affords possibilities advantageously to expand the powers of the group beyond those of individuals. These possibilities relate to several different types of coöperation, some where the emphasis is upon contemporaneous, others upon progressive, perception.

It will be desirable, for brevity and as sufficiently illustrating the essential considerations, to confine our discussion to visual perception. The factors of coöperation are here entirely different from those which we have previously discussed. The cases of contemporaneous coöperative observations are of two principle classes. In the first, the things or events to be observed are *inside* the area bounded by lines drawn between the positions of the observers. The thing observed is more or less centrally located. The differences in position permit the individuals as a group to see the object from all sides at once. This is an important factor in many kinds of observation, of which perhaps the most common is that of men working on machines where movements or adjustments cannot be seen adequately from one position.

The second type of case is the converse of the first. In it the object of observation is *outside* the area bounded by lines joining the positions of observers, so that the observers are more or less centrally located. This accomplishes a great expansion of the range of observations, increasing speed or certainty of detection. A simple example is lookout duty. Between these extreme types there are innumerable combinations in which either speed, range, accuracy, or completeness of observation is the test of superior effectiveness.

When these types of coöperation are effective it is because of the limitations of sense organs and of restricted range of positions which an individual can occupy in a short period of time. In some cases, however, the individual limitation is of endurance of attention. Thus progressive coöperation is required where one person cannot observe a field or a continuing event beyond a limited period and much longer observation is necessary.

(*c*) Obvious as the effectiveness of coöperative observation is under some simple conditions, the offsetting difficulties are great, especially under more complex conditions where the interpretation of mere sight and the verbalization of observation are necessary. Most of the less simple observations require experience to detect the significant, and technical accomplishment to convey it. Thus of what the eye sees in the photographic sense only a part will be perceived, and a smaller part conveyed by abstraction in speech; and the results in error of understanding may be very great. Hence, much important coöperative observation is ineffective except by specially experienced and trained observers, or under a technique derived from experience and invention; that is, it is ineffective if general social factors are excluded. This, I imagine, is so much a matter of everyday experience that it requires no further comment.

The type of analysis just applied is presumably and theoretically applicable to other capacities or faculties which may be found in coöperation; for example, memory, imagination, thought, judgment, decision, determination. In practice, a complete analysis in these respects is hardly possible in the present stage of development of psychology.[3] Nevertheless, that this view is not incorrect is borne out, I think, by the fact that we have numerous specialized organizations whose chief function is coöperation in one or another of these capacities applied in a particular field. Thus we have organizations specialized in manual (unskilled) labor; in observation, as in much marine (and wireless) operation, in biological laboratories, in photography and spectrography, in astronomy; in thinking, as in mathematical work and in army staffs; in imagination, as in much architectural work; in memory, as in historical and accounting work; and in determination, as in the leadership of revolutionary movements and propaganda.

Hence, even under simple conditions, effectiveness of coöperation depends upon adaptation of process in accordance with several quite different principles. To be successful the method must pass a complex of tests. Since ideal conditions are rare, usually ineffective results in one respect must be tolerated to secure desirable results in another respect; but in many cases no net effectiveness can be secured. Even from the limited standpoint of effectiveness, the difficulties of coöperation are evident,

[3] See, however, Chapter XIII, "The Environment of Decision," and Chapter XIV, "The Theory of Opportunism," where coöperative practice in judgment and decision are explained.

and small changes of environment may easily destroy a successful method.

II

The objects of the simplest types of coöperation are similar to the objects of individual action; hence the illusion [4] that the motives of coöperative action are personal. But with very little elaboration of coöperative institutions it will be seen that the objects of coöperative effort change in kind and quality, and that some objects are not susceptible of individual action.

Still leaving out of account social purposes, the objects of individual action are changes in the physical environment recognized as limiting the accomplishment of purposes. These purposes are immediate or remote. When they are remote they involve action upon the present environment intended to facilitate future accomplishments. Remote purposes are of four kinds: (1) those which require a change in the environment deemed convenient for future action, such as removing a stone from a path that is expected to be used; (2) those which require a change which is expected to *develop* a future utility, such as the planting of seed; (3) those which require a change of location of usable material for future use, such as the storing of food; and (4) those which involve the shaping of materials to supplement or make later more effective the biological powers, such as making a club.

These types of roundabout action for remote purposes are all found in coöperative effort, but when coöperative they lose their personal character. Personal purposes cannot be satisfied through coöperative action except as there comes into the action an intermediate process.

This process is distributive. Whatever is accomplished by coöperative action may or may not be distributed to participants in the coöperation. It is frequently never directly distributed,

[4] Discussed in Chapter VII, pp. 88–89.

and rarely all distributed. Moreover there is and can be no direct causal relationship between individual efforts constituting a part of a coöperative system of efforts and either the whole coöperative product or any distributed part of it.[5] In addition two other types of action come into play in coöperative systems that are absent from individual action. One type is that intended to *facilitate* coöperation itself; the second is that intended to *maintain* the coöperative system, for example, the making of anything which can only be useful to a coöperative system, such as a boat too large for one man to use, or the accumulation of material for coöperative operations. In modern economic language the first is largely fixed capital, the second largely working capital.

Such terms are hardly applicable to the results of individual action for remote purposes. Everything that an individual does is for consumption, even though the latter be delayed. It would be a forcing of language for purposes of analogy to give to the objects of individual action listed in the second paragraph of this section such names as (1) capital improvement; (2) agricultural capital; (3) working capital; and (4) equipment or fixed capital. Such concepts become useful only in connection with coöperative systems.

Still confining ourselves to physical operations but turning now to coöperative systems and regarding them as quasi-mechanical systems, we may classify their activities as follows: (*a*) activities to secure consumers' goods; (*b*) activities to distribute consumers' goods; (*c*) activities to secure coöperative equipment; (*d*) activities to secure working capital.

It is apparent that these activities are in mutual dependence, and that the precise combination depends upon the specific conditions for a particular coöperative system. In very simple systems, under favorable conditions, activities *b*, *c*, and *d* are

[5] This is discussed extensively and illustrated in Chapter XVI, "The Executive Process."

minor or negligible; but as I hope has been made evident, the possibilities of effective coöperation are extremely limited for such conditions. We do not ordinarily recognize this truth because most of the systems that we call simple systems of coöperation are in fact interrelated with large complex systems taken for granted; that is, in our simplest systems usually tools made by others, training, education, are all underlying or prior conditions and are themselves coöperative products. Coöperation does not become generally effective (leaving out social factors) until highly developed. "Highly developed" means that elaborate devices for overcoming coöperatively individual biological limitations are present — such as iron levers, wheels, transportation and communication systems, microscopes, machines, etc.

Thus, to become highly effective, coöperation involves activities b, c, and d — to distribute consumers' goods, to secure coöperative equipment, and to secure working capital — until they may become greater in volume than activities a, to secure consumers' goods. This is a familiar situation to those conversant with one of our most effective instrumentalities, engines, in even the most efficient of which the losses of energy through internal friction and heat transfer are much greater than the energy actually converted to useful work.

Thus, assuming discovery and invention of useful coöperative devices (itself a form of activity in the highly developed systems), there is required an accumulation of materials (activities d) before the discoveries or inventions are possible in concrete working form. This, of course, introduces activities of class b, since all the activities, not being of class a, do not make products easily available.

Hence, coöperation once established, the focus of attention alternates among all classes of activities. Each in turn becomes the center of the limitations of the moment or the limiting factors in the situation.

III

It could be assumed that, once established, the alternatives of attention just referred to would be unnecessary unless a desire for progress were present, so that successful systems of coöperation could be considered stable. But whatever other reasons may be present (chiefly of social character), the instability of the physical environment makes such a conception untenable. The conditions of the environment — weather for example — are constantly changing the limitations of the environment with respect to coöperative action. Coöperation is subject in this respect to the same limitations as individuals. The ensuing adjustments that are required in the case of coöperation are unlike the corresponding adjustments of individuals, which are physiological. Adjustments of coöperative systems are adjustments in the balance of the various types of organizational activities. The capacity for making these adjustments is a limiting factor of another kind. Out of this fact develop in such systems adjustment processes and special organs, specialized aspects of the activities designed to maintain coöperation; for if coöperation can not adjust to attack new limitations in the environment it must fail. These adjustment processes become management processes, and the specialized organs are executives and executive organizations. Hence, such processes and organs become in their turn the limitations of coöperation. Barring extraordinary cataclysms, they are in fact the most important limitations in most, and especially in complex, coöperative systems.

IV and V

Instability, however, comes not merely from the changes of the physical environment and from the uncertainty of the adjustment and managerial processes within coöperative systems, but also from the alteration of the character of purposes of action with change of possibilities. This has already been alluded to as respects individuals.[6] As each new limitation is overcome (or conversely with each new failure), new purposes appear or old purposes are abandoned. This is so much a matter of personal experience and common observation that it seems to warrant no further discussion. It should be emphasized that it seems inherent in the conception of free will in a changing environment that the number and range of purposes will expand with the development of coöperation. This expansion of the number or variety of purposes constitutes in itself a factor of instability in coöperation, and probably an increasing one as coöperation develops and becomes more complex.

In this chapter I have attempted to bring out the most elementary aspects of coöperation under conditions of artificial simplicity in which social factors are excluded and a system of coöperation is treated as a quasi-mechanical process. Even so simplified, it appears that there is no meaning to "limitations" and "limiting factor" except a purpose be given. A limitation is a function of the total situation, but must be assigned for operational action to that factor or set of factors which is recognized to be alterable. The primary step in coöperation is to envisage biological characteristics of individuals as limitations which can be overcome by coöperation. To do this we must recognize separate faculties or abilities of individuals. The possibilities of overcoming the limitations of any one faculty by direct coöperation are restricted, especially since faculties are employed in conjunction with each other while conditions favorable to coöperation in one respect may be unfavorable in other respects. In coöperation the objective of action is necessarily removed from the individual, requiring a new form of activities, those of distribution. The ends of coöperative action are of several kinds which are mutually dependent, so that each type of action becomes in turn a limiting

[6] Page 24, above.

condition of coöperation. Systems of coöperation are never stable, because of changes in the environment and the evolution of new purposes. Some of the limitations in coöperation are similar to those of individuals, with additional limitations of an internal character peculiar to coöperation. Finally, adjustment of coöperative systems to changing conditions or new purposes implies special management processes and, in complex coöperation, special organs known as executives or executive organizations.

Into this simplified background of exposition we must now introduce the complexity of the social factors.

CHAPTER IV

PSYCHOLOGICAL AND SOCIAL FACTORS IN SYSTEMS OF COOPERATION

COOPERATIVE systems were discussed in the preceding chapter with psychological and social factors excluded. In all actual coöperative systems, however, factors thus excluded are always present. In this chapter it will be desirable to say what we mean by psychological factors and to discuss those social factors which are peculiarly and directly involved in coöperative systems, so that in Chapter V the principles of coöperative action as observed in actual situations may be set forth.

In Chapter II the psychological factors were defined as combinations, resultants, or residues of physical, biological, and social factors in the behavior of individuals. We imputed to the individual the capacity of experience. This is to say that these factors as they have operated through past time have, jointly, effects upon present behavior. In one aspect these may be given the name "memory," in a broad sense of the word with the emphasis upon these effects. In another aspect the phenomenon may be called "conditioning," in which emphasis is laid upon the process by which the factors are thus effective.

We also imputed to the individual the restricted but important capacity of choice. The restriction or limitations necessary to and within which choice must be exercised are experience — memory or previous conditioning — and the physical, biological, and social factors in the present situation at any given time. This power of choice assigns a meaning to "adaptation" in reference to human behavior that makes it something more than mere "response" to present conditions.

I

The imputation of experience and choice in the individual require two appraisals of him in every situation in which other individuals are implicated. The first appraisal is concerned with the individual's *powers* in the situation. The second appraisal is concerned with his *determination* or volition within the limits set by his powers. In the millions of interactions that daily take place between men these appraisals are not separate in any observable way in most cases. Nevertheless they are so discriminated and separately expressed in numerous instances. The expressions of the first appraisal will be the answers to such questions as these: "Who is he?" "What kind of man is he?" "What can he do?" The second appraisal is expressed in answer to such questions as: "What does he want?" "What is he trying to do?" "What will he do?"

These two appraisals implicit in human relations affect the behavior of persons in two ways in matters of purposeful conduct. What actually may be done by one person to establish satisfactory relationships with another person may be approached either by the attempt to *narrow the limitations* of the second person's choice, or to *expand the opportunities* of his choice. In the first case attempt is made either to change the external situation or to change the person's "state of mind," that is, to restrict either the possibilities or his desires. For example, in a relationship of hostility a man may put an object such as a table between himself and his adversary, thereby restricting the latter's movements, or he may say something that diverts his adversary's attention, thereby changing his "state of mind." These actions restrict or condition the power of choice. In the second case he may put money on the table, thus adding to the alternatives available to his adversary and expanding his power of choice. The equivalent in principle of these processes may be everywhere observed when two or more persons are present.

These two appraisals and the processes related to them suggest that behavior with reference to other persons either takes the form of regarding such persons as *objects* to be *manipulated* by changing the factors affecting them, or as *subjects* to be *satisfied*. In the first case, persons are regarded as functions of continuing processes; in the second, as absolute and independent, at the moment. In either of these cases the treatment is of an individual, isolated from the social situation. In either case he is regarded as a whole; but in the first case approach is to that whole indirectly through operation upon particular external factors, while in the second the approach is to the whole directly, in which all external factors except those of the approach are regarded as given and embodied in the individual or treated as irrelevant. In both cases social factors are included, but they are merged inseparably with others and are only to be distinguished for purposes of analysis. Thus in the terminology we adopt there are no distinguishable social factors operating *from within* the individual *to* the coöperative system; but social factors operate *upon* the individual from a coöperative system as well as from other social relationships.

II

The only social factors which we need to discuss at present are the following: (*a*) the interactions between individuals within a coöperative system; (*b*) the interactions between the individual and the group; (*c*) the individual as the object of coöperative influence; (*d*) social purpose and the effectiveness of coöperation; (*e*) individual motives and coöperative efficiency.

(*a*) When the individual has become associated with a coöperative enterprise he has accepted a position of contact with others similarly associated. From this contact there must arise interactions between these persons individually, and these interactions are social. It may be, and often is, true that these interactions are not a purpose or object either of the coöperative systems or of the individuals participating in them. They nevertheless *cannot be avoided*. Hence, though not sought, such interactions are consequences of coöperation, and constitute one set of social factors involved in coöperation.

These factors operate on the individuals affected; and, in conjunction with other factors, become incorporated in their mental and emotional characters. This is an effect which makes them significant. Hence, coöperation compels changes in the motives of individuals which otherwise would not take place. So far as these changes are in a direction favorable to the coöperative system they are resources to it. So far as they are in a direction unfavorable to coöperation, they are detriments to it or limitations of it.

This is a matter of common observation. Interactions of an unfavorable character may be described as resulting in "incompatibility," which tends to be destructive of coöperation. The reverse condition is compatibility and usually is one condition of coöperation.

(*b*) The interactions encountered in coöperation are not merely between individuals in pairs, but also between individuals and groups. The group can be regarded in this connection in two senses. In the first sense, the group is merely a term for the combined effects of the interactions on the psychology of an individual, A, who is in contact with B, C, D, etc.; in this sense the interactions are included with those discussed in section *a* above. In the second sense, however, the one to which emphasis is given here, the group is a unit with which the individual has interactions, also called social, in that the unit is something more or different from the mere sum of the interactions between the individuals composing it. In this sense the group presents a *system* of social action which *as a whole* interacts with each individual within its scope.

The factors involved in the group relationships in this sense operate on the individual psychology in conjunction with other factors. Hence, the group compels changes in the psychological character of the individual and, therefore, in the motives of individuals, which otherwise would not take place. So far as these changes are in a direction favorable to the coöperative system, the group is a resource. So far as they are unfavorable, the group is a limitation.

The group factors probably are as inescapable in a coöperative system as are those arising from the interaction between individuals, and in many cases they are very important.

(*c*) The social factors just discussed are chiefly not consciously perceived and are non-logical;[1] the relationships are informal and as a whole not deliberate; but a coöperative system may also have a conscious and deliberate relationship to an individual. This relationship has two aspects: first, that of taking specific action to bring the individual within the coöperative system; and second, that of controlling his actions within that system.[2] The first aspect has for its central point a direct appeal to the will of the individual; it is a matter of inducement or coercion. The second relates entirely to the action of the individual as within and as a function of a system of actions. In both aspects, it is clear, effects on the minds and emotions of individuals are inescapable. If these effects are adverse to the continuance of coöperation, the processes to that extent are limitations on coöperation as a continuing enterprise.

(*d*) A formal system of coöperation requires an objective, a purpose, an aim. Such an objective is itself a product of co-

---

[1] This does not mean that there are no conscious logical acts involved.

[2] See Chapter XI, "The Economy of Incentives," and Chapter XII, "The Theory of Authority."

operation and expresses a coöperative discrimination of factors upon which action is to be taken by the coöperative system. It is important to note the complete distinction between the aim of a coöperative effort and that of an individual. Even in the case where a man enlists the aid of other men to do something which he cannot do alone, such as moving a stone, the objective ceases to be personal. It is an objective of the group efforts, from the results of which satisfactions accrue to the members of the group. In most cases, as we shall see, there is no danger of confusion of personal with coöperative aim — the objective obviously could not be personal.[3]

When the purpose of a system of coöperation is attained, we say that the coöperation was effective; if not attained, ineffective. In some cases, of course, no degrees of effectiveness may be recognized — either the objective is completely accomplished or it is not accomplished at all; but in most instances this is not the case and the aim is subject to accomplishment in various degrees. In any event the adequacy of the degree of effectiveness is to be determined from the point of view of the coöperative system; the personal point of view has no pertinence here. It follows that the effectiveness of the effort of an individual in coöperation has two meanings. First, it has reference to the relation of the specific effort to the coöperative result; it is then to be judged from the coöperative point of view with reference to its bearing on the attainment of the coöperative purpose. Second, it has reference to its status as one of an individual's chain of efforts contributed to the coöperative system as a means of satisfying his personal motives; its effectiveness from this point of view is quite a different thing. Usually when coöperation is concerned, effectiveness of a component effort is determined from the coöperative point of view. The personal point of view has no direct relevance.

(e) The situation is quite different as respects efficiency.

[3] This is discussed in Chapter VII, pp. 88 ff.

Coöperative efficiency is the resultant of individual efficiencies, since coöperation is entered into only to satisfy individual motives. The aggregate of the motives of those participating is the total motivation of the coöperative system. It is a complex made up of individual motives that may be highly diverse in character. The efficiency of the coöperative action is the degree to which these motives are satisfied. The only determinant of this efficiency is the individual, since motives are individual. If a person concludes that his action in contributing to the coöperative system is (or would be) inefficient, he ceases (or withholds) that action. If his contribution is essential to the system, then inefficiency as to him is inefficiency of the system, since it cannot continue and therefore must be inefficient to all. Hence, the efficiency of a system of coöperative effort is dependent upon the efficiency of the marginal contribution, or is determined by the marginal contributor. This means that the only measure of the efficiency of a coöperative system is its capacity to survive.

It has already been noted that all purposeful actions of individuals produce consequences not sought for; and that these consequences may result in satisfactions or dissatisfactions whether or not the end sought is attained. This is true of the action of *contributing* to a coöperative system. It inevitably involves consequences which were not the active inducement to that contribution; as a result, motives may be satisfied even though the specific end sought is not attained; and dissatisfactions may arise that are controlling even though the end sought is attained. The principal satisfactions or dissatisfactions arising from participation in coöperation, other than the attainment of a specific end, are social, that is, the result of the personal interactions involved.

Similarly, the coöperative action to achieve a coöperative purpose or objective necessarily as a whole involves consequences not sought for. When the objective is a physical result, such as moving a stone, the unsought-for consequences include those which are social in character. When the objective is social, the unsought-for consequences include physical results. The efficiency of coöperation, like efficiency of individual action, often depends upon the satisfactions and dissatisfactions incident to the process of attaining concrete ends.

The most important general consequence of coöperation, rarely sought for and only occasionally recognized while in process, is the social conditioning of all who participate and often of those who do not. In this way the motives of men are constantly being modified by coöperation, which is itself thereby altered as are the factors of efficiency.

It may be concluded from what has been stated in this chapter that social factors are always present in coöperation, both because of the nature of such a system and because of the effect of social experience upon individuals and their motives. Indeed, the desire of individuals to coöperate, which as to singular individuals is a psychological fact, is as to systems of coöperation a social fact. Conversely, the satisfactions derived from coöperation, which are as to the individual psychological facts, are from the point of view of coöperative systems social effects of coöperation, and they determine coöperation itself.

CHAPTER V

THE PRINCIPLES OF COOPERATIVE ACTION

THERE are no coöperative systems in which physical, biological, personal, and social elements or factors are not all present. In this chapter I shall first give four illustrations of this fact, which will also illustrate a number of the propositions previously presented, in the settings of concrete coöperative situations. With these illustrations in mind, and on the basis of the previous chapters, I shall then focus the attention upon a few generalizations of the first importance; and finally I shall restate in condensed form the principal understandings derived from Part I with which we enter, in Part II, upon the construction of a theory of organization.

I

Often the necessity of operating concretely with regard to one factor or another conceals from us in ordinary thinking the fact that all coöperative action is a synthesis of diverse factors, physical, biological, and social, and affects a total situation in which these factors are all present. To make this as clear as possible is the purpose of the following illustrations:

(a) The most universal form of human coöperation, and perhaps the most complex, is speech. Speech is a physical event; it requires physical energy, converted into sound waves, transmitted in a material medium, limited by physical conditions of the environment. Speech is also a biological act, something done by living beings; it requires lungs, larynx, nose, tongue, teeth, lips, and a nervous system; it also requires ears, etc. Speech is also a social phenomenon; it can only be learned by social contact. It has no use except in a social situation; words have no meaning except in a social usage.

Speech as a coöperative activity ceases to exist if any one of these factors fails. If the wind blows too hard speech ceases. If paralysis, removal of larynx, or death takes place, speech ceases. Also, if there is total deafness speech ceases (except for special methods) or the capacity for speech does not develop. If there is no society, or if the conventional language is not known, there is no speech.

The event to which we give the name speech is an event having inseparable components, physical, biological, social. The event takes place whether we give it a name or not — a child does not. It is an event arising out of or within a total situation that is physical, biological, social. And we know it as an event not merely because we may hear it but also because it produces reactions, changes in the total situation. "See what you are doing" produces action. It changes physical history, biological history, social history. None of these components can be abstracted from the event either in its origin, its process, or its effects, and still leave the event. It is a whole system. It includes many parts that are unknown and for that reason not comprehended in the name we give it. It is possible that all of its physical components are not known; it is certain that all of its biological components are not known; it is still more certain that all of its social components are not known. But it takes place nevertheless, and the conduct of men is affected thereby. That can be observed.[1]

The character of events called speech can be altered by purposive effort. This is now done on an elaborate and complex scale, but it is done only by operations on the components. The only way to affect the whole is by effort applied to the part. We may change the physical conditions. We may remove or bring nearer the communicants, we may introduce electrical waves and electrical apparatus. We may speak louder, or

[1] Cf. Arthur F. Bentley, *Behavior Knowledge Fact* (The Principia Press, Inc., 1935), pp. 146 ff.

softer. We may develop new meanings or new words socially. These are operations intended to overcome limitations imposed by one set of factors or another. Similarly, if we wish to operate on a ball in a given location we can usually only do so by an operation on some part of it. We affect the whole through the part.

(*b*) India is a country inhabited by many millions of persons in a society made up of numerous coöperative systems of which the most important are families. The individuals are biological units requiring food. They are so constituted that they can digest the meat of cattle. The land and the climate permit the raising of cattle. But there is a social force expressed as a controlling aversion to the eating of meat. This social force affects in an important degree the motives, hence conduct, arising from biological needs. This affects the character of the cultivation of the soil and therefore the character of the topographical environment. It may even affect the climate. Specific climatic conditions are said to be in other places a "result" of social coöperation — the increase of rainfall in Australia, the lowering of temperatures in winter in Georgia from the colonization of Alberta.

In India it is evident that both the physical and the biological factors (life and death as affected by famines) are inseparably involved in a social factor. If this situation as a whole is to be attacked it would seem to require action as respects that factor.

(*c*) A house is a concrete assemblage of materials in a specific form. It embodies physical materials and forces and reflects physical conditions such as temperature, winds, etc. It is obvious, however, that they do not produce houses and that a wide variety of houses can be conceived which embody these same factors. The specific house reflects biological facts — the rate of heat loss of human beings, the capacity to work with materials. The house also reflects social factors — notions as to style, comfort, the kind of clothing worn, many other social conditions, including coöperation in building and coöperation in use. It is impossible to find a house that as a whole is not a resultant of all these factors. It is impossible to separate them. But it is only possible to change the whole by operations on one factor at a time.

(*d*) A manual telephone switchboard is an assemblage of physical material through which electrical forces are to be operated. This affects many of its characteristics. Its specific concrete form, however, is likewise determined by social and biological factors. The intercommunication which is its reason for existence is a social function. Its size is determined by the extent of the society and the extent of communication and several other social factors. Its size is provisionally limited by biological factors to 10,500 lines. This is due to the anatomical fact that the length of women's arms is limited. If their arms were as long as monkeys' (relatively) the size of the switchboard and hence the number of lines could be larger, for it is the reach of the operator which limits its height. This limitation, however, only exists if the jacks (devices for terminating telephone circuits in switchboards) are of a certain size. If they were much smaller (as they could be and have been, in Copenhagen for example) the number of lines could be increased. To do this, however, calls for refinements. Such refinements involve biological difficulties of workmen, skill, etc., which obviously involve social factors, most conveniently expressed (also concealed) in terms of money cost. The design is also affected in some details by the biological fact that most women are not color blind, so that colored light signals can be used, and by the fact that women do not have eyesight as good as eagles are said to have, so that signals, jacks, and numeral designations must be larger than would otherwise be necessary. The size in terms of length is also affected by the fact that there are limits to the speed of biological reactions of women at switchboards to the stimuli of lights and sounds, and that they are subject to a biological tendency to fatigue. If they could work twice as fast, switchboards could be much smaller, although this would not affect the number of lines. The speed and skill of operators, however, are materially affected by training and morale. These are social factors. And so on almost indefinitely. Any concrete physical mechanism called a switchboard is in fact without existence except as it embodies physical, biological, and social factors. It never would have been assembled except for all these factors, and it could not be used or useful if it were not designed within the limits imposed jointly by all these factors. Its design as a whole can only be changed, however, by operations on one set of factors at a time. It evolved in fact precisely by that process — a process that was itself social, biological, and physical.

II

The present significance of the preceding generalizations and illustrations lies in their application to four topics: (i) the nature of the joint limitations on coöperation "imposed" by physical, biological, and social factors; (ii) the processes of overcoming those limitations in purposive conduct; (iii) their bearing on effectiveness of coöperative effort; (iv) their bearing on the efficiency of coöperative effort.

i

In very simple circumstances the specific limitations of coöperative accomplishment may often conveniently be stated as arising independently from either the physical, the biological, or the social factors, in the sense that attack on a limitation may be directed to one or another of these. But it is more correct to state that the limitation arises from the total situation or the combination of factors. For example, if a communication cannot adequately be made because one person cannot hear the other, the defect may provisionally be ascribed to lack of loudness; but no statement may be made properly that not-hearing is specifically due to the conditions of the medium (air), or of voice, or of ear, or of distance, or of social factors as governing distances or as governing difficulty of understanding. A change in any one of these factors might change either loudness or the need of it. Similarly, it is not correct to say that certain conditions in India are caused by certain social conventions relative to food. This may be the only aspect regarded as subject to deliberate attack. Nevertheless, if physical conditions such as climate were different, or the total population were less, these particular results might not occur and this factor would lose its significance.[2]

II

Although the limitation is a joint effect of all the factors, from the point of view of attack to serve a purpose it may be ascribed to one factor. This then becomes the strategic factor, the bearing of which on the executive processes will be explained in Chapter XIV. We may say that the lack of loudness in speech is due to fear of communicants, misunderstanding of the loudness required, and distance, but we pick out one factor or another for change as a means of securing the appropriate result. This change in one factor is not the cause of the correction, except in an immediate strategic sense; the correction is due to the change in the total situation. At all times it is the total of all factors, recognized or unrecognized, that determines the relationships or the conditions; the object of effort is to change a total situation favorably by change in a part.

In the initial stage of a coöperative system the choices that

[2] Cf. as to this analysis: Vilfredo Pareto, *Sociologie Générale* (Paris: Payot, 1932), §§ 343, 344, p. 194; also L. J. Henderson, *Pareto's General Sociology* (Harvard University Press, 1935), Notes 3 and 4, beginning on p. 74.

are exercised are personal. It is assumed that the individual situation of each of those coöperating will be improved; that is, it will be more efficient because joint effort will be more effective. The primary opportunities for effectiveness lie in the superiority of the group powers over individual biological powers under the physical and social environments. For example, five men coöperate for defense against strangers who may be enemies by maintaining a continuous watch at two points of observation. It is impossible to do this singly. Note that the nature of the physical terrain is a factor in making *two* points of observation desirable. The *process* of doing this introduces new social factors — the formation of the coöperative system. Thus the physical factors remain constant, the biological factors remain constant, but the social factor changes. This change in the total situation modifies the *effect* of a biological factor. When this change has been accomplished, a purpose is in process of accomplishment. A certain degree of increased security ensues. The efficiency of the enterprise lies in the fact that the satisfactions to the individuals involved are more than sufficient to induce their coöperation. These arise from the increased security, the end sought; and the gratification in social intercourse which was not sought but now becomes desirable.

Now it appears to be generally true that social satisfactions require some objective of activity other than mere personal proximity. Gregariousness calls for coöperative activity. Coöperation requires something to do. In this need lies the frequently observed origin of purposes of action where the motives or satisfactions are described as "social." [3]

In the illustration just given, the immediate danger being relieved, it is determined to obtain more permanent security by building a fort. This is a change in the total situation by a change of the physical environment. Its result will be more

[3] This is developed in Chapter IX, beginning at p. 117.

security, its process provides more social satisfactions. But in the course of the building it appears that some of it cannot be done without additional man power. Accordingly, an additional man is induced to join the group. This is an example of a social method of securing biological power to meet a physical limitation under the conditions. As the work proceeds it soon appears that lack of appropriate coördination of effort is resulting in ineffectiveness. The consideration of this situation results in treating a particular member as the leader for certain coördinations and the assignment of individuals to various correlated tasks. This is an example of the invention of a social method of evading biological limitations in an attack on physical factors.

This illustration serves to show that the operation of a coöperative system requires alternations of objectives. The utilization of biological factors and social factors is required to operate on physical factors, of physical and social factors on biological factors, of physical and biological factors on social factors. The operations, always directed at particular factors as a means of changing a total situation in which all these types of factors are components, have for their *ultimate* ends the satisfaction of individual motives; but their *direct* consequences are either (1) the immediate satisfaction of these motives, or (2) the facilitation of further coöperation.

In the stream of actions of a coöperative system these two classes of consequences are inseparable, and they are frequently not distinguishable objectives of specific acts. But occasionally they are distinguishable. It is convenient to abstract them as distinguishable purposes in the analysis of coöperative action as a whole for the present exposition. We say, then, that we may operate on the physical environment either (1) to secure physical material or forces for immediate satisfactions or (2) to make possible coöperative action not otherwise feasible. We may operate on biological factors either (1) directly to increase "production" or again (2) to facilitate effective coöperation. We may operate on social factors either (1) to give increased social satisfactions, or (2) to facilitate coöperation. In current economic terms we may produce for consumption (consumers' goods) or we may produce for production (production goods).

For the present we may put aside objectives of coöperative effort intended as the means of securing individual satisfaction and restrict our attention to objectives intended directly to facilitate the coöperative system as an immediate end in itself. Such efforts are directed to (a) physical, (b) biological, or (c) social factors.

(a) Operations on the physical factors for the purpose of increasing the possibilities of coöperation take principally the form of purposeful change of the natural environment. We are not accustomed to think of changing the environment as a method of making coöperation possible, but a very large part of our constructive effort nevertheless is for this purpose. Both transportation systems and communication systems largely serve this direct purpose. In their more simple and primitive forms tools often are made for this purpose. For example, the biological limitations of individuals make impossible the power necessary to do certain work; coöperation is required, but the conditions as respects space are such that several men cannot work directly on the objectives. A lever is made or procured to permit this. The making or procuring of a lever is a change in the physical environment to make coöperation possible.

It is evident that much of the accumulation of capital, the invention of mechanical, electrical, optical, auditory, and chemical machines and processes which transcend ordinary human limitations, and the combination of both capital and invention, have for their primary result advances in the power of coöperation. They enormously expand coöperative systems both spatially, that is, over great areas, and temporally, that is, through long time, even many generations. The technique of this general method of expanding coöperative possibilities is widely appreciated, and its economic aspects have received great and relatively excessive attention and development. We shall discuss it further only incidentally.

(*b*) Operations on the biological factors are common and are indispensable to much complex coöperation. They take the forms chiefly of education and training and the specialization of opportunity to develop personal skills. Also, public health programs and much medical and rehabilitation work are operations of this character, either directly or incidentally.

(*c*) We have just referred to what might be called briefly the processes of facilitating coöperation by external developments. But the other, even more important, process, that of operating on the social factors, is in a sense internal and involves the direct invention of effective methods of human relationships. This process as a special technical field has hardly been recognized until recently; and though in fact in innumerable fields of practical endeavor it has been the object of intense detailed effort, it has received little scientific study except, perhaps, in the stage of last refinements, in what was once called "scientific management" or in such systematic technical processes as accounting.

III

What we mean by "effectiveness" of coöperation is the accomplishment of the recognized objectives of coöperative action. The degree of accomplishment indicates the degree of effectiveness.

It is apparent that an objective of coöperation is nonpersonal, that it is an aim of the system of coöperation as a whole. It follows that the definition of effectiveness in any given case is also to be determined in some way by the coöperative system as a whole. The basis of this determination will be whether the action taken *and* the objective result secured prove sufficient to acquire for the system of coöperation the supplies of forces or materials necessary to satisfy personal motives. In either individual action or coöperative action the satisfactions may be secured even though the end is not attained, but the attainment of some end, and belief in the likelihood of attaining it, appears necessary to the continuance of coördinated action. Thus, even though the attainment of a given end is not necessary for itself, it is necessary to keep alive the coöperation. Effectiveness from this point of view is the minimum effectiveness that can be tolerated. Hence it can be seen that the attempt to do what can not be done must result in the destruction or failure of coöperation.

It remains to note here that the effectiveness of coöperative action implies effectiveness, in a special sense, of constituent "individual" actions within the coöperative system. If five men are pushing a stone, the effort of each individual is a constituent action; it has not independent non-coöperative existence; its effectiveness is a function of the total action. The effectiveness of one man can only be appraised on the assumption that the other actions remain equal, that is, effectiveness of constituent efforts has meaning only in a differential sense, its value varying inversely as the values of other efforts vary. For convenience in maintaining effectiveness, however, it is frequent to assign to the constituent effort an artificial or individual objective, such as that man A should exert x pounds of force for y minutes. If he does so he is effective, otherwise not.

IV

Although effectiveness of coöperative effort relates to accomplishment of an objective of the system and is determined with a view to the system's requirements, efficiency relates to the satisfaction of individual motives.[4] The efficiency of a coöpera-

---

[4] In most practical organization work to which the word "efficiency" applies

tive system is the resultant of the efficiencies of the individuals furnishing the constituent efforts, that is, as viewed by them. If the individual finds his motives being satisfied by what he does, he continues his coöperative effort; otherwise he does not. If he does not, this subtraction from the coöperative system may be fatal to it. If five men are required and the fifth man finds no satisfaction in coöperating, his contribution would be inefficient. He would withhold or withdraw his services, so that the coöperation would be destroyed. If he considers it to be efficient, it is continued. Thus, the efficiency of a coöperative system is its capacity to maintain itself by the individual satisfactions it affords. This may be called its capacity of equilibrium, the balancing of burdens by satisfactions which results in continuance.[5]

Efficiency or equilibrium can be secured either by changing motives in individuals (or securing substitute individuals of appropriate motives), which is operation on a social factor, or by its *productive* results which can be distributed to individuals. These productive results are either material or social, or both. As to some individuals, material is required for satisfaction; as to others, social benefits are required. As to most individuals, both material and social benefits are required in different proportions.

The limitations to which coöperative effort must conform imply that even in the case of efficient systems the supplies of material and social benefits are restricted, so that efficiency from the productive viewpoint depends not merely upon what

it is used with reference to a highly restricted section or aspect of coöperation so far removed in most cases from individual motives that it is not seen that ultimately the term relates to them. We shall consider this more extensively later.

[5] Efficiency is not to be conceived as possible only at a single optimum condition. A coöperative system may be inefficient, unable to maintain itself at one stage, but able to do so at either a higher or lower stage, at either a larger or smaller size, in either a more intense or less intense level of activity.

or how much is produced but upon what or how much is given for each individual contribution. If more than sufficient material is given to some, it may be that there will not be enough to go around and only an insufficient amount will be available to others. To the latter the situation would then be unsatisfactory. Similarly, the social benefits are limited, and if they should be improperly distributed there would be a deficiency as to some. Hence, efficiency depends in part upon the distributive process in the coöperative system.

If the distribution were such that benefits just equaled burdens in each case, which would require ideal precision in distribution, each individual would have no margin of inducement as against other alternatives. The coöperative system must create a surplus of satisfaction to be efficient. If each man gets back only what he puts in, there is no incentive, that is, no net satisfaction for him in coöperation. What he gets back must give him advantage in terms of satisfaction; which almost always means return in a different form from that which he contributes. If he puts forth effort, he requires a changed condition for himself, just as he would if he put forth effort individually rather than coöperatively. Efficiency, for the individual, is satisfactory exchange. Thus the process of coöperation also includes that of satisfactory exchange.

From this point of view the process of coöperation could be merely one of exchange, that is, of distribution. Viewed in isolation we are accustomed to this process as a basis for efficient coöperation in the exchanges — stock, commodity, etc. — which are not productive in a direct sense. Much coöperation, especially that of the "social" types, is of this character; in these cases, the formal objective of coöperation is merely a pole around which coöperation organizes. But many important systems of coöperation depend upon a production secured through the accomplishment of a tangible objective. Thus human energy is focused in coöperation upon a physical objective which produces a physical material which may be distributed to individuals in amounts required; as to some individuals these amounts may be more than they could secure by individual efforts; as to others, less. In the latter case, other-satisfactions secured or produced through coöperation are the basis of efficiency. These other satisfactions are social.

The efficiency of coöperation therefore depends upon what it secures and produces on the one hand, and how it distributes its resources and how it changes motives on the other. Everything that it does involves physical, biological, and social forces, applied to particular factors — physical, biological, personal, and social — in the situation as a whole. From the change in this situation it furnishes inducements or satisfactions. The distribution of these satisfactions is itself an application of physical, biological, and social forces to changing the total situation. A coöperative system is incessantly dynamic, a process of continual readjustment to physical, biological, and social environments as a whole. Its purpose is the satisfaction of individuals, and its efficiency requires that its effect be to change the history of its environment as a whole; it does this by changes in the physical, biological, and social components of that environment.

The leading ideas presented in this Part I of this book, and especially in this chapter, are the fundamental assumptions of the exposition of theory and the analysis of practice in the chapters which follow. They will be illustrated repeatedly both in the development of the conceptual scheme in the terms of which I state the theory of coöperative systems and of organization and in the description of the processes of organization, especially the executive processes, by which the life of organizations is maintained. Summarized, the most essential of these assumptions are as follows:

1. The individual human being possesses a limited power of choice. At the same time he is a resultant of, and is narrowly limited by, the factors of the total situation. He has motives, arrives at purposes, and wills to accomplish them. His method is to select a particular factor or set of factors in the total situation and to change the situation by operations on these factors. These are, from the viewpoint of purpose, the limiting factors; and are the strategic points of attack.

2. Among the most important limiting factors in the situation of each individual are his own biological limitations. The most effective method of overcoming these limitations has been that of coöperation. This requires the adoption of a group, or non-personal, purpose. The situation with reference to such a purpose is composed of innumerable factors, which must be discriminated as limiting or non-limiting factors.

3. Coöperation is a social aspect of the total situation and social factors arise from it. These factors may be in turn the limiting factors of any situation. This arises from two considerations: (*a*) the processes of interaction must be discovered or invented, just as a physical operation must be discovered or invented; (*b*) the interaction changes the motives and interest of those participating in the coöperation.

4. The persistence of coöperation depends upon two conditions: (*a*) its effectiveness; and (*b*) its efficiency. Effectiveness relates to the accomplishment of the coöperative purpose, which is social and non-personal in character. Efficiency relates to the satisfaction of individual motives, and is personal in character. The test of effectiveness is the accomplishment of a common purpose or purposes; effectiveness can be measured. The test of efficiency is the eliciting of sufficient individual wills to coöperate.

5. The survival of coöperation, therefore, depends upon two interrelated and interdependent classes of processes: (*a*) those which relate to the system of coöperation as a whole in relation

to the environment; and (*b*) those which relate to the creation or distribution of satisfactions among individuals.

6. The instability and failures of coöperation arise from defects in each of these classes of processes separately, and from defects in their combination. The functions of the executive are those of securing the effective adaptation of these processes.

PART II

THE THEORY AND STRUCTURE OF FORMAL ORGANIZATIONS

CHAPTER VI

THE DEFINITION OF FORMAL ORGANIZATION

A COOPERATIVE system is a complex of physical,[1] biological, personal, and social components which are in a specific systematic relationship by reason of the coöperation of two or more persons for at least one definite end. Such a system is evidently a subordinate unit of larger systems from one point of view; and itself embraces subsidiary systems — physical, biological, etc. — from another point of view. One of the systems comprised within a coöperative system, the one which is implicit in the phrase "coöperation of two or more persons," is called an "organization," and will be defined in this chapter.

I. Development of the Definition

The number of coöperative systems having more or less definite purposes, and of sufficient duration to enlist attention and description or identification, is very large. They may be broadly classified by character of purpose or objective into a few groups which are widely different, such as churches, political parties, fraternal associations, governments, armies, industrial enterprises, schools, families. Between organizations classified in any one of these groups there are also wide differences.

Many similarities in the conduct and attitudes of executives of these systems may be observed, and several students have postulated common elements in these systems. It is evident that if there are uniformities with respect to them generally they will be found in particular aspects or sections of them that

---

[1] The word "physical" as used in this and subsequent chapters includes the biological elements, except in human beings.

are common to all. Effective study of them will therefore require the isolation or definition of these aspects. We shall name one common aspect "organization."

The variations in concrete coöperative situations may be assigned to four preliminary classes: (*a*) those that relate to aspects of the physical environment; (*b*) those that relate to aspects of the social environment; (*c*) those that relate to individuals; (*d*) other variables.

(*a*) An inspection of the concrete operations of any coöperative system shows at once that the physical environment is an inseparable part of it. To the extent that there are variations in the physical aspects of coöperative systems an adjustment or adaptation of other aspects of coöperation is required. Whether such variations are significant for the general study of coöperation, or whether for most purposes the physical environment may be treated as a constant, is the first question at issue. By physical environment so far as we mean geographical aspects — that is, mere location, topography, climate, etc., — it will readily be accepted that it may well be excluded from consideration for nearly all general purposes.[2] That part of the environment, however, which is regarded as the property of an organization is of different status; and that part which consists of structures, improvements, tools, machines, etc., pertains still more specifically to the organization which owns or works with them. For this reason, in many cases the notion of organization evidently includes that of a physical plant; for example, in the case of a railroad or telephone organization. This is also frequently true of a factory. Indeed, the phrase is often used "The *plant* can turn out so much product" when the meaning includes physical plant, a number of men, and the activities or forces of both men and plant. It is apparent

[2] In special cases, however, this is not true; for example, where two manufacturing operations otherwise alike are conducted in two different climates. Climate may then be the most significant variable.

that when one is dealing with a specific enterprise the whole situation comprising physical plant, men, and activities must be the minimum system with which one is primarily concerned. To this system the name organization may be applied, but usually "enterprise," "business," or "operation" is more appropriately used, and "organization" reserved for that part of the coöperative system from which physical environment has been abstracted. All aspects of the physical environment are then regarded or most conveniently treated as the elements of other, physical and technical, systems between which and organizations the significant relationships may be investigated as may be required for the purpose in hand.

(*b*) It is in most cases evident that the social elements are an important aspect likewise of a concrete coöperative situation. The social factors may be regarded as entering into the situation by several routes: (1) through being components of the individual whose activities are included in the system; (2) through their effect upon individuals, whose activities are not included, but who are hostile to the system of coöperation or whose activities potentially are factors in any way; (3) through contact of the system (either coöperative or otherwise) with other collateral coöperative systems and especially with (4) superior systems; and (5) as inherent in coöperation itself. Indirectly, social factors, of course, are also involved in the changes of the physical environment, particularly as effected by prior or other existing coöperative systems.

It appears to be the universal practice to exclude social factors — or to regard them as constants which may be neglected for most purposes — in the working conception of organization, with the single important exception of the state as expressed in law, especially the law of incorporation. This special exception, however, is regarded in two quite opposite ways. By those concerned with the dynamic aspects of coöperation the law is treated as a remote and vague origin of "authority" within the system. By lawyers, on the other hand, the law is treated as the structural element basic to the coöperative system, especially of corporations of various kinds, less so of unincorporated systems. Thus, "to organize" means, from this point of view, to establish the legal conditions necessary to a particular status of a coöperative system. The fact that a coöperative system — industrial or religious or educational for example — of considerable size may operate without incorporation, or with little perceptible change in its character after incorporation, is sufficient to indicate the quite secondary effect of this special aspect of social factors. It will be shown that it is, in fact, minor in comparison with other social factors.[3] Far more important in many cases are the specific contractual relations, in which are involved not merely formal legal circumstances but persistent attitudes and habitual practice of general social character. We shall exclude all of the social environment as such from the definition of organization.

(c) The exclusion of the physical and social environments from the definition of organization for general purposes will on the whole conform to ordinary usage and common sense, and will be accepted without great difficulty as a method of approach to a scientifically useful concept of organization. The question of persons, however, offers greater difficulty and doubt. Though with much vagueness and many exceptions, some of which have been already indicated, the most usual conception of an organization is that of a *group* of persons, some or all of whose activities are coördinated. The concept of the group as the dominant characteristic of coöperative systems is certainly also frequent in the literature of sociology, anthropology, and social psychology, although, as shown by Parsons,[4] systems in which at least the emphasis is upon *action* have been funda-

[3] See Chapter XII.
[4] Talcott Parsons, *The Structure of Social Action* (New York: McGraw-Hill, 1937).

mental in the conceptual schemes of Durkheim, Pareto, and Weber.

As a working concept it may be made clear that "group" contains so many variables as to restrict the number and the firmness of any generalizations. It is unmanageable without the use of some more restricted concept. Hence, to the present writer, discussions of group coöperation often give the impression of vagueness, confusion, and implicit contradiction. The reason for this is apparent from the fact that both group and person require explicit definition. A group is evidently a number of persons plus some interrelationships or interactions to be determined. When the nature of these interrelations or interactions is described or defined, it at once appears that "person" is a highly variable thing, not merely in the sense that persons differ in many respects, but more especially because the extent and character of their participation in groups also widely varies.

This may be shown by reference to concrete "organizations" of various classes. In industrial organizations the group is commonly regarded as "officers and employees," but from some points of view stockholders, the terms of whose participation are radically different, are included. At other times, or in other contexts, creditors, suppliers, and customers must be included — for example in all connections where the vitally important aspect of "good will" is included in organization operation. Thus what is meant by the group, in the aspect of "membership," will be quite variable even for this particular (the industrial) class of coöperative systems.

If one takes religious organizations it is at once evident that except for a few "employees," the definition of both "group" and "membership" is entirely different from that of the industrial organization. But even within religious groups the basis and character of participation is evidently of many kinds. Sometimes "group" means clergy or hierarchy, sometimes it includes orders, sometimes communicants of various degrees of participation.

If we add to these types of organizations military, governmental, political, and fraternal and educational organizations, all of which are "groups," the complexity of the variation of meaning of the membership aspect of the group concept increases rapidly.

The group as a social concept persists because of the fact that the significant[5] relations between persons in groups are regarded as those of systematic personal interactions. In each coöperating group the coöperative acts of persons are coördinated. Those acts of persons who are denominated "members" of the group which are not coördinated with others are not a part of the system of action. It may easily be observed that many acts of persons in a coöperative group are not in any substantial sense a part of the coöperative action even when more or less contemporaneously the individuals contribute coöperative acts. In fact, it is the *system of interactions* which appears to be the basis for the concept of a "group" in the sense in which the word is used in connection with coöperative systems or socially. This concept is implicit in the use of the word, whereas almost invariably the explicit reference is to the persons, rather than to their interactions in coöperation. Thus the word "group" is not applied to three persons who are fighting each other or having nothing to do with each other, although "group" is entirely acceptable for the higher abstraction of arithmetic as implicit in the cardinal number "three" or in special senses such as a "group" of fighters in a painting. It is not its numerical aspect that usually determines the selection of the word "group" in the present context, but a relationship of coöperation, which is a system of interactions.

Now if, with reference to a particular system of coöperative action to which a person contributes, one examines all the

[5] From the point of view of coöperative systems.

acts of any person for even one day it will be at once evident in nearly all cases that many of these acts are outside *any* system of coöperation; and that many of the remainder are distributable among at least several such coöperative systems. The connection of any "member" with an organization is necessarily intermittent, and there is frequent substitution of persons. Again it is almost impossible to discover a person who does not "belong" — taking into account the intermittent character of his participation — at the same time to many organizations. Moreover, often a specific action of a person constitutes a part of the "substance" of two or more organizations simultaneously. In addition it appears necessary to regard as a part of an organization certain efforts of many persons not commonly considered "members," for example, customers; or those of persons that are only treated as members in special senses, for example, stockholders, who in one legal sense *are* the organization; or bondholders, who are important contributors to organization yet who at most are ordinarily viewed as only contingent members. Finally, almost every person regards himself a part of the time as an individual in isolation from and independent of any organization, that is, he assumes the exercise of free will as against all other persons or groups; and he believes that often his biological necessities are quite independent of any present organization as causes of his actions.

Much of the foregoing may be illustrated by a concrete case. I select at random a man who is chiefly identified by his connection with the organization with which I am also ordinarily identified. He is an engineer whose career and living for many years have depended upon that organization. Without special inquiry, I know that he has the following important organization connections also: He is (1) a citizen of the United States, the State of New Jersey, the County of Essex, and the City of Newark — four organizations to which he has many inescapable obligations; he is a member of (2) the Catholic

Church; (3) the Knights of Columbus; (4) the American Legion; (5) the Outanaway Golf Club; (6) the Democratic Party; (7) the Princeton Club of Newark; (8) he is a stockholder in three corporations; (9) he is head of his own family (wife and three children); (10) he is a member of his father's family; (11) he is a member of his wife's family; (12) to judge from his behavior he belongs to other less formal organizations (but often seems not to be aware of it) which affect what he wears, how he talks, what he eats, what he likes to do, how he thinks about many things; and (13) finally he gives evidence of "belonging" also to himself alone occasionally. Lest it be thought that his "major" connection is predominant, and the others trivial, it may be stated that he devotes to it nominally less than 25 per cent of his approximately 8760 hours per annum; and that actually while he thinks he is working, and despite his intentions, he dreams of fishing, reflects on family matters, and replays a part of the previous evening's bridge, etc. Yet he considers himself a hard worker and is properly so regarded.

It is evident from the foregoing that if persons are to be included within the concept "organization," its general significance will be quite limited. The bases or terms upon which persons are included will be highly variable — so much so that even within very restricted fields, such as a particular industry, "organizations" will mean a wide variety of entities. Hence, here again as when we included a part of the physical environment within the definition, the inclusion of persons may be most useful in particular instances, but of limited value for general purposes.

It nevertheless remains to consider whether it would actually be useful to adopt a definition from which persons as well as physical and social environments are excluded as components. If this is done, an organization is defined as *a system of consciously coördinated personal activities or forces*. It is apparent that all the variations found in concrete coöperative systems that are due to physical and social environments, and those that are due to persons or to the bases upon which persons contribute to such systems, are by this definition relegated to the position of external facts and factors,[6] and that the organization as then isolated is an aspect of coöperative systems which is common to all of them.

Organization will then mean a similar thing, whether applied to a military, a religious, an academic, a manufacturing, or a fraternal coöperation, though the physical environment, the social environment, the number and kinds of persons, and the bases of their relation to the organization will be widely different. These aspects of coöperation then become external to organization as defined, though components of the coöperative system as a whole. Moreover, the definition is similarly applicable to settings radically different from those now obtaining, for example, to coöperation under feudal conditions. Such a definition will be of restricted usefulness with reference to any particular coöperative situation, being only one element of such a situation, except as by its adoption we are enabled to arrive at general principles which may be usefully applied in the understanding of specific situations.

It is the central hypothesis of this book that the most useful concept for the analysis of experience of coöperative systems is embodied in the definition of a formal organization as a *system of consciously coördinated activities or forces of two or more persons.* In any concrete situation in which there is coöperation, several different systems will be components. Some of these will be physical, some biological, some psychological, etc., but the

[6] That is, external to the organization but not external to the related coöperative system. It is to be borne in mind that we are dealing with *two* systems: (1) an inclusive coöperative system, the components of which are persons, physical systems, social systems, and organizations; and (2) organizations, which are parts of coöperative systems and consist entirely of coördinated human activities.

element common to all which binds all these other systems into the total concrete coöperative situation is that of organization as defined. If this hypothesis proves satisfactory it will be because (1) an organization, as defined, is a concept valid through a wide range of concrete situations with relatively few variables, which can be effectively investigated; and (2) the relations between this conceptual scheme and other systems can be effectively and usefully formulated. The final test of this conceptual scheme is whether its use will make possible a more effective conscious promotion and manipulation of coöperation among men; that is, whether in practice it can increase the predictive capacity of competent men in this field. It is the assumption upon which this essay is developed that such a concept is implicit in the behavior of leaders and administrators, explaining uniformities observed in their conduct in widely different coöperative enterprises, and that its explicit formulation and development will permit a useful translation of experience in different fields into common terms.

II. Aspects of Formal Organizations as Abstract Systems

It is advisable to present certain considerations regarding organizations as abstract systems, and concerning the use of the definition and associated terms, before proceeding to the discussion of the elements of organization. The matters to be presented are the following: (*a*) terms used to symbolize or personify organizations, and related practice in the remainder of this treatise; (*b*) concepts analogous to "organization" as defined; (*c*) the non-personal character of activities as components of organizations; (*d*) organizations as isolated, as parts of more general systems, and as comprising subordinate systems; (*e*) emergent properties of systems, especially organizations; and (*f*) dimensional characteristics of organizations.

(*a*) When we are obliged in a practical sense to deal with intangible things chiefly characterized by relationships rather than by substance we have to symbolize them by concrete things, or personify them. In the case of organizations the only practicable device for everyday purposes under most circumstances is to symbolize a system called "an organization" by the persons who are connected with it. For example, we think of an army as consisting of men; and in this case it would be so awkward as to be absurd not to do so, whatever in principle an army may be considered to be. Hence, although I define an organization as a *system* of *coöperative activities* of two or more persons — something intangible and impersonal, largely a matter of relationships — nevertheless sometimes for convenience of phraseology, where no confusion of meaning is likely, I shall follow the customary practice of referring to organizations as groups óf persons and shall speak of such persons as "members." Usually, however, in this book, in the interest of clearer understanding and of a consistent conceptual scheme, I shall use the more awkward plan of substituting "contributors" for "members," and "contributions" for the activities constituting organization; but it should be noted that "contributors," though including those whom we would ordinarily call "members" of an organization, is a broader term and may also include others; and that "contributions" is correspondingly a broader term than "membership" or "membership activities."

(*b*) Under the definition of an organization given above, an organization is a "construct" analogous to "field of gravity" or "electromagnetic field" as used in physical science. The hypothesis we follow is that all of the phenomena concerned are usefully explained if we adopt it, and that existing knowledge and experience are consistent with that assumption.[7]

[7] An organization is a field of personal "forces," just as an electromagnetic field is a field of electric or magnetic forces. The evidence of the effects, in both cases, is all that can be used to describe or define these forces; and the dimensions within which those evidences occur are said to define the field of these forces. The evidential effects are observed in certain objective things when certain other forces operate upon or within them *and* certain conditions ob-

(c) What are the actions which are the evidence of the forces of the organization field? Always the action of persons in words, looks, gestures, movements,[8] never physical objects, although things may conveniently be used as evidence of the action, as in the case of writing. This is difficult to keep in mind under ordinary circumstances, because things are constructed by organizations, and property in them or other rights of control are vested in organizations as in individuals. Moreover, sometimes physical things, persons, statements, etc., serve to define or locate an organization, just as magnets and affected metals define or locate magnetic fields. The actions of organization often relate to the use or movement of physical things and to the transfer or retention of ownership or control of them, but as conceived for the present scheme physical things are always a part of the environment, a part of the coöperative system, but never a part of the organization. This is rigorously held to throughout these pages.

For convenience and purposes of simplification, however, I have usually restricted the derivation of organization forces to the persons who would ordinarily be called "members," "communicants," "employees," etc. But I have been unable

tain within the field; but it is not the practice to consider the objective things as constituting the field itself. For example, an electromagnet when actuated by an electric current is said to create an electromagnetic field, the existence of which is only known by phenomena which result when certain other things are put within that field. But none of these objective things are the field, nor is the electric current the electromagnetic force, though it is or carries the electromotive energy essential to it.

Similarly, persons are the objective sources of the organization forces which occupy the organization field. These forces derive from energies that are found only in persons. They become organization forces only when certain conditions obtain within the field, and are evidenced only by certain phenomena such as words and other action, or are inferred by concrete results imputed to such action. But neither the persons nor the objective results are themselves the organization. If they are treated as if they were, inconsistencies and inadequacies of explanation of phenomena ensue.

[8] Also attention and thinking, the latter only to be inferred from other action.

even here to completely restrict myself to this convenience. The actions which are evidence of organization forces include all actions of contribution and receipt of energies, so that a customer making a purchase, a supplier furnishing supplies, an investor furnishing capital, are also contributors. What they contribute is *not* material but the transaction, the transfer, the control of things, or action upon physical things themselves. Thus, usually, the only organization action of an investor is often a simple one of the transfer of money or of credit which he owns or controls. It is so important that an organization agrees to make reciprocal *transfers* of control of money or credit from time to time.

The system, then, to which we give the name "organization" is a system composed of the activities of human beings. What makes these activities a system is that the efforts of different persons are here coördinated. For this reason their significant aspects are not personal. They are determined by the system either as to manner, or degree, or time. Most of the efforts in coöperative systems are easily seen to be impersonal. For example, a clerk writing on a report form for a corporation is obviously doing something at a place, on a form, and about a subject that clearly never could engage his strictly personal interest. Hence, when we say that we are concerned with a system of coördinated human efforts, we mean that although persons are agents of the action, the action is not personal in the aspect important for the study of coöperative systems. Its character is determined by the requirements of the system, or of whatever dominates the system.

(*d*) If organizations are systems, it follows that the general characteristics of systems are also those of organizations. For our purposes we may say that a system is something which must be treated as a whole because each part is related to every other part included in it in a significant way.[9] What is significant is

[9] This "significant way" is that the components are interdependent variables. This will be emphasized again and again in this treatise. The interdependence

determined by order as defined for a particular purpose, or from a particular point of view, such that if there is a change in the relationship of one part to any or all of the others, there is a change in the system. It then either becomes a new system or a new state of the same system.

Usually, if the parts are numerous, they group themselves into subsidiary or partial systems. Where this is the case, each partial system consists of relationships between its own parts which can change, creating a new state of the partial system, without altering the system as a whole in significant degree. But this is true only when the system is viewed from a single or special point of view and the changes of the subsidiary system are within limits. When this is the case we may disregard the larger systems, treating them as constants or the subsidiary system as if it were isolated. Thus the whole physical universe is the single and fundamental system, consisting of parts — which, let us say, are electrons, neutrons, and protons — and relationships between them; but in practice, if our interest is narrow enough, we can deal with the solar system, or the sun, or the earth, or a piece of iron, or a molecule, or an atom, as if each were a complete and final system. This we can do if we do not exceed certain limits. These are determined by whether or not exceeding these limits involves important changes in, or important reactions from, the larger system.

This is similarly true of the systems called organizations. First of all each organization is a component of a larger system which we have called a "coöperative system," the other components of which are physical systems, social systems, biological systems, persons, etc. Moreover, most formal organizations are

---

of the variables is persistently neglected, in my observation, both in the *discussion* of organization in practical affairs, and also in the discussion of concrete systems by social scientists. Cf. L. J. Henderson, *Pareto's General Sociology*, p. 86. "The interdependence of variables in a system is one of the widest inductions from experience that we possess; or we may alternatively regard it as the definition of a system."

partial systems included within larger organization systems. The most comprehensive formal organizations are included in an informal, indefinite, nebulous, and undirected system usually named a "society." In Chapter VII we shall consider the elements of a simple formal organization, and in Chapter VIII the structure of a complex organization.

(e) But we must now refer to one question about systems in general, and about organization systems in particular, the answer to which is of fundamental importance. I refer to the question as to whether the whole is more than the sum of the parts; whether a system should be considered as merely an aggregate of its components; whether a system of coöperative efforts, that is, an organization, is something more or less than or different from its constituent efforts; whether there emerge from the system properties which are not inherent in the parts.

The opinion that governs in this book is that when, for example, the efforts of five men become coördinated in a system, that is, an organization, there is created something new in the world that is more or less than or different in quantity and quality from anything present in the sum of the efforts of the five men.

I will give only one illustration, suggested by an example from Chapter III. If five men are placed at equal distances from each other on a circle to watch an event in the center of the circle, the system of coördinated efforts results in a composite viewing that is impersonal, not the sum of individual views, entirely different from individual views, inferior in some respects, superior in others, reacting on all of the individuals as something different, and having an existence and even a vitality so long as the system is kept alive, that is, so long as the organization persists in this respect.

In this book, therefore, systems of coöperation which we call organizations I regard as social creatures, "alive," just as I regard an individual human being, who himself on analysis is a complex of partial systems, as different from the sum of these constituent systems — if, indeed, the word "sum" has any meaning in this connection.[10]

(*f*) It remains to present a few remarks on the dimensional characteristics of the systems of coöperative interactions which we define as organizations. It perhaps has impressed many executives how indefinitely organizations are located in space. The sense of being "nowhere" is commonly felt. With the great extension of the means of electrical communication this vagueness has increased. To be sure, since the material of organizations is acts of persons, and since they relate in some degree to physical objects or are fixed in some physical environment, they have some degree of physical location. This is especially true of organizations in factories, or connected with railroad or communication systems. But even in these cases location is indirect, by attachment to a system of physical things; and in the case of political and religious organizations even mere location is only feebly conceivable. The notion of spatial dimensions of these systems is hardly applicable.

On the other hand, the dimension of time is of prime importance. Temporal relationship and continuity are primary aspects of organizations. When and how long are the first items of description. As already noted, the persons whose acts are the components of these systems are continually changing, yet the organization persists.

There arises in this connection, however, one question of definition to which reference will again be made, to which no answer is attempted here. It is, whether an organization should be regarded as continuous when all coöperative action ceases, to be resumed at a later time. Many organizations operate intermittently (closing of store or factory for the night, etc.). In such cases it may be held that technically a new organization comes into existence each day, etc., but I have found it more

---

[10] See also the Appendix, at page 314 ff.

convenient to regard these organizations as continuous but "dormant."

The definition of a formal organization which is presented in this chapter is: A system of consciously coördinated activities or forces of two or more persons. In the next chapter we are to consider the elements in the concrete situation that result in a system of activities and order their interrelations — what is essential to the system or necessary to its persistence or duration.

CHAPTER VII

THE THEORY OF FORMAL ORGANIZATION

AN organization comes into being when (1) there are persons able to communicate with each other (2) who are willing to contribute action (3) to accomplish a common purpose. The elements of an organization are therefore (1) communication; (2) willingness to serve; and (3) common purpose. These elements are necessary and sufficient conditions initially, and they are found in all such organizations. The third element, purpose, is implicit in the definition. Willingness to serve, and communication, and the interdependence of the three elements in general, and their mutual dependence in specific coöperative systems, are matters of experience and observation.

For the continued existence of an organization either *effectiveness* or *efficiency* is necessary;[1] and the longer the life, the more necessary both are. The vitality of organizations lies in the willingness of individuals to contribute forces to the coöperative system. This willingness requires the belief that the purpose can be carried out, a faith that diminishes to the vanishing point as it appears that it is not in fact in process of being attained. Hence, when effectiveness ceases, willingness to contribute disappears. The continuance of willingness also depends upon the satisfactions that are secured by individual contributors in the process of carrying out the purpose. If the satisfactions do not exceed the sacrifices required, willingness disappears, and the condition is one of organization inefficiency. If the satisfactions exceed the sacrifices, willingness persists, and the condition is one of efficiency of organization.

In summary, then, the initial existence of an organization

[1] See definitions in Chapters II and V, pp. 19 and 55 ff., also Chapter XVI.

depends upon a combination of these elements appropriate to the external conditions at the moment. Its survival depends upon the maintenance of an equilibrium of the system. This equilibrium is primarily internal, a matter of proportions between the elements, but it is ultimately and basically an equilibrium between the system and the total situation external to it. This external equilibrium has two terms in it: first, the effectiveness of the organization, which comprises the relevance of its purpose to the environmental situation; and, second, its efficiency, which comprises the interchange between the organization and individuals. Thus the elements stated will each vary with external factors, and they are at the same time interdependent; when one is varied compensating variations must occur in the other if the system of which they are components is to remain in equilibrium, that is, is to persist or survive.

We may now appropriately consider these elements and their interrelations in some detail, having in mind the system as a whole. In later chapters we shall consider each element in greater detail with reference to its variability in dependence upon external factors, and the interrelations of the elements as determining the character of the executive functions.

I

I. WILLINGNESS TO COÖPERATE

By definition there can be no organization without persons. However, as we have urged that it is not persons, but the services or acts or action or influences of persons, which should be treated as constituting organizations,[2] it is clear that *willingness* of persons to contribute efforts to the coöperative system is indispensable.

There are a number of words and phrases in common use with reference to organization that reach back to the factor of

---

[2] Page 72 above.

individual willingness. "Loyalty," "solidarity," "*esprit de corps,*" "strength" of organization, are the chief. Although they are indefinite, they relate to intensity of attachment to the "cause," and are commonly understood to refer to something different from effectiveness, ability, or value of personal contributions. Thus "loyalty" is regarded as not necessarily related either to position, rank, fame, remuneration, or ability. It is vaguely recognized as an essential condition of organization.

Willingness, in the present connection, means self-abnegation, the surrender of control of personal conduct, the depersonalization of personal action. Its effect is cohesion of effort, a sticking together. Its immediate cause is the disposition necessary to "sticking together." Without this there can be no sustained personal effort as a contribution to coöperation. Activities cannot be coördinated unless there is first the disposition to make a personal act a contribution to an impersonal system of acts, one in which the individual gives up personal control of what he does.

The outstanding fact regarding willingness to contribute to a given specific formal organization is the indefinitely large range of variation in its intensity among individuals. If all those who may be considered potential contributors to an organization are arranged in order of willingness to serve it, the scale gradually descends from possibly intense willingness through neutral or zero willingness to intense unwillingness or opposition or hatred. The *preponderance of persons in a modern society always lies on the negative side* with reference to any particular existing or potential organization. Thus of the possible contributors only a small minority actually have a positive willingness. This is true of the largest and most comprehensive formal organizations, such as the large nations, the Catholic Church, etc. Most of the persons in existing society are either indifferent to or positively opposed to any single one of them; and if the smaller organizations subordinate to these major organizations are under consideration the minority becomes of course a much smaller proportion, and usually a nearly negligible proportion, of the conceivable total.

A second fact of almost equal importance is that the willingness of any individual cannot be constant in degree. It is necessarily intermittent and fluctuating. It can scarcely be said to exist during sleep, and is obviously diminished or exhausted by weariness, discomfort, etc., a conception that was well expressed by the saying "The spirit is willing, but the flesh is weak."

A corollary of the two propositions just stated is that for any given formal organization the number of persons of positive willingness to serve, but near the neutral or zero point, is always fluctuating. It follows that the aggregate willingness of potential contributors to any formal coöperative system is unstable — a fact that is evident from the history of all formal organizations.

Willingness to coöperate, positive or negative, is the expression of the net satisfactions or dissatisfactions experienced or anticipated by each individual in comparison with those experienced or anticipated through alternative opportunities. These alternative opportunities may be either personal and individualistic or those afforded by other organizations. That is, willingness to coöperate is the net effect, first, of the inducements to do so in conjunction with the sacrifices involved, and then in comparison with the practically available net satisfactions afforded by alternatives. The questions to be determined, if they were matters of logical reasoning, would be, first, whether the opportunity to coöperate grants any advantage to the individual as compared with independent action; and then, if so, whether that advantage is more or less than the advantage obtainable from some other coöperative opportunity. Thus, from the viewpoint of the individual, willingness is the joint effect of personal desires and reluctances; from the viewpoint of organization it is the joint effect of objective inducements offered and burdens imposed. The measure of this net result, however, is entirely individual, personal, and subjective. Hence, organizations depend upon the motives of individuals and the inducements that satisfy them.

II. PURPOSE

Willingness to coöperate, except as a vague feeling or desire for association with others, cannot develop without an objective of coöperation. Unless there is such an objective it cannot be known or anticipated what specific efforts will be required of individuals, nor in many cases what satisfactions to them can be in prospect. Such an objective we denominate the "purpose" of an organization. The necessity of having a purpose is axiomatic, implicit in the words "system," "coördination," "coöperation." It is something that is clearly evident in many observed systems of coöperation, although it is often not formulated in words, and sometimes cannot be so formulated. In such cases what is observed is the direction or effect of the activities, from which purpose may be inferred.

A purpose does not incite coöperative activity unless it is accepted by those whose efforts will constitute the organization. Hence there is initially something like simultaneity in the acceptance of a purpose and willingness to coöperate.

It is important at this point to make clear that every coöperative purpose has in the view of each coöperating person two aspects which we call (a) the coöperative and (b) the subjective aspect, respectively.

(a) When the viewing of the purpose is an *act of coöperation*, it approximates that of detached observers from a special position of observation; this position is that of the interests of the organization; it is largely determined by organization knowledge, but is personally interpreted. For example, if five men are coöperating to move a stone from A to B, the moving of the stone is a different thing in the organization view of each of the five men involved. Note, however, that what moving the stone means to each man personally is not here in question, but what he thinks it means to the organization *as a whole*. This includes the significance of his own effort as an element in coöperation, and that of all others, in his view; but it is not at all a matter of satisfying a personal motive.

When the purpose is a physical result of simple character, the difference between the purpose as objectively viewed by a detached observer and the purpose as viewed by each person coöperating *as an act of coöperation* is ordinarily not large or important, and the different coöperative views of the persons coöperating are correspondingly similar. Even in such cases the attentive observer will detect differences that result in disputes, errors of action, etc., even though no *personal* interest is implicated. But when the purpose is less tangible — for example, in religious coöperation — the difference between objective purpose and purpose as coöperatively viewed by each person is often seen ultimately to result in disruption.

We may say, then, that a purpose can serve as an element of a coöperative system only so long as the participants do not recognize that there are serious divergences of their understanding of that purpose as the object of coöperation. If in fact there is important difference between the aspects of the purpose as objectively and as coöperatively viewed, the divergencies become quickly evident when the purpose is concrete, tangible, physical; but when the purpose is general, intangible, and of sentimental character, the divergencies can be very wide yet not be recognized. Hence, an objective purpose that can serve as the basis for a coöperative system is one that is *believed* by the contributors (or potential contributors) to it to be the determined purpose of the organization. The inculcation of belief in the real existence of a common purpose is an essential executive function. It explains much educational and so-called morale work in political, industrial, and religious organizations that is so often otherwise inexplicable.[3]

[3] This will be expanded in Chapter XVII.

(*b*) Going back to the illustration of five men moving a stone, we have noted "that what moving the stone means to each man personally is not here in question, but what he thinks it means to the *organization as a whole*." The distinction emphasized is of first importance. It suggests the fact that every participant in an organization may be regarded as having a dual personality — an organization personality and an individual personality. Strictly speaking, an organization purpose has directly no meaning for the individual. What has meaning for him is the organization's relation to him — what burdens it imposes, what benefits it confers. In referring to the aspects of purpose as coöperatively viewed, we are alluding to the *organization* personality of individuals. In many cases the two personalities are so clearly developed that they are quite apparent. In military action individual conduct may be so dominated by organization personality that it is utterly contradictory of what personal motivation would require. It has been observed of many men that their private conduct is entirely inconsistent with official conduct, although they seem completely unaware of the fact. Often it will be observed that participants in political, patriotic, or religious organizations will accept derogatory treatment of their personal conduct, including the assertion that it is inconsistent with their organization obligations, while they will become incensed at the slightest derogation of the tenets or doctrines of their organization, even though they profess not to understand them. There are innumerable other cases, however, in which almost no organization personality may be said to exist. These are cases in which personal relationship with the coöperative system is momentary or at the margin of willingness to participate.

In other words we have clearly to distinguish between organization purpose and individual motive. It is frequently assumed in reasoning about organizations that common purpose and individual motive are or should be identical. With the exception noted below, this is never the case; and under modern conditions it rarely even appears to be the case. Individual motive is necessarily an internal, personal, subjective thing; common purpose is necessarily an external, impersonal, objective thing even though the individual interpretation of it is subjective. The one exception to this general rule, an important one, is that the accomplishment of an organization purpose becomes itself a source of personal satisfaction and a motive for many individuals in many organizations. It is rare, however, if ever, and then I think only in connection with family, patriotic, and religious organizations under special conditions, that organization purpose becomes or can become the *only* or even the major individual motive.

Finally it should be noted that, once established, organizations change their unifying purposes. They tend to perpetuate themselves; and in the effort to survive may change the reasons for existence. I shall later make clearer that in this lies an important aspect of executive functions.[4]

III. COMMUNICATION

The possibility of accomplishing a common purpose and the existence of persons whose desires might constitute motives for contributing toward such a common purpose are the opposite poles of the system of coöperative effort. The process by which these potentialities become dynamic is that of communication. Obviously a common purpose must be commonly known, and to be known must be in some way communicated. With some exceptions, verbal communication between men is the method by which this is accomplished. Similarly, though under crude and obvious conditions not to the same extent, inducements to persons depend upon communication to them.

The method of communication centers in language, oral and written. On its crudest side, motions or actions that are of

[4] See also Chapters II and III.

obvious meaning when observed are sufficient for communication without deliberate attempt to communicate; and signaling by various methods is an important method in much coöperative activity. On the other side, both in primitive and in highly complex civilization "observational feeling" is likewise an important aspect of communication.[5] I do not think it is generally so recognized. It is necessary because of the limitations of language and the differences in the linguistic capacities of those who use language. A very large element in special experience and training and in continuity of individual association is the ability to understand without words, not merely the situation or conditions, but the *intention*.

The techniques of communication are an important part of any organization and are the preëminent problems of many. The absence of a suitable technique of communication would eliminate the possibility of adopting some purposes as a basis for organization. Communication technique shapes the form and the internal economy of organization. This will be evident at once if one visualizes the attempt to do many things now accomplished by small organizations if each "member" spoke a different language. Similarly, many technical functions could

[5] The phrase "observational feeling" is of my coining. The point is not sufficiently developed, and probably has not been adequately studied by anyone. I take it to be at least in part involved in group action not incited by any "overt" or verbal communication. The cases known to me from the primitive field are those reported by W. H. R. Rivers on pages 94–97 of his *Instinct and the Unconscious* (2nd edition Cambridge University Press, 1924), with reference to Polynesia and Melanesia. One case is summarized by F. C. Bartlett, in *Remembering* (Cambridge University Press, 1932), at p. 297. Rivers states in substance that in some of the relatively small groups decisions are often arrived at and acted upon without having ever been formulated by anybody.

I have observed on innumerable occasions apparent unanimity of decision of equals in conferences to quit discussion without a word to that effect being spoken. Often the action is initiated apparently by someone's rising; but as this frequently occurs in such groups *without* the termination of the meeting, more than mere rising is involved. "Observational feeling," I think, avoids the notion of anything "occult."

hardly be carried on without special codes; for example, engineering or chemical work. In an exhaustive theory of organization, communication would occupy a central place, because the structure, extensiveness, and scope of organization are almost entirely determined by communication techniques. To this aspect of communication much of the material in subsequent chapters will be devoted.[6] Moreover, much specialization in organization originates and is maintained essentially because of communication requirements.

II

I. EFFECTIVENESS OF COÖPERATION

The continuance of an organization depends upon its ability to carry out its purpose. This clearly depends jointly upon the appropriateness of its action and upon the conditions of its environment. In other words, effectiveness is primarily a matter of technological[7] processes. This is quite obvious in ordinary cases of purpose to accomplish a physical objective, such as building a bridge. When the objective is non-physical, as is the case with religious and social organizations, it is not so obvious.

It should be noted that a paradox is involved in this matter. An organization must disintegrate if it cannot accomplish its purpose. It also destroys itself by accomplishing its purpose. A very large number of successful organizations come into being and then disappear for this reason. Hence most continuous organizations require repeated adoption of new purposes. This is concealed from everyday recognition by the practice of generalizing a complex series of specific purposes under one term, stated to be *"the* purpose" of this organization. This is strikingly true in the case of governmental and public

[6] Especially in Chapter XII, latter half.
[7] Using "technological" in the broad sense emphasized in Chapter III.

utility organizations when the purpose is stated to be a particular kind of service through a period of years. It is apparent that their real purposes are not abstractions called "service" but specific acts of service. A manufacturing organization is said to exist to make, say, shoes; this is its "purpose." But it is evident that not making shoes in general but making specific shoes from day to day is its series of purposes. This process of generalization, however, provides in advance for the approximate definition of new purposes automatically — so automatically that the generalization is normally substituted in our minds for the concrete performances that are the real purposes. Failure to be effective is, then, a real cause of disintegration; but failure to provide for the decisions resulting in the adoption of new purposes would have the same result. Hence the generalization of purpose which can only be defined concretely by day-to-day events is a vital aspect of permanent organization.

II. ORGANIZATION EFFICIENCY

It has already been stated that "efficiency" as conceived in this treatise is not used in the specialized and limited sense of ordinary industrial practice or in the restricted sense applicable to technological processes. So-called "practical" efficiency has little meaning, for example, as applied to many organizations such as religious organizations.

Efficiency of effort in the fundamental sense with which we are here concerned is efficiency relative to the securing of necessary personal contributions to the coöperative system. The life of an organization depends upon its ability to secure and maintain the personal contributions of energy (including the transfer of control of materials or money equivalent) necessary to effect its purposes. This ability is a composite of perhaps many efficiencies and inefficiencies in the narrow senses of these words, and it is often the case that inefficiency in some respect can be treated as the cause of total failure, in the sense that if corrected success would then be possible. But certainly in most organization — social, political, national, religious — nothing but the absolute test of survival is significant objectively; there is no basis for comparison of the efficiencies of separate aspects.

A more extensive consideration of the inducements that result in personal willingness to coöperate will be had in Chapter XI. The emphasis now is on the view that efficiency of organization is its capacity to offer effective inducements in sufficient quantity to maintain the equilibrium of the system. It is efficiency in this sense and not the efficiency of material productiveness which maintains the vitality of organizations. There are many organizations of great power and permanency in which the idea of productive efficiency is utterly meaningless because there is no material production. Churches, patriotic societies, scientific societies, theatrical and musical organizations, are cases where the original flow of *material* inducements is toward the organization, not from it — a flow necessary to provide resources with which to supply material inducements to the small minority who require them in such organizations.

In those cases where the primary purpose of organization is the production of material things, insufficiency with respect to the non-material inducements leads to the attempt to substitute material inducements for the non-material. Under favorable circumstances, to a limited degree, and for a limited time, this substitution may be effective. But to me, at least, it appears utterly contrary to the nature of men to be sufficiently induced by material or monetary considerations to contribute enough effort to a coöperative system to enable it to be productively efficient to the degree necessary for persistence over an extended period.

If these things are true, then even in purely economic enterprises efficiency in the offering of non-economic inducements may be as vital as productive efficiency. Perhaps the word efficiency as applied to such non-economic inducements as I have given for illustration will seem strange and forced. This, I think, can only be because we are accustomed to use the word in a specialized sense.

The non-economic inducements are as difficult to offer as others under many circumstances. To establish conditions under which individual pride of craft and of accomplishment can be secured without destroying the material economy of standardized production in coöperative operation is a problem in real efficiency. To maintain a character of personnel that is an attractive condition of employment involves a delicate art and much insight in the selection (and rejection) of personal services offered, whether the standard of quality be high or low. To have an organization that lends prestige and secures the loyalty of desirable persons is a complex and difficult task in efficiency — in all-round efficiency, not one-sided efficiency. It is for these reasons that good organizations — commercial, governmental, military, academic, and others — will be observed to devote great attention and sometimes great expense of money to the non-economic inducements, because they are indispensable to fundamental efficiency, as well as to effectiveness in many cases.[8]

The theory of organization set forth in this chapter is derived from the study of organizations which are exceedingly complex, although it is stated in terms of ideal simple organizations. The temptation is to assume that, in the more complex organizations which we meet in our actual social life, the effect of complexity is to modify or qualify the theory. This appears not to be the case. Organization, simple or complex, is always *an impersonal system of coördinated human efforts*; always

[8] The economics of coöperative systems and their relation to organizations is presented in Chapter XVI.

there is purpose as the coördinating and unifying principle; always there is the indispensable ability to communicate, always the necessity for personal willingness, and for effectiveness and efficiency in maintaining the integrity of purpose and the continuity of contributions. Complexity appears to modify the quality and form of these elements and of the balance between them; but fundamentally the same principles that govern simple organizations may be conceived as governing the structure of complex organizations, which are composite systems. We shall discuss them in the next chapter.

CHAPTER VIII

THE STRUCTURE OF COMPLEX FORMAL ORGANIZATIONS

IT is the purpose of this chapter to present a general description of complex organization, especially from a structural standpoint, and to indicate the way in which the elementary features of organization govern the evolution and growth of these complex systems.

I. COMPLETE, INCOMPLETE, SUBORDINATE, AND DEPENDENT ORGANIZATIONS

I

Overlaying or embedded in the complex of informal organizations, which in the aggregate we call great national and local societies, is a network of formal organizations. If we examine this network it quickly appears that there are a few strands of formal organization that are clearly dominant and relatively comprehensive, all other formal organizations being directly or indirectly attached to and subordinate to them.[1] They are of two types, now known as churches, that is, formally organized religions; and states, formally organized political interests. In barbarous and primitive peoples, and in the earlier history of more advanced peoples, such as that of the early

---

[1] It must be noted here that the use of the word "superior" and "subordinate" in this presentation follows the conventional practice; by "superior" we mean "more comprehensive"; by "subordinate" we mean "of a lower or more restricted order." The terms as used at present are legitimate for the structural point of view, where the parts of the whole complex of organized society as a static presentation are classified in accordance with order of generality. "Superior" organizations from the dynamic or organic point of view are dependent upon "subordinate" organizations, and are controlled by the latter; or more strictly they are in a state of mutual dependence.

Greek City States, one formal organization covered both types of consciously organized interests. Even then, except in the case of isolated peoples, it was not true that this single dominant organization was coextensive with society; and in modern western civilization not only are church and state separated, but no church and no state is coextensive with the society or great complex of informal organizations within which it lives. All states are smaller in territorial or popular limits than their related societies; and coexistence of more than one church is the usual condition in all countries even where there is a state religion.[2]

We, therefore, conclude that there are no single formal organizations that are dominant, except in primitive isolated societies; but that there exist in any territory or among any people churches and states to which all other organizations are formally subordinate. This subordination may be exclusive either to a church or to the state, or it may relate to both simultaneously. Frequently, at least, the latter is the case, a local subsidiary organization being subordinate in some respects to the state, in other respects to a superior church.

II

The subordination of organizations to these supreme organizations is direct or indirect, and in most cases it is both.

[2] It is unnecessary to enter into the question of the subordination of churches to states; or of states to churches, or their partnership by concordats, etc., either from a political, legal, or ecclesiastical standpoint. These questions are perhaps of interest in the United States only as to churches which are formally limited by their own constitutions to the United States. It would appear that the Church of England is formally, in the temporal sense at least, subordinate to the government of the United Kingdom. But such questions from the organization standpoint have no place here. The fact is that churches whose formal organizations are international in scope are necessarily independent of governments in principle. This does not mean that they may not affect or limit each other — they do; but that the relation is an external one, not one of inherent superiority or inferiority of position. The relations between them are chiefly regulated by informal organization.

Where it is direct, some rights and privileges or limitations of the subordinate organization as such are prescribed and guaranteed by the superior organizations, as, for example, in the relation of the state to corporations. When it is indirect, permission to exist is implied, and it is within the rights and privileges of individuals to contribute their services to these subordinate organizations. Thus all individuals are subordinate to a state,[3] and may also be subordinate to a corporation or other organization.

This process of subordination is manifestly quite complex, often involving many intermediate stages. Thus, government has several branches and many departments, sub-departments, and local organizations. Churches have archdioceses, dioceses, parishes, districts, and departments; corporations and associations have similar subdivisions and specializations, functional and territorial.

The effect of subordination of organizations is to limit their purposes or the ways in which they may operate, and sometimes also to limit the number or the character or the status of persons who may "belong" to them. It is for this reason that all subordinate organizations may be described as incomplete and dependent. This is the point upon which major emphasis is required here. In the language used in Chapter VI,[4] disregarding society altogether, all organizations except the state or a church are partial systems, being parts of larger systems, and can only be regarded as in isolation and independent within special limits. Always when this is the case the relationships with the superior organizations are treated as a constant, the changes or phenomena under consideration being equally affected by these general and superior conditions.[5]

---

[3] But they are only subordinate in fact either through concrete formal organizations or through the individual "state of mind." This will be developed in Chapters XII and XVII.

[4] Page 77.

[5] It will be recalled that an organization is a subordinate system of a specific

In dealing with the ordinary subordinate organizations to which we give direct everyday attention, it is rarely safe to disregard the superior organizations, that is, to assume they are constant. Not only are the characteristics of subordinate systems of coöperation in large measure directly or indirectly determined by prescription of superior organizations, but these superior organizations themselves are composed of the complex of subordinate organizations, so that what takes place within the latter, their existence, their success or failure, react upon the superior organization. Thus a state as a formal organization depends in its functions and in its success or failure on the character and vitality not only of its citizens but also, and chiefly, of the organizations to which those citizens contribute, that is, of which they are "members." In fact, the organized activity of citizens as such is almost entirely contained within those subordinate organizations. Moreover, it appears quite impossible that a citizen should have any concrete interaction with his government, or the latter with him, except through subordinate organizations.[6]

---

larger system, the coöperative system, whose components are physical, biological, and personal systems. The relations with other organizations which are now being discussed are outside this specific coöperative system. Other organizations are a part of the social environment of the organization. It is for this reason I have used the phrase "complex of organizations" rather than "system." Usually the most significant relationships of a unit organization are those with the specific coöperative system of which it is a part. It is this system which primarily and on the whole in most instances determines the chief conditions of the organization's existence. This may be true in more limited degree, however, where a superior organization is a process of integration with a corresponding coöperative system of larger scope. For example, a telephone complex of organizations relates to a complex of physical systems, so that each local coöperative system is definitely a part of this larger coöperative system. Under such conditions a local organization is subordinate in an important sense which does not apply in high degree at least to the relations between it and a government organization, for example.

[6] Important indirect relationships of the citizen with government are through informal organization of society, in establishing norms of conduct which re-

III

This takes us to another observation of importance, namely, that complex organization involves competition for the contribution of individuals, and makes conflicts of loyalties unavoidable.[7] This competition is not merely between subordinate organizations of the same rank — for example, for employees by several corporations — but also between superior and subordinate organizations. Thus the state and a subordinate corporation both compete for the support of the same individual; and similarly the corporation competes with its own department for the loyalty of the men assigned to it, and cannot tolerate much more or much less than a certain combination of loyalties to itself directly and indirectly through its department. Similarly, a church may be built on the doctrine that it is one indivisible body of believers, directly subordinate to fundamental dogma and canons that are general, and yet also prescribe and in practice inculcate limited obligations and loyalty to subdivisions, or diocesan and parochial bodies or authorities.

This means that no complex organization is similar to a mechanical agglomeration of groups of mechanisms in which the parts are related to the whole only through a single group. Individuals stand outside all organizations and have multiple relationships with them. As the complex of formal organization becomes more extensive and more intricate, the choice of the individual becomes enlarged; in the exercise of choice, informal organizations[8] serve the function relatively of practical guides in freedom, whereas in simpler, primitive societies they appear to be more definitely prescribers of action.

---

quire, broadly, acceptance of abstract governmental propositions (laws). See Chapter XII, "The Theory of Authority."

[7] This conflict of loyalties is, in part, what is called conflict of moral codes in Chapter XVII, "The Nature of Executive Responsibility."

[8] Discussed more fully in Chapter IX.

II. The Origin and Growth of Organizations

So far we have discussed complex organization without reference to its history or its processes of growth; but the nature of its structure and the limitations upon it are only to be properly understood by reference to the genesis and growth of organizations. In fact, the analysis of the existing complex of formal organizations with its superior and subordinate classifications may be misleading in that it implies progress from the superior to the inferior, from the top down, or a process of division of a whole instead of one of growth. This erroneous impression is emphasized by our historical knowledge of organizations that have endured through long periods. For example, many of the superior formal organizations of western civilization are traceable to the early Christian Church, the empire of Charlemagne, and the government of William the Conqueror. History restricted to these starting points suggests in the main that all existing governmental and religious organizations in western civilization have originated either by subdivision attendant upon growth, or by segmentation of existing organizations as a result of schism, rebellion, or revolution. But back of these is also a long history of formal organizations extending into prehistoric times in the case of government, and to the small group of Apostles in the case of the Church. What the actual origins were may be inferred only from what occurs now; and what the processes of growth may be may similarly be surmised.

I

Now if new organizations be observed, it will be found that they have originated by one or another of four different methods. Either they are (*a*) spontaneous; or they are (*b*) the direct result of an individual's effort to organize; or they are (*c*) infant bodies set off by an existing parent organization; or they are (*d*) the result of segmentation of existing organizations caused by schism, rebellion, or the interposition of an external force.

(*a*) Spontaneous organization is of very frequent occurrence. It takes place when two or more persons simultaneously contribute efforts, without the leadership or initiative of any one of them, to the accomplishment of a common purpose. A considerable number of family organizations are of this origin; but the most frequent cases of spontaneous organization that can be readily observed and unequivocally classified occur in connection with accidents. For example, if someone is knocked down on a public street, it will invariably happen that several persons not previously in contact and unknown to each other will rush to the rescue. Without a recognized leader they will unite their efforts for first aid; or similarly, to extinguish a fire, or to rescue a drowning person, etc. Less frequent but undoubted cases arise where several persons are threatened with a common danger. Coöperation for amusement among strangers not infrequently develops similarly; and there is no doubt that occasional fixed groupings for constructive effort, exploration, or adventure arise in this way also. Certainly these spontaneous organizations in most cases are facilitated by knowledge, in the minds of the participants, of similar coöperative efforts of themselves or others on previous occasions, so that there may be nothing original in the *character* of the coöperation; but the organizations themselves are nevertheless new and spontaneous. No doubt also such organizations are almost always of very short life, so that they ordinarily do not impress us as being organizations, especially because we so persistently regard organizations as fixed groups of men instead of systems of efforts of men. But occasionally, out of perhaps many thousands of cases, one will last for a considerable period. It would only be necessary for one or at most a few such spontaneous organizations to have endured in prehistoric times to have been possibly the origin of much existing organization.

(*b*) Probably a more frequent origin of enduring organizations lies in the deliberate intention of a single person. He conceives and formulates a purpose, transmits it to others, and induces them to coöperate with him.

(*c*) Often quite similar is the germination of subsidiary organization by a parent organization, which sends one man forth to organize a new unit. This is the essence of the expansion of church organization by individual missionary effort; and it is frequent in commercial organizations, for example, when one man is sent to a distant point to organize a branch.

(*d*) While originations of these types are always occurring and in the aggregate constitute an important part of the current organization of purposeful effort at any given time, the many generations during which a considerable amount of complex organization has continued makes it probable that many of the new organizations that persist for long arise out of other organizations by segmentation. This may be caused by the effect of growth; or by schism. In one type of situation this is often described as reorganization required by expansion. In others it is the effect of centrifugal personal forces or the development of conflicting purposes. Sometimes it is the effect of superior external force operating on the principle of "divide and rule." Not infrequently schism and the effect of superior force may proceed so far as to destroy, in any straightforward sense, the original organization.

The use of the word "new" in this connection, however, is subject to important qualification. Often when there is segmentation, the splitting off of subsidiary units in a complex organization, what takes place is not the creation of new organizations but a new complex or grouping of existing organizations. This is neither creation nor even growth. Occasionally there are very radical rearrangements, such as the creation of "new" divisions; but it will be found on examination that these "new" divisions are merely new groups of previous smaller organizations.

II

Now it will be noted that when the origin of organization is spontaneous, or is the result of the initiative of one man, or is the deliberate creation of a parent organization, the beginning is small. The organization comes into being when two or more persons begin to coöperate to a common end. Where there is division by schism, rebellion, this is likewise true, but is usually not so recognized because attention is given to the final breakup of a large complex organization. What takes place beforehand is the growth of a new counter organization or independent organization supported by the efforts of individuals who may in part still continue to support the older organization. So far as I have learned, this beginning is always small; that is, it results from the spontaneous acceptation of a new purpose, independent of and perhaps definitely conflicting with the older purpose, by a small group; or it is prompted by one individual who associates others with himself. Hence, all organizations of complex character grow out of small, simple organizations.[9] It is impossible for formal organizations to grow except by the process of combining unit organizations already existing, or the creation of new units of organization to be added to those in an existing complex.

It may, therefore, be said that all large formal organizations are constituted of numbers of small organizations.[10] It is im-

[9] Perhaps this will be clearer if the process is visualized of trying to organize a group of one hundred or five hundred men. Under the most favorable circumstances, i.e., when they are willing to be organized because there has come about some consensus of opinion as to purpose or objective, the mass must be broken up into small groups with group leaders. Only when by this process unit organizations have been created is it possible to combine these units into a complex organization that can manage itself.

In this connection, I should regard a mob not as a formal organization, simple or complex, but a special type of informal organization, until it has formal leaders.

[10] I exclude the very extreme and special case of large audiences as being of limited pertinence to a discussion of the functions of the executive.

possible to create a large organization except by combining small organizations.[11]

The basic organization, if measured by the number of persons simultaneously contributing to it, is usually quite small — from two to fifteen or twenty persons, and probably not having an average of more than ten. Certain special types of simple organization, however, are very large, just as in biology some cells, such as birds' eggs, are very large. The largest of such organizations which I have observed are a full orchestra or orchestra and chorus; and a public speaker and his audience, which under radio technique reaches enormous size.[12]

The clue to the structural requirements of large complex organizations lies in the reason for the limitations of the size of simple organizations. The limitations are inherent in the

[11] The origins of the major organizations being historically so remote, and the processes of reorganization being apparently often directed from central points or by central authority, we are much under the delusion that large mass organizations are subdivided as a secondary process, the mass having first been created. This is the order in which intellectually we approach the understanding of most large complex organizations; it is the method of analysis, of breaking down a whole into parts. Thus, if we wish to study a government organization or a large telephone system, we may often effectively begin with the constitution, the major departments, the parent company, etc. But this procedure is as if we subdivided a trunk of a tree or a piece of flesh into fibres and membranes and finally into cells, being misled into thinking that these subdivisions developed after the existence of an undifferentiated protoplasm of the same mass.

Many theoretical and practical errors arise from employing this analytical approach except for immediate limited purposes. For it is, I think, as true of organization as it is of all living things that they grow by the multiplication of cells and begin with single cells. It is true that quite often a fusion of two existing simple or complex organizations into one complex organization takes place; but fundamentally the growth is from single-cell organizations.

[12] A descriptive catalogue and classification of organizations from the standpoint of unit size would be of interest in a more exhaustive treatment. For example, clubs furnish an illustration of rather large units which are partly structured by "working" units (staff, officers, committees and official meetings of members), and temporary "playing" or "social" units.

necessities of intercommunication.[13] In Chapter VII we discussed communication between persons as an essential element of coöperative systems; it is also the limiting factor in the size of simple organizations and, therefore, a dominant factor in the structure of complex organizations. We must now consider why this is true.

III

Under most ordinary conditions, even with simple purposes, not many men can see what each is doing or the whole situation; nor can many communicate essential information regarding or governing specific action without a central channel or leader. But a leader likewise is limited in time (and capacity) in communicating with many persons contemporaneously, especially if they are widely separated so that he must move about. In practice a limit of usually less than fifteen persons obtains, and for many types of coöperation five or six persons is the practicable limit.

These limits are widely exceeded in certain special cases, chiefly those where the action involved is that of extreme habitual practice within narrow limits, as in military drill and orchestral performance, where there are both individual and collective habituation and a precise special system of language or some other special means of communication; and those where the action is limited substantially to one person, the others being relatively passive, as in an audience. In this case the organization is practically limited (at least for the time being) to communication in one direction only.[14] Moreover, in the case of audiences and speakers, this communication is an end in itself.

Fundamentally, communication is necessary to translate pur-

[13] These limitations, therefore, arise out of the joint effect of physical, biological, and social factors. See Chapter V.

[14] Where not limited to one direction, a leader — moderator, chairman, i.e., an executive — is required.

pose into terms of the concrete action required to effect it — what to do and when and where to do it. This necessitates knowledge of the conditions of the environment, and of the action under way. Under very simple and usually temporary conditions and with small numbers of persons the communication problem often appears simple, but under many conditions, even with small numbers, a special channel of communication is required. For if all talk at once there is confusion; and there is indecision particularly as to timing of actions. This creates the necessity for a leader. The size of the unit, therefore, usually is determined by the limitations of effective leadership. These limitations depend upon (*a*) the complexity of purpose and technological conditions; (*b*) the difficulty of the communication process; (*c*) the extent to which communication is necessary; (*d*) the complexity of the personal relationships involved, that is, of the social conditions.

(*a*) It is clear that when the purpose is not simple — that is, when its requirements are complex and not obvious, or the conditions require precision of coördinated movements, or the nature of the individual action necessary is difficult to grasp by the actor (or by the leader) — much more communication is necessary than under the contrary conditions.

(*b*) It is also evident that the difficulty of the communication process has an important bearing on the size of the organization unit. There are many things that are difficult to communicate by words — in some matters it is impossible. When the difficulty is great it is evident that the time required may limit the number between whom communication may be effectively had; for example, communication perhaps must be accomplished by demonstration.

(*c*) It is apparent that if each actor can see what the other is doing and can see the situation as a whole, the amount of positive communication is reduced. Thus, if five men are working together on a simple task (say pulling a boat into the water) little communication is required; but if five men are coördinating efforts under conditions such that they cannot see each other and the whole situation, constant communication is often necessary. Moreover, if men know what to do from previous experience and can work on the basis of habit and acquired skill, a minimum of communication is required; or if they are accustomed to working together, a special language which they evolve cuts down the time of communication.

(d) The complexity of the relationships in any group increases with great rapidity as the number of persons in the group increases. If the simplest possible relationship between two persons is that of "knowing" each other as accomplished by a mutual introduction, then the relational complexity at the very least increases as follows:

Number in Group	Number of Relationships	Increase in Relationships with Each Addition to Group
2	1	..
3	3	2
4	6	3
5	10	4
6	15	5
7	21	6
8	28	7
9	36	8
10	45	9
15	105	..
20	190	..
50	1225	..

The relationships between persons in a group will be "active" in a great variety of subgroupings which may constantly change. If A, B, C, D, and E constitute a group of five, then subgroups may be made as follows: ten pairs, ten triplets, five groups of four, one of five. If only one person be added to the group of

five, the possible subgroups become: fifteen pairs, twenty triplets, fifteen groups of four, six groups of five, and one of six.

A person has relationships not only with others individually
and with groups, but groups are related to groups. As the
number of possible groups increases, the complexity of group
relationship increases in greater ratio.[15]

The complexity of relationships within groups is important
in two aspects: technologically and socially. Technologically,
the burden of coördination, that is, the communication function
of a leader, will increase in the proportion that the relationships
increase; and the ability of individuals and groups without leadership to coördinate is also quickly outrun with increase in the
size of groups. The same is true of the social or informal
organization relationships. The capacity of persons to maintain social relationships is obviously limited. If the technological
group is larger than is adapted to social limitations, the social
organization groupings cannot correspond to the technological
requirements. Since a large part of the communication of
organizations is informal, the burden on formal channels is
thereby increased.[16]

These factors, and probably others also, limit the size of the
fundamental organization cell. I shall call the simple basic
organization form a "unit" organization. It differs from the
ideal organization of Chapter VII in that it is never found
isolated from other organizations and is always subordinate to
some other formal organization directly or indirectly, being

[15] A suggestive exposition of this subject in quantitative terms is given by
V. A. Graicunas' "Relationship in Organization," reprinted in *Papers on the
Science of Administration*, edited by Gulick & Urwick (New York: Institute of
Public Administration, 1937).

[16] See also discussion on p. 225. I have strongly the opinion that there may
be substantial variations in social satisfactions related to disparities between the
size of organizations as determined technologically by organization purpose
and the size of "natural" social groups. "Natural" would be affected by the
personalities involved.

ultimately subordinate to and dependent upon either a church or a state or both.

IV

The size of a unit organization being usually restricted very narrowly by the necessities of communication, it follows that growth of organization beyond the limits so imposed can only be accomplished by the creation of new unit organizations, or by grouping together two or more unit organizations already existing. When an organization grows by the addition of the services of more persons it is compelled, if it reaches the limit of size, to establish a second unit; and henceforward it is a complex of two unit organizations. All organizations except unit organizations are a group of two or more unit organizations. Hence, a large organization of complex character consists not of the services of individuals directly but of those of subsidiary unit organizations. Nowhere in the world, I think, can there be found a large organization that is not composed of small units. We think of them as having descended from the mass, whereas the mass can only be created from the units.[17]

Usually when two and always when several unit organizations are combined in one complex organization, the necessities of communication impose a super-leader, who becomes, usually

[17] A group of two or more unit organizations may coöperate as a whole without a formal superior organization or leader. Under many conditions this is observed, especially where two small organizations (or a large and a small) work together under contract for specified purposes. The method of communication is primarily that of conference. Because of our habit of considering an organization as a group of persons rather than as systems of coöperative services of persons, the usually temporary combinations that are made as a result of contracts or agreements are not recognized as organizations, since they have no name or common officials. Most large building operations are so organized, however; and it will be readily seen that a very large part of the organized activities of today are carried on by temporary limited combinations under contracts without a general coördinating "authority." The state, through the law of contracts and the provisions of courts, is a general formal executive in these cases in limited degree; but the real general executive is custom, etc.

with assistants, an "overhead" unit of organization. Similarly, groups of groups are combined into larger wholes. The most obvious case of complex structure of this type is an army. The fact that these large organizations are built up of small unit organizations is neglected in the spectacular size that ensues, and we often pass from the whole or major divisions to "men." The resulting dismissal from the mind of the inescapable practice of unit organization often leads to utterly unrealistic attitudes regarding organization problems.

III. The Executive Organization

In a unit organization there are executive functions to be performed, but not necessarily by a single individual continuously. They may be performed alternately by the several persons who contribute to the organization. In complex organizations, on the other hand, the necessities of communication result almost invariably in the localization of the executive functions of the subordinate unit organizations normally in one person. This is necessary for reasons of formal communication; but it is also necessary to establish executive organizations, that is, those units specializing in the executive functions. The executives of several unit organizations as a group, usually with at least one other person as a superior, form an executive organization. Accordingly, persons specializing in the executive functions in most cases are "members" of, or contributors to, two units of organization in one complex organization — first, the so-called "working" unit, and second, the executive unit. This is clearly seen in practice, it being customary to recognize a foreman, or a superintendent of a shop section, or a captain, at one time or from one point of view as a "member" of his gang, shop crew, or company, at another time or from another point of view as a member of a "district management group," or the "shop executives' group," or the "regimental organization." Under such condition a single concrete action or decision is an activity of two different unit organizations. This simultaneous contribution to two organizations by a single act appears to be the critical fact in all complex organization; that is, the complex is made an organic whole by it. Here again, it will be noted that the definition of formal organization as an impersonal system of efforts and influences is supported by the facts more closely in accord with concrete phenomena than the "group membership" idea. One person often functions in or contributes services to several different units of the same complex organization, as well as to different external organizations. For payroll, and many other formal purposes, it is convenient to regard every person as being "in" only one unit organization; but this is merely a matter of convenience for certain purposes, and is misleading as to the actual operation of organizations even for many other practical purposes.

The size of executive units of organizations is limited generally by the same conditions that govern the size of unit organizations of other kinds. When there are many basic working units, therefore, there must be several primary executive unit organizations, from the heads of which will be secured the personnel of superior executive units. And so on, in extensive pyramids of executive units in very large complex organizations.[18]

[18] Professor Philip Cabot, in a published address, once quoted my opinion that organizations are best regarded as circular or spherical, with the chief executive positions in the center. This was based on discussions with him and an unpublished manuscript which he was kind enough to examine. I have, however, followed the conventional figures here, because they are well established, and because there appears to be no practicable way to diagram the system of authoritative communication that does not result in a "pyramid" (usually in two-dimensional perspectives, however) which put the chief executive positions at the top. They also are frequently located on top floors. Probably all spatial figures for organization are seriously misleading; but if they are used to cover the functioning of organizations as distinguished from its structural aspects, either the center of a circle or of a sphere better suggests the relationships. The nearest approach to this, I think, is the practice of regarding the location of G.H.Q. in field armies as *behind* the lines centrally.

In summary, we may say that historically and functionally all complex organizations are built up from units of organization, and consist of many units of "working" or "basic" organizations, overlaid with units of executive organizations; and that the essential structural characteristics of complex organizations are determined, by the effect of the necessity for communication upon the size of a unit organization.

CHAPTER IX

INFORMAL ORGANIZATIONS AND THEIR RELATION TO FORMAL ORGANIZATIONS

IT has already been necessary several times to mention informal organizations, and in two of the succeeding chapters it will be seen that they are important aspects of the subjects treated.[1] It is therefore advisable to discuss informal organizations very briefly, chiefly to show their relationship to formal organizations and to the operations of the latter. I propose to present the following: I, The nature of informal organizations; II, Certain important effects and consequences of informal organizations; III, The creation of informal by formal organizations; and IV, The functions of informal in formal organizations.

I. What Informal Organizations Are

It is a matter of general observation and experience that persons are frequently in contact and interact with each other when their relationships are not a part of or governed by any formal organization. The magnitude of the numbers involved varies from two persons to that of a large mob or crowd. The characteristic of these contacts or interactions is that they occur and continue or are repeated without any specific conscious *joint* purpose. The contact may be accidental, or incidental to organized activities, or arise from some personal desire or gregarious instinct; it may be friendly or hostile. But whatever the origins, the fact of such contacts, interactions, or groupings changes the experience, knowledge, attitudes, and emotions of the individuals affected. Sometimes we are aware of the fact

---

[1] Chapter XII, "The Theory of Authority," *passim* and especially at p. 169; and Chapter XV, "The Executive Functions," especially at pp. 223–224.

that our emotions are affected, for example, by being in a crowd; more often we observe effects of such relationships in others; still more frequently we are not aware of any permanent effects either in ourselves or in others by direct observation. But we nevertheless currently show that we infer such effects by using the phrase "mob psychology," by recognizing imitation and emulation, by understanding that there are certain attitudes commonly held, and very often by our use of the phrases "consensus of opinion" and "public opinion." The persistence of such effects is embodied in "states of mind" and habits of action which indicate the capacities of memory, experience, and social conditioning. As a result of these capacities some of the effects of contacts of persons with limited numbers of persons can spread through very large numbers in a sort of endless chain of interaction over wide territories and through long periods of time.

By informal organization I mean the aggregate of the personal contacts and interactions and the associated groupings of people that I have just described. Though common or joint purposes are excluded by definition, common or joint results of important character nevertheless come from such organization.

Now it is evident from this description that informal organization is indefinite and rather structureless, and has no definite subdivision. It may be regarded as a shapeless mass of quite varied densities, the variations in density being a result of external factors affecting the closeness of people geographically or of formal purposes which bring them specially into contact for conscious joint accomplishments. These areas of special density I call informal organizations, as distinguished from societal or general organization in its informal aspects. Thus there is an informal organization of a community, of a state. For our purposes, it is important that there are informal organizations related to formal organizations everywhere.

II. Consequences of Informal Organizations

Informal organization, although comprising the processes of society which are unconscious as contrasted with those of formal organization which are conscious, has two important classes of effects: (*a*) it establishes certain attitudes, understandings, customs, habits, institutions; and (*b*) it creates the condition under which formal organization may arise.

(*a*) The most general direct effects of informal organization are customs, mores, folklore, institutions, social norms and ideals — a field of importance in general sociology and especially in social psychology and in social anthropology. No discussion of these effects is necessary here, except on two points. The first is that as a result, as I think, of the inadequate attention to formal organization there is much confusion between formal institutions, resulting directly from formal organizational processes, and informal institutions resulting from informal organization; for example, a practice established by legal enactment, and a custom, the latter usually prevailing in the event of conflict. Not only locally, in restricted collectivities, but in broad areas and large collectivities, there is a divergence, and a corrective interaction, between institutions informally developed and those elaborated through formal organization practices. The first correspond to the unconscious or non-intellectual actions and habits of individuals, the second to their reasoned and calculated actions and policies. The actions of formal organizations are relatively quite logical.[2]

(*b*) Informal association is rather obviously a condition which necessarily precedes formal organization. The possibility of accepting a common purpose, of communicating, and of attaining a state of mind under which there is willingness to coöperate, requires prior contact and preliminary interaction. This is especially clear in those cases where the origin of formal

[2] See Chapter XIII for the discussion of this fact.

organization is spontaneous. The informal relationship in such cases may be exceedingly brief, and of course conditioned by previous experience and knowledge of both informal and formal organization.

The important consideration for our purposes, however, is that informal organization compels a certain amount of formal organization, and probably cannot persist or become extensive without the emergence of formal organization. This partly results from the recognition of similarity of needs and interests which continuation of contact implies. When these needs and interests are material and not social, either combination and coöperation — at least to the extent of the development of a distributive purpose [3] — or conflict of interest, antagonism, hostility, and disorganization ensue.

Even when the needs and interests are not material but are social — that is, there is a gregarious need of interaction for its own sake — it likewise requires a considerable concentration upon definite purposes or ends of action to maintain the association. This is especially true if instead of gregarious impulses one goes back to a *need of action* as a primary propensity or instinct. It is an observable fact that men are universally active, and that they seek objects of activity. Correlative with this is the observation that enduring social contact, even when the object is exclusively social, seems generally impossible without activity. It will be generally noted that a purely passive or bovine kind of association among men is of short duration. They seem impelled to *do something*. It is frequently the case that the existence of organizations depends upon satisfactions in mere association, and that this is the uniform and only motive of all participants. In these cases, nevertheless, we can, I think, always observe a purpose, or concrete object of action, which may be of minor importance or even trivial. In these cases it may make no difference in a direct and substantial sense whether

[3] See Chapter III, pp. 32–33.

the objective is accomplished or not. For example, the discussion of some subject (or subjects) is essential to conversation which is socially desirable, yet the participants may be and frequently are rather indifferent to the subject itself. But the personal associations which give the satisfactions depends upon discussing *something*. This is easily observed in ordinary social affairs.

Thus a concrete object of action is necessary to social satisfactions. The simplest form of doing something together is, of course, conversation, but it is evident that any particular form of activity for one reason or another is exhausted usually in a short time and that alternative methods of activity are on the whole not easy to devise either by individuals or groups. Hence, the great importance of established patterns of activity. Where circumstances develop so that a variety of outlets for activity involving associations are not readily available — as is often the case, for example, with unemployed persons — the situation is one in which the individual is placed in a sort of social vacuum, producing a feeling and also objective behavior of being "lost." I have seen this a number of times. Where the situation affects a number of persons simultaneously they are likely to do any sort of mad thing. The necessity for action where a group of persons is involved seems to be almost overwhelming. I think this necessity underlies such proverbs as "Idle hands make mischief," and I have no doubt that it may be the basis for a great deal of practice within armies.

The opposite extreme to lack of concrete objectives of action is a condition of social complexity such that action may take a great many different forms involving the possibilities of association with many different groups. In such situations the individual may be unable to decide which activity he wishes to indulge in, or what groups he wishes to be associated with. This may induce a sort of paralysis of action through inability to make choice, or it may be brought about by conflict of obligations. The resulting condition was described by the

French sociologist Durkheim as "anomie." This I take to be a state of individual paralysis of social action due to the absence of effective norms of conduct.

The activities of individuals necessarily take place within local immediate groups. The relation of a man to a large organization, or to his nation, or to his church, is necessarily through those with whom he is in *immediate* contact. Social activities cannot be action at a distance. This seems not to have been sufficiently noted. It explains, or justifies, a statement made to me that comradeship is much more powerful than patriotism, etc., in the behavior of soldiers.[4] The essential need of the individual is association, and that requires local activity or immediate interaction between individuals. Without it the man is lost. The willingness of men to endure onerous routine and dangerous tasks which they could avoid is explained by this necessity for action at all costs in order to maintain the sense of social integration, whether the latter arises from "instinct," or from social conditioning, or from physiological necessity, or all three. Whether this necessity for action in a social setting arises exclusively from biological factors, or is partly inherent in gregarious association, need not be considered.

Finally, purposive coöperation is the chief outlet for the logical or scientific faculties of men, and is the principal source of them as well. Rational action is chiefly a purposive coöperative action, and the personal capacity of rational action is largely derived from it.

For these reasons, either small enduring informal organizations or large collectivities seem always to possess a considerable number of formal organizations. These are the definite structural material of a society. They are the poles around which personal associations are given sufficient consistency to retain continuity. The alternative is disintegration into hostile groups, the hostility itself being a source of integrating purposes (defense and offense) of the groups which are differentiated

[4] See footnote 4, p. 148.

by hostility. Thus as formal organization becomes extended in scope it permits and requires an expansion of societal cohesiveness. This is most obviously the case when formal organization complexes of government expand — government itself is insufficient, except where economic and religious functions are included in it. Where with the expansion of formal government complexes there is correlative expansion of religious, military, economic, and other formal organizations, the structure of a large-scale society is present. When these formal complexes fail or contract, social disintegration sets in. There appear to be no societies which in fact are not completely structured by formal organizations — beginning with families and ending in great complexes of states and religions.

This is not to deny, but to reaffirm, that the attitudes, institutions, customs, of informal society affect and are partly expressed through formal organization. They are interdependent aspects of the same phenomena — a society is structured by formal organizations, formal organizations are vitalized and conditioned by informal organization. What is asserted is that there cannot be one without the other. If one fails the other disintegrates. Nor is this to say that when disintegrated the separated or conflicting societies (except isolated societies) have no affect upon each other. Quite the contrary; but the effect is not coöperative but polemic; and even so requires formal organization within the conflicting societies. Complete absence of formal organization would then be a state of nearly complete individualism and disorder.

III. The Creation of Informal by Formal Organizations

Formal organizations arise out of and are necessary to informal organization; but when formal organizations come into operation, they create and require informal organizations.

It seems not easily to be recognized without long and close observation that an important and often indispensable part of a formal system of coöperation is informal. In fact, more often than not those with ample experience (officials and executives of all sorts of formal organizations) will deny or neglect the existence of informal organizations within their "own" formal organizations. Whether this is due to excessive concentration on the problems of formal organization, or to reluctance to acknowledge the existence of what is difficult to define or describe, or what lacks in concreteness, it is unnecessary to consider. But it is undeniable that major executives and even entire executive organizations are often completely unaware of widespread influences, attitudes, and agitations within their organizations. This is true not only of business organizations but also of political organizations, governments, armies, churches, and universities.

Yet one will hear repeatedly that "you can't understand an organization or how it works from its organization chart, its charter, rules and regulations, nor from looking at or even watching its personnel." "Learning the organization ropes" in most organizations is chiefly learning who's who, what's what, why's why, of its informal society. One could not determine very closely how the government of the United States works from reading its Constitution, its court decisions, its statutes, or its administrative regulations. Although ordinarily used in a derogatory sense, the phrase "invisible government" expresses a recognition of informal organization.

Informal organizations as associated with formal organization, though often understood intuitively by managers, politicians, and other organization authorities, have only been definitely studied, so far as I know, at the production level of industrial organizations.[5] In fact, informal organization is so

[5] See especially the following: Elton Mayo, *The Human Problems of an Industrial Civilization* (New York: The Macmillan Co., 1933); T. N. Whitehead, *Leadership in a Free Society* (Cambridge: Harvard University Press, 1936) and *The Industrial Worker*, 2 vols. (Cambridge: Harvard University Press, 1938);

much a part of our matter-of-course intimate experience of everyday association, either in connection with formal organizations or not, that we are unaware of it, seeing only a part of the specific interactions involved. Yet it is evident that association of persons in connection with a formal or specific activity inevitably involves interactions that are incidental to it.

IV. The Functions of Informal in Formal Organizations

One of the indispensable functions of informal organizations in formal organizations — that of communication — has already been indicated.[6] Another function is that of the maintenance of cohesiveness in formal organizations through regulating the willingness to serve and the stability of objective authority.[7] A third function is the maintenance of the feeling of personal integrity, of self-respect, of independent choice. Since the interactions of informal organization are not consciously dominated by a given impersonal objective or by authority as the organization expression, the interactions are apparently characterized by choice, and furnish the opportunities often for reinforcement of personal attitudes. Though often this function is deemed destructive of formal organization, it is to be regarded as a means of maintaining the personality of the individual against certain effects of formal organizations which tend to disintegrate the personality.

The purpose of this chapter has been to show (1) that those interactions between persons which are based on personal rather

F. J. Roethlisberger and W. J. Dickson, *Management and the Worker*, Business Research Studies No. 9 (Harvard Graduate School of Business Administration, 1938). See also works of Mary P. Follett, who had great insight into the dynamic elements of organization; see especially her paper reprinted in *Papers on the Science of Administration*, edited by Gulick & Urwick (New York: Institute of Public Administration, 1937).

[6] Chapter VIII, "The Structure of Complex Formal Organizations," p. 96.

[7] See Chapter XII, "The Theory of Authority," especially at p. 169 ff.

than on joint or common purposes, because of their repetitive character become systematic and organized through their effect upon habits of action and thought and through their promotion of uniform states of mind; (2) that although the number of persons with whom any individual may have interactive experience is limited, nevertheless the endless-chain relationship between persons in a society results in the development, in many respects, over wide areas and among many persons, of uniform states of mind which crystallize into what we call mores, customs, institutions; (3) that informal organization gives rise to formal organizations, and that formal organizations are necessary to any large informal or societal organization; (4) that formal organizations also make explicit many of the attitudes, states of mind, and institutions which develop directly through informal organizations, with tendencies to divergence, resulting in interdependence and mutual correction of these results in a general and only approximate way; (5) that formal organizations, once established, in their turn also create informal organizations; and (6) that informal organizations are necessary to the operation of formal organizations as a means of communication, of cohesion, and of protecting the integrity of the individual.

This completes the difficult presentation of the theory of cooperative systems and organizations. Parts III and IV which follow are concerned with the behavior of organizations and of people in them, especially of executives. The presentation is largely in terms of this theory and expresses the theory more concretely, but is based closely on experience and direct observation rather than on general knowledge and reasoning.

PART III
THE ELEMENTS OF FORMAL ORGANIZATIONS

CHAPTER X

THE BASES AND KINDS OF SPECIALIZATIONS

THREE terms are in current use to denominate the same subject: "division of labor," "specialization," "functionalization." Each of these terms implies the other at least in considerable degree, with some variations in meaning of local or personal preference. There is, however, some approach to consistency of usage in that "division of labor" seems usually to connote a *general social setting* and an aspect of large economic systems, whereas "functionalization" is used within large organizations with emphasis upon a particular kind of work as a function of an organic system of work; and "specialization" places the emphasis upon the *person* or groups of persons. Thus men specialize, but work is functionalized. In either event, there is division of labor — and of necessity a corresponding division of work.

Unfortunately, all of these terms fail to mark important distinctions which, if possible, must be secured from the context in which they are used. For example, specialization may relate to the *kind of thing* done, where the reference is to differences in material, or it may relate to the *way* in which work is done. Often one aspect implies the other. Digging potatoes and digging coal relate to different processes, but it is also true that often different methods of working at the same material produce either different products or the same products more "efficiently" or "effectively."

Thus, "specialization" more and more with the growth of technology has implied difference of process. This tendency has been reinforced by the fact that two of the bases of specialization — superior natural personal adaptation to the task (broadly, skill), and the effect of repetitive experience — connote differences in "ways" or processes, though often of subtle character.

With this tendency there has been a shift farther and farther from the explicit recognition of two of the important bases of specialization, place and time. Both have been so bound up with the conception of the individual who was "specializing," and who always had to be somewhere at some time while working, that they have been taken for granted and their significance missed. Yet both place and time are bases of specializations or division of labor prior to, and perhaps even in modern times more important than, specializations based on technical process, or even on kinds of material worked on.

It is probable that place and time can without great consequence be neglected in most instances where *personal* specialization is considered without reference to organization; that is, where place, time, and organization for limited purposes may be disregarded. This is not true when the specialization of *organizations* is itself in question. One has only to consider railroad and communication or military organizations to perceive that specialization of subsidiary organizations by both time and place is of critical importance. The utmost skill and the most refined differentiation of processes will instantly wither if there is failure in time or place.

But this does not exhaust the factors of specialization. Wherever organization is present what I shall call "associational specialization" is at once initiated. By this I mean the repeated mutual adjustment of persons to persons in coöperative effort.

I

Thus the bases of specialization of organizations (and of individuals also) are five: (*a*) the place where work is done; (*b*) the time at which work is done; (*c*) the persons with whom work is done; (*d*) the things upon which work is done; and (*e*) the method or process by which work is done. Usually a complete statement of objective or purpose of coöperation will require reference to the first four of these items and often to all five. On the foundation of these elements the extreme division of labor and the minute specializations of western civilizations rest. They are not stated here in an effort to attain theoretical completeness, but because they are all essential to the understanding of concrete conditions of organizations and coöperative systems. Whether from the aspect of definition of purpose, or from that of the deliberate construction of complex organizations, or from that of the "pathology" of unit organizations or groups of them, these bases of specialization, which are largely interdependent, both as a whole and in particular are of first importance theoretically and practically.

Because this is certainly not recognized generally, it will be in order to be more explicit.

(*a*) It is generally impossible to avoid geographical specialization. Work must be done somewhere, not everywhere. Since the coöperative system or unit organization is a system of efforts of individuals who have physical location, such a system is usually so obviously local and so frequently described in local terms that the significance of this fact escapes attention, despite practical problems that not infrequently arise from it. Thus, if two organizations are doing identical kinds of work (digging a ditch, for example) they must be digging ditches in separate locations. The difference is often not significant; but it often is. Those who occupy positions in the management of organizations often compare the effectiveness or efficiency of two organizations doing the same kind of work, and are well aware that the "differences" in conditions are frequent explanations of differences in apparent results. Often these explanations are not adequate, but they frequently are and always may be. In fact the "same kind" of work is always different when the location is different. Farming one quarter section may be the same kind of work as farming the adjacent section; but any farmer knows that as a system of concrete activities it may be radically different, and, moreover, that effective and efficient work may depend upon a "specialized" knowledge of terrain.

Geographical specialization is in fact more fundamental and precedes specialization of function or processes in the usual sense. Thus, if a large number of persons contribute to a complex organization, doing the same type of work, they must function in organizational units at different locations; and the coördination of effort will be a geographical coördination in its primary aspects. Hence the universal use of geographical description in identifying organizations.[1]

Reference has already been made in Chapter III to the fact that one of the alternatives of coöperative effort is to facilitate further coöperation by deliberate alteration of the physical factors of the situation. This is done by carrying on improvements and the construction of tools and machinery. Much of this relates to process; but much of it is a matter of adapting location to other factors of specialization. Thus shelter, heating, etc., are methods of securing freedom in one sense from geographical specialization, accomplished by still greater geographical restriction in another sense; for example, confinement to a particular building.

(*b*) The relations between seasons and between night and day are obvious bases of specialization of work. The limitations of the endurance of human beings is another basis, of even greater importance in modern industrial organization.

Specialization of organizations with respect to time is one of the most obvious bases of division of labor in continuous-service enterprises, and the scheduling of such specializations is among the most complex of the processes of coördination in them. Because the method of work, especially of individuals,

---

[1] For example, the Central Division, the Boston District, the Newark Diocese, the Pacific Fleet.

seems the same in most cases in different hours of the day or days of the week or seasons, it has been much overlooked in the general consideration of specialization; yet the capacity, or disposition, to adhere to time-schedule assignments is possibly the most important single basis of selection of persons — the factor being called "dependability" as respects punctuality and continuity of function.

(c) Specialization with reference to the persons doing work in organizational relations and with reference to the organization itself I have called "associational specialization." Some common expressions of the existence and function of associational specialization are: "They are used to working together," "You don't know people until you work with them," "He knows his men," etc. Every relatively stable or enduring unit organization is an associational specialization in itself.

Specialization in this sense is one of the most important aspects of executive organization, and to it considerable attention will be given in Chapter XV.[2] It is also an aspect of small informal organizations, as presented in Chapter IX.

(d) It is obvious that objectives of effort or purposes of work are specializations. In many cases this will be expressed in terms of the materials to be used, when commodities or material products are the objects of effort. In other cases the end to be accomplished, especially where "services" are to be performed, will express the specialization. In either event, there is usually some implication of differences in process, but the emphasis is not on such differences. The question of emphasis is, however, one of interest or point of view. In most cases "functionalization" is an expression of "specialization" where the emphasis is upon the end to be accomplished, differences of process being implicit and taken for granted.

(e) Finally there is specialization of process, particularly stressed when several methods of accomplishing the same char-

[2] Pages 223 ff.

acter of results is in mind. These specializations rest upon either superior natural adaptation of persons — that is, a selective process precedes the working process — or upon increase in skill from repetitive experience, or upon increase of knowledge by study and experience.

II

This very brief statement regarding specialization is given here as a convenient background for the presentation of the following general propositions: (1) that the effectiveness of coöperative systems depends almost entirely upon the invention or adoption of *innovations* of specialization; and (ii) that the primary aspect of specialization is the *analysis of purpose* or general ends into intermediate or detailed ends which are means to the more remote ends.

I

In Chapter III, it was shown that the primary aspect of coöperative systems was the effect of coördination of the activities of two or more persons on the overcoming of the limitations involved in the relations between the biological capacities of individuals and the natural environment. This coördination may proceed on one of two principles: on the principle of simultaneity of effort, or on that of efforts in series. The first was called contemporaneous coöperation and the second progressive coöperation. In cases where the power factor is the significant individual limitation, or where limitations of the range of individual sense organs or of individual position are important, approximate simultaneity of effort is used to increase power, or to extend range of perception. In cases where endurance of effort or attention or limitation of speed of individual movement are important, a progressive application of energy or attention among two or more persons is required to overcome individual limitations.

It is evident that in either class of cases the dominant factor of order is that of time and that each activity is specialized in terms of time. It is of course true that the effectiveness of the action of the isolated individual also depends upon the same factor of order. In some cases doing two different things at the *same* time is necessary, and in almost all cases the *order* of acts in a time series is the decisive factor. But as respects the individual the spatial aspects of the situation are of equal relevance and time-order is an aspect of spatial factors. In order to do something requiring change of position, time is necessary. In the coöperative situation, however, although of course the spatial dimensions are inherent in the physical conditions, time-order is predominant. This is so implicit in all successful coöperation that it is taken for granted and its fundamental significance is missed. In unsuccessful coöperative attempts, however, a major cause of failure is error of temporal coördination. If there is failure of simultaneity of effort, the power factor is not increased over that of the individual, nor is the range of observation widened. When the limitations to be overcome are of power or range of observation this is usually apparent. When continuity of effort or periodic action is required, failure of order in the time series is more frequently not noted as a cause of failure. The right things are done in the wrong time-order very often.

The discovery or invention of the correct order of coöperative acts is the first step in the development of coöperative systems. But temporal order will be only one indispensable element. Another for any series of concrete acts will be spatial. The act will take place somewhere; and since the acts of organization are those of persons (by definition), they will take place where the acting persons are. This is sometimes true only in a limited sense, particularly when the act is one of communication. But as to those activities which relate to work done on the physical environment, the acts must be specialized to the effective locations.

Thus action at the "right" place and at the "right" time, that is, double coördination by time and place, where either or both exceed the capacities of the individual, is the clue to effectiveness of coöperation. The perception of what is "right" and of the "right" combination, that is, the recognition of what means may be effectively employed coöperatively, that is, what specialization of activity will work, is the preliminary necessity.

In this type of specialization there is not necessarily involved either special skill or aptitudes, knowledge or practice. But it always depends upon a special group of persons who are (1) willing to submit to the requirements of coördination and who (2) are able adequately to communicate. The first requisite lies outside organization as defined, and is a specialization of individuals. The second is internal to organization. It is social specialization, the effective function of which is to facilitate communication, and to create social conditions which are attractive to such persons. Proper associational specialization is essential — on the one side as an inducement to participation in organization, which will be discussed in Chapter XI, and on the other in an aspect of suitable informal organization already presented in Chapter IX.

Suitable associational specialization even for the most elementary cases of organization is only partly fortuitous — good fortune. In most cases it depends upon selection, inducements, and the maintenance of the coöperative disposition in the group and appropriate conditions of communication. The ingenuities of "tactics" essential to this end are requisites to the accomplishment of the coördination of activities at proper places and times.

It is apparent that even when limited to these three factors — specialization in time, by place, and of association — the possible number of concrete specializations is exceedingly large, and that the three factors are in part interdependent. Hence the organizational inventiveness required relates not merely to the factors separately but also to combinations of them.

The specialization introduced by the determination of specific objectives of coöperation is more than that involved in the idea that each specific end involves a specialization of means. It includes the interaction of the feasible specializations in other respects upon the choice of the ends of coöperation. Thus objectives of coöperation for which it is evident it is not possible to "organize," that is, to secure the appropriate combinations of specializations, will generally be rejected. Those for which appropriate specialization may be secured may be selected. Hence, in considerable measure specialization is a reflection of desired ends, and conversely the latter reflect the status of the arts of organization.

This is most evident with respect to the fifth type of specialization — that of process or method. Here it is often apparent that not only is the end dependent on the discovery or invention of specialized processes, or skill, or knowledge and experience, but that conversely the aim results, by its effect upon selection of talents, repetitive practice, etc., in the development of special processes and skills. What is less obvious in most cases is that these special processes and skills themselves depend upon refinements and precision of coördination — temporal, spatial, and associational. Most of the specialization of process of modern industry and government are not within the range of feasibility without high development of specialization in other respects.

Thus, though each aspect of specialization in some conditions may be regarded as independent of other aspects, in general these aspects are elements inseparable from each other in the concrete case. They are mutually dependent.

On a primary level, then, specialization depends upon the variation in persons, upon the conditions of coöperation (chiefly physical environment), and upon the inventions and innovations of the arts of organizing. Beyond the primary level, however, though these factors do not completely disappear as independent factors, there is progressive reaction of organization upon objectives, persons, and physical environment, all of which are altered as means of elaborating specializations of organization. It is these elaborated specializations of organization which more and more transcend the biological limitations of individuals.

It may therefore be said that the significant concrete stage of specialization is the unit organization rather than the "specialized" individual. Each unit organization has a specific objective, specific locational characteristics, specific time schedule, and involves a specific associational situation which determines the selection of individual contributors.

In a complex of organizations, the specializations are described most frequently in geographical terms and in functional terms; but in certain organizations, especially families, the specific personal associational character is emphasized by the use of a common surname, though often geography or function were originally combined with a baptismal name (John Kent, John Smith).

II

Thus, in an important aspect, "organization" and "specialization" are synonyms. The ends of coöperation cannot be accomplished without specialization. The coördination implied is a functional aspect of organization. This function is to correlate the efforts of individuals in such a way with the conditions of the coöperative situation as a whole that purpose may be accomplished.

The way in which this correlation is accomplished is to analyze purpose into parts or detailed purposes or ends, the accomplishment of which in proper order will permit the attainment of the final objective; and to analyze the situation as a whole into parts which may be specifically coördinated by organization activity with detailed ends. These when accomplished become means toward the final attainment. The nature of this process and the function of specialization are of critical importance in the understanding of executive work.[3]

A final observation may now be made. Since every unit organization in a complex organization is a specialization, the general purpose of the complex must be broken into specific purposes for each unit of organization. Since purpose is the unifying element of formal organization, it is this detailed purpose at the unit level that is effective in maintaining the unit. It is this purpose which must be accepted first of all in each unit in order that there may be units of which a complex may be composed. If this local or detailed purpose is not understood or accepted, disintegration of the unit organization follows. This is not more than an induction from my personal experience and observation, as is what now follows: and it is obvious in any event that much qualification for time elements and degrees of disintegration would be required for a complete statement.[4]

Understanding or acceptance of the *general* purpose of the complex is not, however, essential. It may be, and usually but not always is, desirable as explaining or making acceptable a detailed purpose; and if this is possible it no doubt in most cases strengthens the unit organization. But in general complex organizations are characterized by obvious lack of complete understanding and acceptance of *general* purposes or aims. Thus it is not essential and usually impossible that the company should know the specific objectives of the army as a whole; but it is essential that it know and accept *an* objective of its own, or it cannot function. If it feels that the whole depends upon

[3] The principles of this process of double analysis will be discussed in Chapter XIV.

[4] Compare, however, statements in Chapter XII, "The Theory of Authority," p. 165, as to the impossibility of accepting an order that does not conform to purpose as understood.

the achievement of this objective, which it is more likely to do if it understands what the whole objective is, the intensity of its action will ordinarily be increased. It is belief in the cause rather than intellectual understanding of the objective which is of chief importance. "Understanding" by itself is rather a paralyzing and divisive element.

CHAPTER XI

THE ECONOMY OF INCENTIVES

IT has already been demonstrated that an essential element of organizations is the willingness of persons to contribute their individual efforts to the coöperative system. The power of coöperation, which is often spectacularly great when contrasted with that even of large numbers of individuals unorganized, is nevertheless dependent upon the willingness of individuals to coöperate and to contribute their efforts to the coöperative system. The contributions of personal efforts which constitute the energies of organizations are yielded by individuals because of incentives. The egotistical motives of self-preservation and of self-satisfaction are dominating forces; on the whole, organizations can exist only when consistent with the satisfaction of these motives, unless, alternatively, they can change these motives. The individual is always the basic strategic factor in organization. Regardless of his history or his obligations he must be induced to coöperate, or there can be no coöperation.

It needs no further introduction to suggest that the subject of incentives is fundamental in formal organizations and in conscious efforts to organize. Inadequate incentives mean dissolution, or changes of organization purpose, or failure of coöperation. Hence, in all sorts of organizations the affording of adequate incentives becomes the most definitely emphasized task in their existence. It is probably in this aspect of executive work that failure is most pronounced, though the causes may be due either to inadequate understanding or to the breakdown of the effectiveness of organization.

I

The net satisfactions which induce a man to contribute his efforts to an organization result from the positive advantages as against the disadvantages which are entailed.[1] It follows that a net advantage may be increased or a negative advantage made positive either by increasing the number or the strength of the positive inducements or by reducing the number or the strength of the disadvantages. It often occurs that the positive advantages are few and meager, but the burdens involved are also negligible, so that there is a strong net advantage. Many "social" organizations are able to exist under such a state of affairs. Conversely, when the burdens involved are numerous or heavy, the offsetting positive advantages must be either numerous or powerful.

Hence, from the viewpoint of the organization requiring or seeking contributions from individuals, the problem of effective incentives may be either one of finding positive incentives or of reducing or eliminating negative incentives or burdens. For example, employment may be made attractive either by reducing the work required — say, by shortening hours or supplying tools or power, that is, by making conditions of employment less onerous — or by increasing positive inducement, such as wages.

In practice, although there are many cases where it is clear which side of the "equation" is being adjusted, on the whole specific practices and conditions affect both sides simultaneously or it is impossible to determine which they affect. Most specific factors in so-called working conditions may be viewed either as making employment positively attractive or as making work

---

[1] The method of statement convenient for this exposition should not be allowed to mislead. Only occasionally as to most persons and perhaps as to all persons is the determination ot satisfactions and dissatisfactions a matter of logical thought.

less onerous. We shall, therefore, make no attempt to treat specific inducements as increasing advantages or as decreasing disadvantages; but this underlying aspect is to be kept in mind.

More important than this is the distinction between the objective and the subjective aspects of incentives. Certain common positive incentives, such as material goods and in some senses money, clearly have an objective existence; and this is true also of negative incentives like working hours, conditions of work. Given a man of a certain state of mind, of certain attitudes, or governed by certain motives, he can be induced to contribute to an organization by a given combination of these objective incentives, positive or negative. It often is the case, however, that the organization is unable to offer objective incentives that will serve as an inducement to that state of mind, or to those attitudes, or to one governed by those motives. The only alternative then available is to change the state of mind, or attitudes, or motives, so that the available objective incentives can become effective.

An organization can secure the efforts necessary to its existence, then, either by the objective inducements it provides or by changing states of mind. It seems to me improbable that any organization can exist as a practical matter which does not employ both methods in combination. In some organizations the emphasis is on the offering of objective incentives — this is true of most industrial organizations. In others the preponderance is on the state of mind — this is true of most patriotic and religious organizations.

We shall call the processes of offering objective incentives "the method of incentives"; and the processes of changing subjective attitudes "the method of persuasion." Using these new terms, let us repeat what we have said: In commercial organizations the professed emphasis is apparently almost wholly on the side of the method of incentives. In religious and political organizations the professed emphasis is apparently almost wholly on the side of persuasion. But in fact, especially if account be taken of the different kinds of contributions required from different individuals, both methods are used in all types of organizations. Moreover, the centrifugal forces of individualism and the competition between organizations for individual contributions result in both methods being ineffective, with few exceptions, for more than short periods or a few years.

I. THE METHOD OF INCENTIVES

We shall first discuss the method of incentives. It will facilitate our consideration of the subject if at the outset we distinguish two classes of incentives; first those that are specific and can be specifically offered to an individual; and second, those that are general, not personal, that cannot be specifically offered. We shall call the first class specific inducements, the second general incentives.

The specific inducements that may be offered are of several classes, for example: (*a*) material inducements; (*b*) personal non-material opportunities; (*c*) desirable physical conditions; (*d*) ideal benefactions. General incentives afforded are, for example: (*e*) associational attractiveness; (*f*) adaptation of conditions to habitual methods and attitudes; (*g*) the opportunity of enlarged participation; (*h*) the condition of communion. Each of these classes of incentives is known under various names, and the list does not purport to be complete, since our purpose now is illustrative. But to accomplish this purpose it is necessary briefly to discuss the incentives named.

(*a*) Material inducements are money, things, or physical conditions that are offered to the individual as inducements to accepting employment, compensation for service, reward for contribution. Under a money economy and the highly specialized production of material goods, the range and profusion of material inducements are very great. The complexity of schedules of money compensation, the difficulty of securing the monetary means of compensation, and the power of exchange which money gives in organized markets, have served to exaggerate the importance of money in particular and material inducements in general as incentives to personal contributions to organized effort. It goes without elaboration that where a large part of the time of an individual is devoted to one organization, the physiological necessities — food, shelter, clothing — require that material inducements should be present in most cases; but these requirements are so limited that they are satisfied with small quantities. The unaided power of material incentives, when the minimum necessities are satisfied, in my opinion is exceedingly limited as to most men, depending almost entirely for its development upon persuasion. Notwithstanding the great emphasis upon material incentives in modern times and especially in current affairs, there is no doubt in my mind that, unaided by other motives, they constitute weak incentives beyond the level of the bare physiological necessities.

To many this view will not be readily acceptable. The emphasis upon material rewards has been a natural result of the success of technological developments — relative to other incentives it is the material things which have been progressively easier to produce, and therefore to offer. Hence there has been a forced cultivation of the love of material things among those above the level of subsistence. Since existing incentives seem always inadequate to the degree of coöperation and of social integration theoretically possible and ideally desirable, the success of the sciences and the arts of material production would have been partly ineffective, and in turn would have been partly impossible, without inculcating the desire of the material. The most significant result of this situation has been the expansion of population, most of which has been necessarily at the bare subsistence level, at which level material inducements are, on the whole, powerful incentives. This has perpetuated the illusion that beyond this subsistence level material incentives are also the most effective.[2]

A concurrent result has been the creation of sentiments in individuals that they *ought* to want material things. The inculcation of "proper" ambitions in youth have greatly stressed material possessions as an evidence of good citizenship, social adequacy, etc. Hence, when underlying and governing motives have not been satisfied, there has been strong influence to rationalize the default as one of material compensation, and not to be conscious of the controlling motives or at least not to admit them.

Yet it seems to me to be a matter of common experience that material rewards are ineffective beyond the subsistence level excepting to a very limited proportion of men; that most men neither work harder for more material things, nor can be induced thereby to devote more than a fraction of their possible contribution to organized effort. It is likewise a matter of both present experience and past history that many of the most effective and powerful organizations are built up on incentives in which the materialistic elements, above bare subsistence, are either relatively lacking or absolutely absent. Military organizations have been relatively lacking in material incentives. The greater part of the work of political organizations is without material incentive. Religious organizations are characterized on the whole by material sacrifice. It seems to me to be definitely a general fact that even in purely commercial organizations material incentives are so weak as to be almost negligible except when reinforced by other incentives, and then only because of wholesale general persuasion in the form of salesmanship and advertising.

---

[2] It has been suggested to me that the illusion is also a result of the neglect of motives and the excessive imputation of logical processes in men by the earlier economists, and in purely theoretical economics. This was associated with the deterministic and especially the utilitarian doctrines of the greater

It will be noted that the reference has been to material incentives rather than to money. What has been said requires some, but not great, qualification with reference to money as an incentive — solely for the reason that money in our economy may be used as the indirect means of satisfying non-materialistic motives — philanthropic, artistic, intellectual, and religious motives for example — and because money income becomes an index of social status, personal development, etc.

(b) Inducements of a personal, non-materialistic character are of great importance to secure coöperative effort above the minimum material rewards essential to subsistence. The opportunities for distinction, prestige, personal power,[3] and the attainment of dominating position are much more important than material rewards in the development of all sorts of organizations, including commercial organizations. In various ways this fact applies to many types of human beings, including those of limited ability and children. Even in strictly commercial organizations, where it is least supposed to be true, money without distinction, prestige, position, is so utterly ineffective that it is rare that greater income can be made to serve even temporarily as an inducement if accompanied by suppression of prestige. At least for short periods inferior material rewards are often accepted if assurance of distinction is present; and usually the presumption is that material rewards ought to follow or arise from or even are made necessary by the attainment of distinction and prestige. There is unlimited experience to show that among many men, and especially among women, the real value of differences of money rewards lies in the recognition or distinction assumed to be conferred thereby, or to be procured therewith — one of the reasons why differentials either in money income or in material possessions are a source of

---

part of the nineteenth century, and with the materialistic philosophies of Marx and others.

[3] Largely an illusion, but a very dear one to some.

jealousy and disruption if not accompanied by other factors of distinction.

(*c*) Desirable physical conditions of work are often important conscious, and more often important unconscious, inducements to coöperation.

(*d*) Ideal benefactions as inducements to coöperation are among the most powerful and the most neglected. By ideal benefaction I mean the capacity of organizations to satisfy personal ideals usually relating to non-material, future, or altruistic relations. They include pride of workmanship, sense of adequacy, altruistic service for family or others, loyalty to organization in patriotism, etc., aesthetic and religious feeling. They also include the opportunities for the satisfaction of the motives of hate and revenge, often the controlling factor in adherence to and intensity of effort in some organizations.

All of these inducements — material rewards, personal non-material opportunities, desirable physical conditions, and ideal benefactions — may be and frequently are definitely offered as inducements to contribute to organizations. But there are other conditions which cannot usually be definitely offered, and which are known or recognized by their absence in particular cases. Of these I consider associational attractiveness as exceedingly, and often critically, important.

(*e*) By associational attractiveness I mean social compatibility. It is in many cases obvious that racial hostility, class antagonism, and national enmities absolutely prevent coöperation, in others decrease its effectiveness, and in still others make it impossible to secure coöperation except by great strengthening of other incentives. But it seems clear that the question of personal compatibility or incompatibility is much more far-reaching in limiting coöperative effort than is recognized, because an intimate knowledge of particular organizations is usually necessary to understand its precise character. When such an intimate knowledge exists, personal compatibility or incompatibility is so thoroughly sensed, and the related problems are so difficult to deal with, that only in special or critical cases is conscious attention given to them. But they can be neglected only at peril of disruption. Men often will not work at all, and will rarely work well, under other incentives if the social situation *from their point of view* is unsatisfactory. Thus often men of inferior education cannot work well with those of superior education, and vice versa. Differences not merely of race, nation, religion, but of customs, morals, social status, education, ambition, are frequently controlling. Hence, a powerful incentive to the effort of almost all men is favorable associational conditions from their viewpoint.

Personal aversions based upon racial, national, color, and class differences often seem distinctly pernicious; but on the whole they are, in the immediate sense, I believe, based upon a sound feeling of organization necessities. For when there is incompatibility or even merely lack of compatibility, both formal communication and especially communication through informal organization become difficult and sometimes impossible.

(*f*) Another incentive of the general type is that of customary working conditions and conformity to habitual practices and attitudes. This is made obvious by the universal practice, in all kinds of organization, of rejecting recruits trained in different methods or possessing "foreign" attitudes. It is taken for granted that men will not or cannot do well by strange methods or under strange conditions. What is not so obvious is that men will frequently not attempt to coöperate if they recognize that such methods or conditions are to be accepted.

(*g*) Another indirect incentive that we may regard as of general and often of controlling importance is the opportunity for the feeling of enlarged participation in the course of events. It affects all classes of men under some conditions. It is sometimes, though not necessarily, related to love of personal distinction and prestige. Its realization is the feeling of importance of result of effort because of the importance of the coöperative effort as a whole. Thus, *other things being equal*, many men prefer association with large organizations, organizations which they regard as useful, or organizations they regard as effective, as against those they consider small, useless, ineffective.

(*h*) The most intangible and subtle of incentives is that which I have called the condition of communion. It is related to social compatibility, but is essentially different. It is the feeling of personal comfort in social relations that is sometimes called solidarity, social integration, the gregarious instinct, or social security (in the original, not in its present debased economic, sense). It is the opportunity for comradeship, for mutual support in personal attitudes. The need for communion is a basis of informal organization that is essential to the operation of every formal organization. It is likewise the basis for informal organization within but hostile to formal organization.[4]

It is unnecessary for our purpose to exhaust the list of inducements and incentives to coöperative contributions of individuals to organization. Enough has been said to suggest that the subject of incentives is important and complex when viewed in its objective aspects. One fact of interest now is that different men are moved by different incentives or combinations of incentives,

---

[4] Referring to this paragraph, one of my valued correspondents, an army officer of long experience in active service, writes to the effect that I do not relatively emphasize this incentive sufficiently. Speaking of comradeship he says: "I was impressed, somewhat to my innocent surprise, during 1918, by the influence of this factor. I came out of the war with the definite impression that it was perhaps the strongest constructive moral factor, stronger than patriotism, and in many cases stronger than religion." He quotes Professor Joergensenson of Denmark, in his treatise appearing (with other contributions) in the Interparliamentary Union's book *What Would Be the Character of a New War?* as saying: "In the opinion of many experts these feelings [of brotherhood and comradeship among the troops] constituted the most important source of inner strength from a psychological point of view, and helped the soldiers to bear the sufferings and perils of the battlefield."

and by different incentives or combinations at different times. Men are unstable in their desires, a fact partly reflecting the instability of their environments. A second fact is that organizations are probably never able to offer *all* the incentives that move men to coöperative effort, and are usually unable to offer adequate incentives. To the reasons for this fact we shall advert later; but a result of it to which we shall turn our attention now is the necessity of persuasion.

II. THE METHOD OF PERSUASION

If an organization is unable to afford incentives adequate to the personal contributions it requires it will perish unless it can by persuasion so change the desires of enough men that the incentives it can offer will be adequate. Persuasion in the broad sense in which I am here using the word includes: (*a*) the creation of coercive conditions; (*b*) the rationalization of opportunity; (*c*) the inculcation of motives.

(*a*) Coercion is employed both to exclude and to secure the contribution of individuals to an organization. Exclusion is often intended to be exclusion permanently and nothing more. It is an aspect of competition or hostility between organizations or between organizations and individuals with which we shall not further be concerned, except to note that exclusion of undesirables is a necessary method of maintaining organization efficiency. But forced exclusion is also employed as a means of persuasion *by example*, to create fear among those not directly affected, so that they will be disposed to render to an organization certain contributions. It presents realistically the alternative either of making these contributions or of foregoing the advantages of association. The grades of exclusion are numerous, beginning with homicide, outlawing, ostracism, corporal punishment, incarceration, withholding of specific benefits, discharge, etc.

Contributions secured by force seem to have been often a

necessary process of coöperation. Thus slavery is the creation of conditions by force under which bare subsistence and protection are made sufficient incentives to give certain contributions to the organization; although often it has been the result of conditions not purposely created, that is, slavery has been sometimes a voluntary means to being admitted to benefits of coöperation otherwise withheld. However, usually slavery is evidence of an unstable efficiency, except when it can be combined with other incentives (as in forced military service). But it has undoubtedly often been an effective process of persuasion to those not directly affected. Those who observe homicide, ostracism, outlawing, incarceration, discharge, and other expressions of the power of organizations to persuade by force have unquestionably been affected in their views of the adequacy of offered incentives. Nevertheless, I suppose it is generally accepted that no superior permanent or very complex system of coöperation can be supported to a great extent merely by coercion.

(*b*) The rationalization of opportunity is a method of persuasion of much greater importance in most modern activities. Even under political and economic regimes in which coercion of individuals is at least temporarily and in some degree the basic process of persuasion, as in Russia, Germany, and Italy, it is observed that the processes of rationalization of other incentives, that is, propaganda, are carried on more extensively than anywhere else.

The rationalization of incentives occurs in two degrees; the general rationalization that is an expression of social organization as a whole and has chiefly occurred in connection with religious and political organizations, and the specific rationalization that consists in attempting to convince individuals or groups that they "ought," "it is to their interest," to perform services or conform to requirements of specific organizations.

The general rationalization of incentives on a noteworthy

scale has occurred many times. The rationalization of religious motives as a basis of the Crusades is one of the most striking. The rationalization of communist doctrine in Russia is another. The rationalization of hate as a means of increasing organization (national) "solidarity" is well known. One of the most interesting of these general rationalizations is that of materialistic progress, to which we have already referred. It is an important basis of the characteristic forms of modern western organization. In its most general form it consists in the cult of science as a means to material ends, the glorification of inventions and inventive talent, including patent legislation; and the exaltation of the exploitation of land, forests, mineral resources, and of the means of transportation. In its more obvious current forms it consists in extensive and intensive salesmanship, advertising, and propaganda concerning the satisfactions to be had from the use of material products.

It is the pleasure of many idealists to decry this rationalization of the material. If materialism is to be made an incentive to coöperation as an alternative to other incentives, there is grave reason to question its social value except as it may be the process whereby many millions are enabled to survive and live on a bare subsistence level who otherwise would have perished. But if it is regarded as in the nature of making an *additional* incentive effective, with the result of more effective social coöperation, its justification is not, in my opinion, questionable. It is then the process by which, to use current economic phraseology, purchasing power in material things and services is created. In everyday language, people will not work for what they are not convinced is "worth while"; if the conviction that material things are worth while detracts from other non-material things as incentives it may be harmful; but if it succeeds in capturing waste effort or wasted time or in minimizing harmful incentives, such as hate, it is clearly advantageous.

Specific rationalization of incentives is the process of personal appeal to "join" an organization, to accept a job or position, to undertake a service, to contribute to a cause. It is the process of proselyting or recruiting that is commonly observed in connection with industrial, military, political, and religious organizations. It consists in emphasizing opportunities for satisfaction that are offered, usually in contrast with those available otherwise; and in attempting to elicit interest in those incentives which are most easily or most outstandingly afforded.

The background of the individual to whom incentives are rationalized consists of his physiological requirements, his geographical and social location, and the general rationalization and especially the social influences to which he has previously been subjected by his society, his government, and his church.

Thus specific rationalization is concerned usually with a small marginal area of choice and with competition. This background differs so widely among individuals that at any given time only a few individuals are deemed to be within range of specific rationalization; and for those that are within that range there are wide differences in the composition of incentives that will be effective.

(c) The form of persuasion that is most important is the inculcation of motives. In its formal aspects this is a process of deliberate education of the young, and propaganda for adults. Thus the persuasion of religious incentives, except at comparatively infrequent intervals, is chiefly accomplished by religious instruction of children. Similarly, the inculcation of ideas of patriotism and much of the other incentives to co-operation are a part of the family and general educational process.

Associated with these formal processes are those which are informal and indirect. Precept, example, suggestion, imitation and emulation, habitual attitudes, chiefly condition the motives and the emotional response of individuals to incentives. These are the controlling and fundamental conditions of whole peoples and of groups and classes with respect to the power of incentives. They furnish the greatest limitations to which organizations must adapt their processes both of offering incentives and of persuading individuals.

This brief [5] discussion of the incentives has been a necessary introduction to the considerations that are important to our study of the subject of organization and the executive functions. The processes concerned are each of them difficult in themselves, and are subject to highly developed techniques and skills. Their importance as a whole arises from the inherent difficulty that organizations experience either in supplying incentives or in exercising persuasion. The most appropriate phrase to apply to this inherent difficulty is "economy of incentives"; but it should be understood that "economy" is used in a broad sense and refers not merely to material or monetary economy.

II

In the economy of incentives we are concerned with the net effects of the income and outgo of things resulting from the production of objective incentives and the exercise of persuasion. An organization which makes material things the principal incentive will be unable long to offer this kind of incentive if it is unable to secure at least as much material or money as it pays out. This is the ordinary economic aspect

[5] Among other matters it has not been necessary to develop here are those of fraud, trickery, and "economic compulsion," as related either to force or social pressures. At periods or in specific situations all have been important, and in the aggregate at any time no doubt are substantial. In principle, however, it is usually evident that, like direct coercion, they all involve disadvantages or sacrifices that offset their advantages; and it is doubtful if they often are the dominant factors in coöperation. On the contrary they arise from and are chiefly evidence of non-coöperation. They are disruptive, not integrating, methods.

which is well understood. But the same principle applies to other incentives. The possibilities of offering non-material opportunities, desirable conditions, ideal benefactions, desirable associations, stability of practice, enlarged participation, or communion advantages are limited and usually insufficient, so that the utmost economy is ordinarily essential not only in the material sense but in the broader sense as well. The limitations are not alone due to the relationship of the organization to the external physical environment, but also to its relationship to the social environment, and to its internal efficiency.

A complete exposition of the economy of incentives would among other things involve some duplication of the theories of general economics, rewritten from the point of view of organization. This is not the place to attempt such an exposition; but as the economy of incentives as a whole in terms of organization is not usually stressed in economic theory [6] and is certainly not well understood, I shall attempt to indicate the outlines of the theory. It will be convenient to do this with reference to organizations of three radically different purposes: (a) an industrial organization; (b) a political organization; and (c) a religious organization.

(a) In an industrial organization the purpose [7] is the production of material goods, or services. For the sake of simplicity we may assume that it requires no capital. It secures

---

[6] I think it doubtful that many of the aspects of the economy of incentives have any place in theoretical economics.

[7] The purpose is *not* profit, notwithstanding that business men, economists, ecclesiastics, politicians, labor unions, persistently misstate the purpose. Profit may be essential to having a supply of inducements to satisfy the motives of that class of contributors usually called owners or investors whose contributions in turn were essential to the supply of inducements to other classes of contributors. The possibilities of profit and their realization in some degree are necessary in some economies as conditions under which a continuing supply of incentives is possible; but the objective purpose of no organization is profit, but services. Among industrialists this has been most emphasized by Mr. Ford and some utility organizations.

material production by applying the energies of men to the physical environment. These energies will result in a gross production; but if the inducements offered to secure these energies are themselves material, and are sufficient, then it will pay out of its production something on this account. If the amount paid out is no more than the production the organization can survive; but if the amount paid out is more than the production, it must cease, since it cannot then continue to offer inducements.

Whether this occurs depends upon the combined effect of four factors; the difficulties of the environment, the effectiveness of organization effort, the internal efficiency of organization, and the amount of inducements paid. Obviously many coöperative efforts fail because the environment is too resistant, others because the organization is ineffective, others because internal losses are large, others because the price paid for services is too large. Within the range of ordinary experience, these are mutually dependent variables, or mutually interacting factors. Under very favorable environmental conditions, relative ineffectiveness and relative internal inefficiency with high outgo for inducements are possible. Under unfavorable conditions, effectiveness, efficiency, and low inducements are necessary.

In most cases the limitations of conditions, of effectiveness, and of efficiency permit only limited material inducements; and both effectiveness and efficiency require an output of individual energies that cannot be elicited from most men by material inducements in any event. Hence, in practice other inducements also must be offered. But in such an organization such inducements in some degree, and usually to a considerable degree, require again material inducements. Thus, satisfactory physical conditions of work mean material inducements to factors not directly productive; satisfactory social conditions mean the rejection of some of those best able to contribute the material production and acceptance of some less able. Almost every type of incentive that can be, or is, necessary will itself in some degree call for material outgo, so that the question is one of choice of methods and degree of emphasis upon different incentives to find the most efficient combination of incentives determined from the material viewpoint. Hence, the various incentives are in competition with each other even from the material point of view.

But the economy of incentives in an industrial organization only begins with the analysis of incentives from the standpoint of material; that is, dollars and cents, costs. The non-material incentives often conflict with each other or are incompatible. Thus opportunity for personal prestige as an incentive for one person necessarily involves a relative depression of others; so that if this incentive is emphasized as to one person, it must be in conjunction with other persons to whom personal prestige is relatively an unimportant inducement.

The difficulties of finding the workable balance of incentives is so great that recourse must be had to persuasion. But persuasion in connection with an industrial effort itself involves material outgo. Thus if coercion is the available method of persuasion, the maintenance of force for this purpose is involved; and if the contribution that can be secured by coercion is limited, as it usually is, except for short periods, the cost of coercion exceeds its effect. The limited efficiencies of slavery systems is an example.

If the method of persuasion is rationalization, either in the form of general propaganda [8] or that of specific argument to individuals (including processes of "selection"), again the overhead cost is usually not negligible. When the general social conditioning is favorable, of course, it is a windfall like favorable physical environment.

(b) A political organization is not ordinarily productive in

[8] General propaganda of industrial concerns usually relates to that class of contributors to organizations known as consumers.

the materialistic sense. The motives which lie at its roots are ideal benefactions and community satisfactions. Such organizations appear not to survive long unless they can afford these incentives; yet it is obvious that every extensive political organization requires the use of "inferior" incentives. Of these, opportunity for personal prestige and material rewards are most prominent. Hence the necessity, under all forms of political organization, for obtaining great supplies of material inducements for use either in the form of direct payments or of "paying jobs." Accordingly, a striking characteristic of political organizations has been the necessity for securing material contributions from "members" either to capture the opportunities to secure additional material (through taxation) or for direct payment (as in campaigns). But here again the balancing of incentives is necessary. For the limitations of material resources, the impossibility of giving more than is received, the discrimination between recipients as respects either material benefits or prestige granted, all tend either to destroy the vital idealism upon which political organization is based or to minimize the *general* material advantages which are perhaps an alternative basis of political organization in many cases.

It is hardly necessary to add that persuasion in its many forms is an important aspect of political recruiting — and that much of the material expenditure goes for this purpose; but this thereby decreases the material available as an incentive to intensive efforts of the "faithful."

(*c*) In religious organizations the predominant incentives [9] appear to be ideal benefactions and the communion of "kindred spirits," although inferior incentives no doubt often are effective. The fundamental contributions required of members are intensity of faith and loyalty to organization. A most important effort of religious organizations has been persuasion, known as missionary or proselyting effort. But both the maintenance of

[9] That is, without taking into account supernatural benefactions.

organization and missionary effort (and coercion when this is used) require material means, so that superficially, and often primarily, members are required by various methods to make material contributions to permit great material expenditures. The material aspects of religious organizations have been often prominent and always inescapable. As a result, the combination and adjustment of incentives in religious organizations appear even more delicate and difficult to administer than in political, military, or industrial organizations. Consider, for example, the conflict between sacrifice by individuals on one hand as a means of intensifying faith and loyalty — which it does in many cases — and sacrifice as a deterrent to adherence and membership, and the resulting dilemma as respects both quality and numbers of communicants. Or the necessity for prestige and display — which are both individual and group incentives — and humility, which is a contrary ideal benefaction.

It will be evident, perhaps, without more elaborate illustration, that in every type of organization, for whatever purpose, several incentives are necessary, and some degree of persuasion likewise, in order to secure and maintain the contributions to organization that are required. It will also be clear that, excepting in rare instances, the difficulties of securing the means of offering incentives, of avoiding conflict of incentives, and of making effective persuasive efforts, are inherently great; and that the determination of the precise combination of incentives and of persuasion that will be both effective and feasible is a matter of great delicacy. Indeed, it is so delicate and complex that rarely, if ever, is the scheme of incentives determinable in advance of application. It can only evolve; and the questions relating to it become chiefly those of strategic factors from time to time in the course of the life of the organization. It is also true, of course, that the scheme of incentives is probably the most unstable of the elements of the coöperative system, since invariably external conditions affect the possibilities of material incentives; and human motives are likewise highly variable. Thus incentives represent the final residual of all the conflicting forces involved in organization, a very slight change in underlying forces often making a great change in the power of incentives; and yet it is only by the incentives that the effective balancing of these forces is to be secured, if it can be secured at all.

Two general consequences of this inherent instability are to be noted. One is the innate propensity of all organizations to expand. The maintenance of incentives, particularly those relating to prestige, pride of association, and community satisfaction, calls for growth, enlargement, extension. It is, I think, the basic and, in a sense, the legitimate reason for bureaucratic aggrandizement in corporate, governmental, labor, university, and church organizations everywhere observed. To grow seems to offer opportunity for the realization of all kinds of active incentives — as may be observed by the repeated emphasis in all organizations upon size as an index of the existence of desirable incentives, or the alternative rationalization of other incentives when size is small or growth is discouraged. The overreaching which arises from this cause is the source of destruction of organizations otherwise successful, since growth often so upsets the economy of incentives, through its reactions upon the effectiveness and efficiency of organization, that it is no longer possible to make them adequate.

A second and more important result of the inherent difficulty of securing an adequate scheme of incentives is the highly selective character of the organizational recruiting practice. This has two aspects, the acceptance of desirable and the rejection of undesirable contributions or contributors; and its chief process is the maintenance of differential incentives. Since all incentives are costly to organization, and the costs tend to prevent its survival, and since the balancing of organization outgo and income is initially to be regarded as impossible without the utmost economy, the distribution of incentives must be proportioned to the value and effectiveness of the various contributions sought.[10]

This is only too much accepted as respects material incentives, that is, material things or money payment. No enduring or complex formal organization of any kind seems to have existed without differential material payments, though material compensation may be indirect to a considerable extent. This seems true up to the present even though contrary to the expressed attitude of the organization or not in harmony with its major purpose, as often in the case of churches and socialistic states.

The same doctrine applies in principle and practice even more to non-material incentives. The hierarchy of positions, with gradation of honors and privileges, which is the universal accompaniment of all complex organization, is essential to the adjustment of non-material incentives to induce the services of the most able individuals or the most valuable potential contributors to organization, and it is likewise necessary to the maintenance of pride of organization, community sense, etc., which are important general incentives to all classes of contributors.

[10] The function of distribution has already been described as peculiar to co-operative systems, in Chapter III, pp. 32–33, and will be discussed again in Chapter XVI, pp. 253 ff.

CHAPTER XII

THE THEORY OF AUTHORITY

IN this chapter we consider a subject which in one aspect relates to the "willingness of individuals to contribute to organizations," the element of organization presented in the preceding chapter; and in a second aspect is the most general phase of the element "communication."

I. The Source of Authority

If it is true that all complex organizations consist of aggregations of unit organizations and have grown only from unit organizations, we may reasonably postulate that, whatever the nature of authority, it is inherent in the simple organization unit; and that a correct theory of authority must be consistent with what is essentially true of these unit organizations. We shall, therefore, regard the observations which we can make of the actual conditions as at first a source for discovering what is essential in elementary and simple organizations.

I

Now a most significant fact of general observation relative to authority is the extent to which it is ineffective in specific instances. It is so ineffective that the violation of authority is accepted as a matter of course and its implications are not considered. It is true that we are sometimes appalled at the extent of major criminal activities; but we pass over very lightly the universal violations, particularly of sumptuary laws, which are as "valid" as any others. Even clauses of constitutions and statutes carrying them "into effect," such as the Eighteenth Amendment, are violated in wholesale degrees.

Violation of law is not, however, peculiar to our own country.

I observed recently in a totalitarian state under a dictator, where personal liberty is supposed to be at a minimum and arbitrary authority at a maximum, many violations of positive law or edict, some of them open and on a wide scale; and I was reliably informed of others.

Nor is this condition peculiar to the authority of the state. It is likewise true of the authority of churches. The Ten Commandments and the prescriptions and prohibitions of religious authority are repeatedly violated by those who profess to acknowledge their formal authority.

These observations do not mean that all citizens are lawless and defy authority; nor that all Christians are godless or their conduct unaffected by the tenets of their faith. It is obvious that to a large extent citizens are governed; and that the conduct of Christians is substantially qualified by the prescriptions of their churches. What is implied is merely that which specific laws will be obeyed or disobeyed by the individual citizen are decided by him under the specific conditions pertinent. This is what we mean when we refer to individual responsibility. It implies that which prescriptions of the church will be disobeyed by the individual are determined by him at a given time and place. This is what we mean by moral responsibility.

It may be thought that ineffectiveness of authority in specific cases is chiefly exemplified in matters of state and church, but not in those of smaller organizations which are more closely knit or more concretely managed. But this is not true. It is surprising how much that in theory is authoritative, in the best of organizations in practice lacks authority — or, in plain language, how generally orders are disobeyed. For many years the writer has been interested to observe this fact, not only in organizations with which he was directly connected, but in many others. In all of them, armies, navies, universities, penal institutions, hospitals, relief organizations, corporations, the same conditions prevail — dead laws, regulations, rules, which no one dares bury but which are not obeyed; obvious disobedience carefully disregarded; vital practices and major institutions for which there is no authority, like the Democratic and Republican parties, not known to the Constitution.

II

We may leave the secondary stages of this analysis for later consideration. What we derive from it is an approximate definition of authority for our purpose: Authority is the character of a communication (order) in a formal organization by virtue of which it is accepted by a contributor to or "member" of the organization as governing the action he contributes; that is, as governing or determining what he does or is not to do so far as the organization is concerned. According to this definition, authority involves two aspects: first, the subjective, the personal, the *accepting* of a communication as authoritative, the aspects which I shall present in this section; and, second, the objective aspect — the character in the communication by virtue of which it is accepted — which I present in the second section, "The System of Coördination."

If a directive communication is accepted by one to whom it is addressed, its authority for him is confirmed or established. It is admitted as the basis of action. Disobedience of such a communication is a denial of its authority for him. Therefore, under this definition the decision as to whether an order has authority or not lies with the persons to whom it is addressed, and does not reside in "persons of authority" or those who issue these orders.

This is so contrary to the view widely held by informed persons of many ranks and professions, and so contradictory to legalistic conceptions, and will seem to many so opposed to common experience, that it will be well at the outset to quote two opinions of persons in a position to merit respectful attention. It is not the intention to "argue from authorities"; but before attacking the subject it is desirable at least to recognize that prevalent notions are not universally held. Says Roberto Michels in the monograph "Authority" in the *Encyclopaedia of the Social Sciences*,[1] "Whether authority is of personal or institutional origin it is created and maintained by public opinion, which in its turn is conditioned by sentiment, affection, reverence or fatalism. Even when authority rests on mere physical coercion it is *accepted*[2] by those ruled, although the acceptance may be due to a fear of force."

Again, Major-General James G. Harbord, of long and distinguished military experience, and since his retirement from the Army a notable business executive, says on page 259 of his *The American Army in France*:[3]

A democratic President had forgotten that the greatest of all democracies is an Army. Discipline and morale influence the inarticulate vote that is instantly taken by masses of men when the order comes to move forward — a variant of the crowd psychology that inclines it to follow a leader, but the Army does not move forward until the motion has "carried." "Unanimous consent" only follows cooperation between the *individual* men in the ranks.

These opinions are to the effect that even though physical force is involved, and even under the extreme condition of battle, when the regime is nearly absolute, authority nevertheless rests upon the acceptance or consent of individuals. Evidently such conceptions, if justified, deeply affect an appropriate understanding of organization and especially of the character of the executive functions.

Our definition of authority, like General Harbord's democracy in an army, no doubt will appear to many whose eyes are fixed only on enduring organizations to be a platform of chaos. And so it is — exactly so in the preponderance of attempted

[1] New York: Macmillan.
[2] Italics mine.
[3] Boston: Little, Brown and Co., 1936.

organizations. They fail because they can maintain no authority, that is, they cannot secure sufficient contributions of personal efforts to be effective or cannot induce them on terms that are efficient. In the last analysis the authority fails because the individuals in sufficient numbers regard the burden involved in accepting necessary orders as changing the balance of advantage against their interest, and they withdraw or withhold the indispensable contributions.

III

We must not rest our definition, however, on general opinion. The necessity of the assent of the individual to establish authority *for him* is inescapable. A person can and will accept a communication as authoritative only when four conditions simultaneously obtain: (*a*) he can and does understand the communication; (*b*) *at the time of his decision* he believes that it is not inconsistent with the purpose of the organization; (*c*) *at the time of his decision,* he believes it to be compatible with his personal interest as a whole; and (*d*) he is able mentally and physically to comply with it.

(*a*) A communication that cannot be understood *can* have no authority. An order issued, for example, in a language not intelligible to the recipient is no order at all — no one would so regard it. Now, many orders are exceedingly difficult to understand. They are often necessarily stated in general terms, and the persons who issued them could not themselves apply them under many conditions. Until interpreted they have no meaning. The recipient either must disregard them or merely do anything in the hope that that is compliance.

Hence, a considerable part of administrative work consists in the interpretation and reinterpretaion of orders in their application to concrete circumstances that were not or could not be taken into account initially.

(*b*) A communication believed by the recipient to be in-

compatible with the purpose of the organization, as he understands it, could not be accepted. Action would be frustrated
by cross purposes. The most common practical example is that
involved in conflicts of orders. They are not rare. An intelligent person will deny the authority of that one which contra-
dicts the purpose of the effort as *he* understands it. In extreme
cases many individuals would be virtually paralyzed by conflicting orders. They would be literally unable to comply — for
example, an employee of a water system ordered to blow up
an essential pump, or soldiers ordered to shoot their own com-
rades. I suppose all experienced executives know that when
it is necessary to issue orders that will appear to the recipients
to be contrary to the main purpose, especially as exemplified in
prior habitual practice, it is usually necessary and always advisable, if practicable, to explain or demonstrate why the appearance of conflict is an illusion. Otherwise the orders are likely
not to be executed, or to be executed inadequately.

(*c*) If a communication is believed to involve a burden that
destroys the net advantage of connection with the organization,
there no longer would remain a net inducement to the individual to contribute to it. The existence of a net inducement is the
only reason for accepting *any* order as having authority. Hence,
if such an order is received it must be disobeyed (evaded in the
more usual cases) as utterly inconsistent with personal motives
that are the basis of accepting any orders at all. Cases of voluntary resignation from all sorts of organizations are common
for this sole reason. Malingering and intentional lack of
dependability are the more usual methods.

(*d*) If a person is unable to comply with an order, obviously
it must be disobeyed, or, better, disregarded. To order a man
who cannot swim to swim a river is a sufficient case. Such extreme cases are not frequent; but they occur. The more usual
case is to order a man to do things only a little beyond his
capacity; but a little impossible is still impossible.

IV

Naturally the reader will ask: How is it possible to secure such important and enduring coöperation as we observe if in principle and in fact the determination of authority lies with the subordinate individual? It is possible because the decisions of individuals occur under the following conditions: (a) orders that are deliberately issued in enduring organizations usually comply with the four conditions mentioned above; (b) there exists a "zone of indifference" in each individual within which orders are acceptable without conscious questioning of their authority; (c) the interests of the persons who contribute to an organization as a group result in the exercise of an influence on the subject, or on the attitude of the individual, that maintains a certain stability of this zone of indifference.

(a) There is no principle of executive conduct better established in good organizations than that orders will not be issued that cannot or will not be obeyed. Executives and most persons of experience who have thought about it know that to do so destroys authority, discipline, and morale.[4] For reasons to be

[4] Barring relatively few individual cases, when the attitude of the individual indicates in advance likelihood of disobedience (either before or after connection with the organization), the connection is terminated or refused before the formal question arises.

It seems advisable to add a caution here against interpreting the exposition in terms of "democracy," whether in governmental, religious, or industrial organizations. The dogmatic assertion that "democracy" or "democratic methods" are (or are not) in accordance with the principles here discussed is not tenable. As will be more evident after the consideration of objective authority, the issues involved are much too complex and subtle to be taken into account in *any* formal scheme. Under many conditions in the political, religious, and industrial fields democratic processes create artificial questions of more or less logical character, in place of the real questions, which are matters of feeling and appropriateness and of informal organization. By oversimplification of issues this may destroy objective authority. No doubt in many situations formal democratic processes may be an important element in the maintenance of authority, i.e., of organization cohesion, but may in other situations be disruptive, and probably

stated shortly, this principle cannot ordinarily be formally admitted, or at least cannot be professed. When it appears necessary to issue orders which are initially or apparently unacceptable, either careful preliminary education, or persuasive efforts, or the prior offering of effective inducements will be made, so that the issue will not be raised, the denial of authority will not occur, and orders will be obeyed. It is generally recognized that those who least understand this fact — newly appointed minor or "first line" executives — are often guilty of "disorganizing" their groups for this reason, as do experienced executives who lose self-control or become unbalanced by a delusion of power or for some other reason. Inexperienced persons take literally the current notions of authority and are then said "not to know how to use authority" or "to abuse authority." Their superiors often profess the same beliefs about authority in the abstract, but their successful practice is easily observed to be inconsistent with their professions.

(b) The phrase "zone of indifference" may be explained as follows: If all the orders for actions reasonably practicable be arranged in the order of their acceptability to the person affected, it may be conceived that there are a number which are clearly unacceptable, that is, which certainly will not be obeyed; there is another group somewhat more or less on the neutral line, that is, either barely acceptable or barely unacceptable; and a

---

never could be, in themselves, sufficient. On the other hand the solidarity of some coöperative systems (General Harbord's army, for example) under many conditions may be unexcelled, though requiring formally autocratic processes.

Moreover, it should never be forgotten that authority in the aggregate arises from *all* the contributors to a coöperative system, and that the weighting to be attributed to the attitude of individuals varies. It is often forgotten that in industrial (or political) organizations measures which are acceptable at the bottom may be quite unacceptable to the substantial proportion of contributors who are executives, and who will no more perform their essential functions than will others, if the conditions are, to them, impossible. The point to be emphasized is that the maintenance of the contributions necessary to the endurance of an organization requires the authority of *all* essential contributors.

third group unquestionably acceptable. This last group lies within the "zone of indifference." The person affected will accept orders lying within this zone and is relatively indifferent as to what the order is so far as the question of authority is concerned. Such an order lies within the range that in a general way was anticipated at time of undertaking the connection with the organization. For example, if a soldier enlists, whether voluntarily or not, in an army in which the men are ordinarily moved about within a certain broad region, it is a matter of indifference whether the order be to go to A or B, C or D, and so on; and goings to A, B, C, D, etc., are in the zone of indifference.

The zone of indifference will be wider or narrower depending upon the degree to which the inducements exceed the burdens and sacrifices which determine the individual's adhesion to the organization. It follows that the range of orders that will be accepted will be very limited among those who are barely induced to contribute to the system.

(c) Since the efficiency of organization is affected by the degree to which individuals assent to orders, denying the authority of an organization communication is a threat to the interests of all individuals who derive a net advantage from their connection with the organization, unless the orders are unacceptable to them also. Accordingly, at any given time there is among most of the contributors an active personal interest in the maintenance of the authority of all orders which to them are within the zone of indifference. The maintenance of this interest is largely a function of informal organization. Its expression goes under the names of "public opinion," "organization opinion," "feeling in the ranks," "group attitude," etc. Thus the common sense of the community informally arrived at affects the attitude of individuals, and makes them, as individuals, loath to question authority that is within or near the zone of indifference. The formal statement of this common sense is the fiction that authority comes down from above, from the general to the particular. This fiction merely establishes a presumption among individuals in favor of the acceptability of orders from superiors, enabling them to avoid making issues of such orders without incurring a sense of personal subserviency or a loss of personal or individual status with their fellows.

Thus the contributors are willing to maintain the authority of communications because, where care is taken to see that only acceptable communications in general are issued, most of them fall within the zone of personal indifference; and because communal sense influences the motives of most contributors most of the time. The practical instrument of this sense is the fiction of superior authority, which makes it possible normally to treat a personal question impersonally.

The fiction [5] of superior authority is necessary for two main reasons:

(1) It is the process by which the individual delegates upward, or to the organization, responsibility for what is an organization decision — an action which is depersonalized by the fact of its coördinate character. This means that if an instruction is disregarded, an executive's risk of being wrong must be accepted, a risk that the individual cannot and usually will not take unless in fact his position is at least as good as that of another with respect to correct appraisal of the relevant situation. Most persons are disposed to grant authority because they dislike the personal responsibility which they otherwise accept, especially when they are not in a good position to accept it. The practical difficulties in the operation of organization seldom lie in the excessive desire of individuals to assume responsibility for the organization action of themselves or others,

---

[5] The word "fiction" is used because from the standpoint of logical construction it merely explains overt acts. Either as a superior officer or as a subordinate, however, I know nothing that I actually regard as more "real" than "authority."

but rather lie in the reluctance to take responsibility for their own actions in organization.

(2) The fiction gives impersonal notice that what is at stake is the good of the organization. If objective authority is flouted for arbitrary or merely temperamental reasons, if, in other words, there is deliberate attempt to twist an organization requirement to personal advantage, rather than properly to safeguard a substantial personal interest, then there is a deliberate attack on the organization itself. To remain outside an organization is not necessarily to be more than not friendly or not interested. To fail in an obligation intentionally is an act of hostility. This no organization can permit; and it must respond with punitive action if it can, even to the point of incarcerating or executing the culprit. This is rather generally the case where a person has agreed in advance in general what he will do. Leaving an organization in the lurch is not often tolerable.

The correctness of what has been said above will perhaps appear most probable from a consideration of the difference between executive action in emergency and that under "normal" conditions. In times of war the disciplinary atmosphere of an army is intensified — it is rather obvious to all that its success and the safety of its members are dependent upon it. In other organizations, abruptness of command is not only tolerated in times of emergency, but expected, and the lack of it often would actually be demoralizing. It is the sense of the justification which lies in the obvious situation which regulates the exercise of the veto by the final authority which lies at the bottom. This is a commonplace of executive experience, though it is not a commonplace of conversation about it.[6]

---

[6] It will be of interest to quote a statement which has appeared since these lines were written, in a pamphlet entitled "Business — Well on the Firing Line" (No. 9 in the series "What Helps Business Helps You," in *Nation's*

II. The System of Coördination

Up to this point we have devoted our attention to the subjective aspect of authority. The executive, however, is predominantly occupied not with this subjective aspect, which is fundamental, but with the objective character of a communication which induces acceptance.

I

Authority has been defined in part as a "character of a communication in a formal organization." A "superior" is not in our view an authority nor does he have authority strictly speaking; nor is a communication authoritative except when it is an effort or action of organization. This is what we mean when we say that individuals are able to exercise authority only when they are acting "officially," a principle well established in law, and generally in secular and religious practice. Hence the importance ascribed to time, place, dress, ceremony, and authentication of a communication to establish its official character. These practices confirm the statement that authority relates to a communication "in a formal organization." There often occur occasions of compulsive power of individuals and of hostile groups; but authority is always concerned with something *within* a definitely organized system. Current usage conforms to the definition in this respect. The word "authority" is seldom employed except where formal organization connection is

---

Business). It reads in part: "Laws don't create Teamplay. It is not called into play by law. For every written rule there are a thousand unwritten rules by which the course of business is guided, which govern the millions of daily transactions of which business consists. These rules are not applied from the top down, by arbitrary authority. They grow out of actual practice — from the bottom up. They are based upon mutual understanding and compromise, the desire to achieve common ends and further the common good. They are observed *voluntarily*, because they have the backing of experience and common sense."

stated or implied (unless, of course, the reference is obviously figurative).

These circumstances arise from the fact that the character of authority in organization communications lies in the *potentiality of assent* of those to whom they are sent. Hence, they are only sent to contributors or "members" of the organization. Since all authoritative communications are official and relate only to organization action, they have no meaning to those whose actions are not included within the coöperative system. This is clearly in accord with the common understanding. The laws of one country have no authority for citizens of another, except under special circumstances. Employers do not issue directions to employees of other organizations. Officials would appear incompetent who issued orders to those outside their jurisdiction.

A communication has the presumption of authority when it originates at sources of organization information — a communications center — better than individual sources. It loses this presumption, however, if not within the scope or field of this center. The presumption is also lost if the communication shows an absence of adjustment to the actual situation which confronts the recipient of it.

Thus men impute authority to communications from superior positions, provided they are reasonably consistent with advantages of scope and perspective that are credited to those positions. This authority is to a considerable extent independent of the personal ability of the incumbent of the position. It is often recognized that though the incumbent may be of limited personal ability his advice may be superior solely by reason of the advantage of position. This is the *authority of position*.

But it is obvious that some men have superior ability. Their knowledge and understanding regardless of position command respect. Men impute authority to what they say in an organization for this reason only. This is the *authority of leadership*.

When the authority of leadership is combined with the authority of position, men who have an established connection with an organization generally will grant authority, accepting orders far outside the zone of indifference. The confidence engendered may even make compliance an inducement in itself.

Nevertheless, the determination of authority remains with the individual. Let these "positions" of authority in fact show ineptness, ignorance of conditions, failure to communicate what ought to be said, or let leadership fail (chiefly by its concrete action) to recognize implicitly its dependence upon the essential character of the relationship of the individual to the organization, and the authority if tested disappears.

This objective authority is only maintained if the positions or leaders continue to be adequately informed. In very rare cases persons possessing great knowledge, insight, or skill have this adequate information without occupying executive position. What they say ought to be done or ought not to be done will be accepted. But this is usually personal advice at the risk of the taker. Such persons have influence rather than authority. In most cases genuine leaders who give advice concerning organized efforts are required to accept positions of responsibility; for knowledge of the applicability of their special knowledge or judgment to concrete *organization* action, not to abstract problems, is essential to the worth of what they say as a basis of organization authority. In other words, they have an organization personality, as distinguished from their individual personality,[7] commensurate with the influence of their leadership. The common way to state this is that there cannot be authority without corresponding responsibility. A more exact expression would be that objective authority cannot be imputed to persons in organization positions unless subjectively they are dominated by the organization as respects their decisions.

It may be said, then, that the maintenance of objective au-

[7] See Chapter VII, p. 88.

thority adequate to support the fiction of superior authority and able to make the zone of indifference an actuality depends upon the operation of the system of communication in the organization. The function of this system is to supply adequate information to the positions of authority and adequate facilities for the issuance of orders. To do so it requires commensurate capacities in those able to be leaders. High positions that are not so supported have weak authority, as do strong men in minor positions.

Thus authority depends upon a coöperative personal attitude of individuals on the one hand; and the system of communication in the organization on the other. Without the latter, the former cannot be maintained. The most devoted adherents of an organization will quit it, if its system results in inadequate, contradictory, inept orders, so that they cannot know who is who, what is what, or have the sense of effective coördination.

This system of communication, or its maintenance, is a primary or essential continuing problem of a formal organization. Every other practical question of effectiveness or efficiency — that is, of the factors of survival — depends upon it. In technical language the system of communication of which we are now speaking is often known as the "lines of authority."

II

It has already been shown [8] that the requirements of communication determine the size of unit organizations, the grouping of units, the grouping of groups of unit organizations. We may now consider the controlling factors in the character of the communication system as a system of objective authority.

(*a*) The first is that *channels of communication should be definitely known*. The language in which this principle is ordinarily stated is, "The lines of authority must be definitely es-

[8] Chapter VIII, "The Structure of Complex Formal Organizations," beginning at p. 106.

tablished." The method of doing so is by making official appointments known; by assigning each individual to his position; by general announcements; by organization charts; by educational effort, and most of all by habituation, that is, by securing as much permanence of system as is practicable. Emphasis is laid either upon the position, or upon the persons; but usually the fixing of authority is made both to positions and, less emphatically, to persons.

(*b*) Next, we may say that *objective authority requires a definite formal channel of communication to every member of an organization.* In ordinary language this means "everyone must report to someone" (communication in one direction) and "everyone must be subordinate to someone" (communication in the other direction). In other words, in formal organizations everyone must have definite formal relationship to the organization.[9]

(*c*) Another factor is that *the line of communication must be as direct or short as possible.* This may be explained as follows: Substantially all formal communication is verbal (written or oral). Language as a vehicle of communication is limited and susceptible of misunderstanding. Much communication is necessarily without preparation. Even communications that are carefully prepared require interpretation. Moreover, communications are likely to be in more general terms the more general — that is, the higher — the position. It follows that something may be lost or added by transmission at each stage of the process, especially when communication is oral, or when at each stage there is combination of several communications. Moreover, when communications go from high positions down they often must be made more specific as they proceed; and when in the

---

[9] In some types of organizations it is not unusual, however, for one person to report to and to be subordinate to two or three "superiors," in which case the functions of the superiors are defined and are mutually exclusive in principle.

reverse direction, usually more general. In addition, the speed of communication, other things equal, will be less the greater the number of centers through which it passes. Accordingly, the shorter the line the greater the speed and the less the error.

How important this factor is may be indicated by the remarkable fact that in great complex organizations the number of levels of communication is not much larger than in smaller organizations. In most organizations consisting of the services of one or two hundred men the levels of communication will be from three to five. In the Army the levels are: President, (Secretary of War), General, Major-General, Brigadier-General, Colonel, Major, Captain, Lieutenant, Sergeant, men — that is, nine or ten. In the Bell Telephone System, with over 300,000 working members, the number is eight to ten.[10] A similar shortness of the line of communication is noteworthy in the Catholic Church viewed from the administrative standpoint.

Many organization practices or inventions are used to accomplish this end, depending upon the purpose and technical conditions. Briefly, these methods are: The use of expanded executive organizations at each stage; the use of the staff department (technical, expert, advisory); the division of executive work into functional bureaus; and processes of delegating responsibility with automatic coördination through regular conference procedures, committees for special temporary functions, etc.

(d) Another factor is that, in principle, *the complete line of communication should usually be used.* By this is meant that a communication from the head of an organization to the bottom should pass through every stage of the line of authority. This is due to the necessity of avoiding conflicting communications (in either direction) which might (and would) occur if there were any "jumping of the line" of organization. It is

---

[10] Disregarding the corporate aspects of the organization, and not including boards of directors.

also necessary because of the need of interpretation, and to maintain responsibility.[11]

(*e*) Again, the *competence of the persons serving as communication centers, that is, officers, supervisory heads, must be adequate*. The competence required is that of more and more *general* ability with reference to the work of the entire organization the more central the office of communication and the larger the organization. For the function of the center of communication in an organization is to translate incoming communications concerning external conditions, the progress of activity, successes, failures, difficulties, dangers, into outgoing communications in terms of new activities, preparatory steps, etc., all shaped according to the ultimate as well as the immediate purposes to be served. There is accordingly required more or less mastery of the technologies involved, of the capabilities of the personnel, of the informal organization situation, of the character and status of the subsidiary organizations, of the principles of action relative to purpose, of the interpretation of environmental factors, and a power of discrimination between communications that can possess authority because they are recognizably compatible with *all* the pertinent conditions and those which will not possess authority because they will not or cannot be accepted.

It is a fact, I think, that we hardly nowadays expect individual personal ability adequate to positional requirements of communication in modern large-scale organization. The limitations of individuals as respects time and energy alone preclude such personal ability, and the complexity of the technologies or other special knowledge involved make it impossible. For these reasons each major center of communication is itself organized, sometimes quite elaborately. The immediate staff of the executive (commanding officer), consisting of deputies, or chief

---

[11] These by no means exhaust the considerations. The necessity of maintaining personal prestige of executives as an *inducement to them* to function is on the whole an important additional reason.

clerks, or adjutants, or auxiliaries with their assistants, constitute an executive unit of organization only one member of which is perhaps an "executive," that is, occupies the *position* of authority; and the technical matters are assigned to staff departments or organizations of experts. Such staff departments often are partly "field" departments in the sense that they directly investigate or secure information on facts or conditions external to the organizations; but in major part in most cases they digest and translate information from the field, and prepare the plans, orders, etc., for transmission. In this capacity they are advisory or adjutant to the executives. In practice, however, these assistants have the function of semi-formal advice under regulated conditions to the organizations as a whole. In this way, both the formal channels and the informal organization are supplemented by intermediate processes.

In some cases the executive (either chief or some subordinate executive) may be not a person but a board, a legislature, a committee. I know of no important organizations, except some churches and some absolute governments in which the highest objective authority is not lodged in an *organized* executive group, that is, a "highest" unit of organization.

(*f*) Again, *the line of communication should not be interrupted during the time when the organization is to function.* Many organizations (factories, stores) function intermittently, being closed or substantially so during the night, Sundays, etc. Others, such as army, police, railroad systems, telephone systems, never cease to operate. During the times when organizations are at work, in principle the line of authority must never be broken; and practically this is almost, if not quite, literally true in many cases. This is one of the reasons which may be given for the great importance attached to hereditary succession in states, and for the elaborate provision that is made in most organizations (except possibly small "personal" organizations) for the temporary filling of offices automatically during incapacity or absence of incumbents. These provisions emphasize the non-personal and communication character of organization authority, as does the persistent emphasis upon the *office* rather than the *man* that is a matter of indoctrination of many organizations, especially those in which "discipline" is an important feature.

The necessity for this is not merely that specific communications cannot otherwise be attended to. It is at least equally that the *informal* organization disintegrates very quickly if the formal "line of authority" is broken. In organization parlance, "politics" runs riot. Thus, if an office were vacant, but the fact were not known, an organization might function for a considerable time without serious disturbance, except in emergency. But if known, it would quickly become disorganized.

(*g*) The final factor I shall mention is that *every communication should be authenticated*. This means that the person communicating must be known actually to occupy the "position of authority" concerned; that the position includes the type of communication concerned — that is, it is "within its authority"; and that it actually is an authorized communication from this office. The process of authentication in all three respects varies in different organizations under different conditions and for different positions. The practice is undergoing rapid changes in the modern technique, but the principles remain the same. Ceremonials of investiture, inaugurations, swearing-in, general orders of appointment, induction, and introduction, are all essentially appropriate methods of making known who actually fills a position and what the position includes as authority. In order that these *positions* may function it is often necessary that the filling of them should be dramatized, an essential process to the creation of authority *at the bottom*, where only it can be fundamentally — that is, it is essential to inculcate the "sense of organization." This is merely stating that it is essential to "organization loyalty and solidarity" as it may be otherwise expressed. Dignifying the superior position is an important method of dignifying *all* connection with organization, a fact which has been well learned in both religious and political organizations where great attention to the subjective aspects of the "membership" is the rule.

This statement of the principles of communication systems of organizations from the viewpoint of the maintenance of objective authority has necessarily been in terms of complex organizations, since in a simple unit organization the concrete applications of these principles are fused. The principles are with difficulty isolated under simple conditions. Thus, as a matter of course, in unit organizations the channels of communication are known, indeed usually obvious; they are definite; they are the shortest possible; the only lines of authority are complete lines; there is little question of authentication. The doubtful points in unit organization are the competence of the leader, never to be taken for granted even in simple organizations; and whether he is functioning when the organization is in operation. Yet as a whole the adequately balanced maintenance of these aspects of simple leadership is the basis of objective authority in the unit organization, as the maintenance of the more formal and observable manifestations of the same aspects is the basis of authority in the complex organizations.

III. Reconciliation with Legalistic Conceptions

Legalistic conceptions of authority, at least somewhat different from those we have presented, seem to have support in the relations between superior and subsidiary organizations. A corporate organization, for example, is subject to the law of the state. Is not this a case where authority actually does come down from the top, from the superior organizations? Only in exactly the same sense that individuals accept objective authority, as we have described it. A subsidiary or dependent organization must accept law to give law its authority. Units of organization, integrated complexes of organization, and dependent organizations, make and must make the subjective decision of authority just as individuals do. A corporation may and often does quit if it cannot obey the law and still have a net reason for existence. It is no more able to carry out an unintelligible law than an individual, it can no more do the impossible than an individual, it will show the same inability to conform to conflicting laws as the individual. The only difference between subsidiary, or dependent, unit and group organizations and individuals is that the denial of authority can be made directly by the individual, and either directly or indirectly by the unit, group, or dependent or subsidiary complex. When it is direct, the effect of the law or order upon the organization as a whole is in point; when it is indirect the effect is on the individuals of whose efforts the whole is made up. Thus no complex can carry out a superior order if its members (either unit organizations or individuals) will not enable it to do so. For example, to order by law working conditions which will not be accepted by individual employees, even though the employer is willing, is futile; its authority is in fact denied. The employees quit, then the organization ends.

But in the final analysis the differences are not important, except occasionally in the concrete case. The subsidiary organization in point of fact derives most of its authority for most of its action from its own "members" individually. They may quit if they do not accept the orders, no matter what the "ultimate" authority; and no absolute or external authority can compel the necessary effort beyond a minimum insufficient to maintain efficient or effective organization performance. An important effect of the ascription of legalistic origin of a part of the formal authority of subsidiary and independent organizations has been its obscuring of the nature of the real authority that governs the greater part of the coöperative effort of such organizations.

There is, however, a considerable quantitative difference in the factor of informal organization, that is, the factor of public opinion, general sentiment. This is not a difference of principle, but merely one of the relationship of the size of the informal organization relative to the individual or formal group. A strong individual can resist the domination of opinion if it is confined to a small number; but rarely if there is in question the opinion of an overwhelming number, actively and hostilely expressed. Now the size of any subsidiary organization is small compared with the informal organization that permeates the State; and this wide informal organization will usually support "law and order" regardless of merits if the question at issue is minor from its point of view. The pressure on the subjective attitude of individuals or on that of subsidiary or dependent organizations is strong ordinarily to induce acceptance of law in an "orderly" society.

But this informal support of objective authority of the State depends upon essentially the same principles as in the case of ordinary organizations. Inappropriateness of law and of government administration, lack of understanding of the ultimate basis of authority, indifference to the motives governing individual support, untimely or impossible legislation, as is well known destroy "respect for law and order," that is, destroy objective political authority. In democracies the normal reaction is to change law and administration through political action. But when majorities are unable to understand that authority rests fundamentally upon the consent of minorities as well as of majorities, or when the system is autocratic or absolute, the liquidation of attempted tyranny is through revolution or civil war. Authority lies always with him to whom it applies. Coercion creates a contrary illusion; but the use of force *ipso facto* destroys the authority postulated. It creates a new authority, a new situation, a new objective, which is granted when the force is accepted. Many men have destroyed all authority as to themselves by dying rather than yield.

At first thought it may seem that the element of communication in organization is only in part related to authority; but more thorough consideration leads to the understanding that communication, authority, specialization, and purpose are all aspects comprehended in coördination. All communication relates to the formulation of purpose and the transmission of coördinating prescriptions for action and so rests upon the ability to communicate with those willing to coöperate.

Authority is another name for the willingness and capacity of individuals to submit to the necessities of coöperative systems. Authority arises from the technological and social limitations of coöperative systems on the one hand, and of individuals on the other. Hence the status of authority in a society is the measure both of the development of individuals and of the technological and social conditions of the society.

CHAPTER XIII

THE ENVIRONMENT OF DECISION

THE acts of individuals may be distinguished in principle as those which are the result of deliberation, calculation, thought, and those which are unconscious, automatic, responsive, the results of internal or external conditions present or past. In general, whatever processes precede the first class of acts culminate in what may be termed "decision." Involved in acts which are ascribed to decision are many subsidiary acts which are themselves automatic, the processes of which are usually unknown to the actor.

When decision is involved there are consciously present two terms — the end to be accomplished and the means to be used. The end itself may be the result of logical processes in which the end is in turn a means to some broader or more remote end; or the immediate end, and generally the ultimate end, may not be a result of logical processes, but "given" — that is, unconsciously impressed — by conditions, including social conditions past or present, including orders of organizations. But whenever the end has been determined, by whatever process, the decision as to means is itself a logical process of discrimination, analysis, choice — however defective either the factual basis for choice or the reasoning related to these facts.

The acts of organizations are those of persons dominated by organizational, not personal, ends. These ends, especially those which are most general or remote, since they represent a consensus of opinion, may be arrived at by non-logical processes; but since they must usually be formulated in some degree, whereas individual ends more rarely need to be formulated, the ends of organization to a relatively high degree involve logical processes, not as rationalizations after decision but as processes of decision. Moreover, when ends have been adopted, the coördination of acts as means to these ends is itself an essentially logical process. The discrimination of facts and the allocation of acts by specialization which coördination implies may quite appropriately be regarded as logical or deliberate thinking processes of organization, though not necessarily logical processes of thought of the individual participants. Generally, however, it will be observed that the more important *organization* acts of individuals are likely also to be logical — in that they require deliberate choice of means to accomplish ends which are not personal, and therefore cannot be directly automatic or responsive reactions.

This does not mean that unconscious, automatic, responsive, action is not involved in organization. On the contrary, the discussion of informal organization in Chapter IX has suggested that non-logical organization processes are indispensable to formal organization. Moreover, much of the action of individuals as participating in organization is habitual, repetitive, and may be merely responsive by *organization design* — a result, for example, of specialization intended to enhance this non-logical process. What is important here, however, is the superlative degree to which logical processes must and can characterize organization action as contrasted with individual action, and the degree to which decision is specialized in organization. It is the deliberate adoption of means to ends which is the essence of formal organization. This is not only required in order to make coöperation superior to the biological powers and senses of individuals, but it is possibly the chief superiority of coöperative to individual action in most of the important cases of enduring organizations.

From this analysis it follows that acts of decision are characteristic of organization behavior as contrasted with individual behavior, and that the description of the processes of decision are relatively more important to the understanding of organization behavior than in the case of individuals. Moreover, whereas these processes in individuals are as yet matters of speculation rather than of science in the various psychologies, they are in organizations much more open to empirical observation. In fact they are themselves matters of deliberate attention and subject to intentional specialization, as will appear later. The formulation of organization purposes or objectives and the more general decisions involved in this process and in those of action to carry them into effect are distributed in organizations, and are not, nor can they be, concentrated or specialized to individuals except in minor degree. The facts in this regard are obscured to many by the formal location of objective authority in various organization positions, the reasons for which have been discussed in Chapter XII; but it has already been indicated in that chapter that underlying the formal structure of authority and intraorganization communication are processes of interacting decisions distributed throughout the positions in the lines of communication. This may be regarded as the essential process of organization action which continually synthesizes the elements of coöperative systems into concrete systems.

Every effort that is a constituent of organization, that is, every coördinated coöperative effort, may involve two acts of decision. The first is the decision of the person affected as to whether or not he will contribute this effort as a matter of personal choice. It is a detail of the process of repeated personal decisions that determine whether or not the individual will be or will continue to be a contributor to the organization. The personal result here in question we have discussed in the chapters on the Economy of Incentives and the Theory of Authority. This act of decision is *outside* the system of efforts constituting organization, as it has been defined in Chapter VI, although it is, as we have seen, a subject for organized attention.

The second type of decisions has no direct or specific relation to personal results, but views the effort concerning which decision is to be made non-personally from the viewpoint of its organization effect and of its relation to organization purpose. This second act of decision is often made in a direct sense by individuals, but it is impersonal and organizational in its intent and effect. Very often it is also organizational in its process, as, for example, in legislatures, or when boards or committees determine action. The act of decision is a part of the organization itself.

This distinction between the two types of decision is frequently recognized in ordinary affairs. We very often say or hear sentences similar to this: "If this were my business, I think I would decide the question this way — but it is not my personal affair"; or, "I think the *situation* requires such and such an answer — but I am not in a position to determine what ought to be done"; or, "The decision should be made by someone else." This is in effect a restatement, with a different emphasis, of the suggestion in Chapter VII that a sort of dual personality is required of individuals contributing to organization action — the private personality, and the organization personality.

These two kinds of decisions — organization decisions and personal decisions — are chiefly to be distinguished as to process by this fact: that personal decisions cannot ordinarily be delegated to others, whereas organization decisions can often if not always be delegated. For example, what may be called a major decision by an individual may require numerous subsidiary decisions (or judgments) which he also must make. A similar important decision by an organization may in its final form be enunciated by one person and the corresponding subsidiary decisions by several different persons, all acting organizationally, not personally. Similarly, the execution of a decision by one person may require subsequent detailed decision by him as to various steps, whereas the execution of a similar decision in an organization almost always requires subsequent detailed decision by several different persons. Indeed, it may be said that often the responsibility for an organization decision is not a personal responsibility until assigned. Responsibility for organization decision must be assigned positively and definitely in many cases because the aptness of decision depends upon knowledge of facts and of organization purpose, and is therefore bound up with organization communication. Thus central or general organization decisions are best made at centers of the communication system of the organization, so that such decisions must be assigned to those located at these central positions. Persons located at such positions are known as executives; so that the necessities of communication as an essential element in organization imposes the assignment of responsibility for some kinds of organization decision to executives. In short, a characteristic of the services of executives is that they represent a specialization of the process of making organization decisions — and this is the essence of their functions.

The circumstances surrounding the making of concrete decisions are of course of indefinitely large variety, but we will give attention here only to certain general conditions, which may be presented under three headings: the occasions of decision, the evidences of decision, and the environment of decision.

I. The Occasions of Decision

The making of decisions, as everyone knows from personal experience, is a burdensome task. Offsetting the exhilaration that may result from correct and successful decision and the relief that follows the terminating of a struggle to determine issues is the depression that comes from failure or error of decision and the frustration which ensues from uncertainty. Accordingly, it will be observed that men generally try to avoid making decisions, beyond a limited degree when they are rather uncritical responses to conditions. The capacity of most men to make decisions is quite narrow,[1] although it is a capacity that may be considerably developed by training and especially by experience.

The executive is under the obligation of making decisions usually within approximately defined limits related to the position he has accepted; and is under the necessity of keeping within the limits of his capacity if he is continuously to discharge this obligation. He must, therefore, to be successful, distinguish between the occasions of decision in order to avoid the acceptance of more than he can undertake without neglecting the fields to which his position relates. For the natural reluctance of other men to decide, their persistent disposition to avoid responsibility, and their fear of criticism, will lead them to overwhelm the executive who does not protect himself from excessive burdens of decision if he is not already protected by a well regulated and habitual distribution of responsibilities.

It is for this reason necessary in the making of decisions to maintain a balance between the fields from which the occasions of them arise. I suppose this is rarely a matter of conscious selection, and is probably subject to no general rules. It involves in itself important decisions. For our purposes, however, it may be helpful to note that the occasions for decision originate in three distinct fields: (*a*) from authoritative communications from superiors; (*b*) from cases referred for decision by subordinates; (*c*) from cases originating in the initiative of the executive concerned.

(*a*) Occasions for decision are frequently furnished by instructions or by general requirements of superior authority. Such decisions relate to the interpretation, application, and distribution of instructions. These occasions cannot be avoided, though the burden may be reduced by delegation of responsibility to subordinates. They involve serious decisions when the

[1] Why this is so will be presented at length in Chapter XVII.

instructions seem morally wrong, harmful to the organization, or impossible of execution.

(*b*) The cases referred for decision may be called appellate cases. They arise from incapacity of subordinates, uncertainty of instructions, novelty of conditions, conflict of jurisdiction or conflicts of orders, or failure of subjective authority. The control of the number of appellate cases lies in adequacy of executive organization, of personnel, of previous decision; and the development of the processes of informal organization. The test of executive action is to make these decisions when they are important, or when they cannot be delegated reasonably, and to decline the others.

(*c*) The occasions of decision on the initiative of the executive are the most important test of his capacity. Out of his understanding of the situation, which depends upon his ability and initiative, and on the character of the communication system of his organization, it is to be determined whether something needs to be done or corrected. To decide that question involves not merely the ordinary elements but the executive's specific justification for deciding. For when the occasions for decision arise from above or below the position of the executive, others have in advance granted him authority; but when made on his own initiative, this always may be (and generally is) questioned, at least tacitly (in the form whether decision was necessary, or related to scope of obligations, etc.). Moreover, failure to decide is usually not specifically subject to attack, except under extreme conditions. Hence there is much incentive to avoid decision. Pressure of other work is the usual self-justification. Yet it is clear that the most important obligation is to raise and decide those issues which no one else is in a position to raise effectively.

From the point of view of the *relative* importance of specific decisions, those of executives properly call for first attention. From the point of view of *aggregate* importance, it is not decisions of executives but of non-executive participants in organization which should enlist major interest. Indeed it is precisely for this reason that many executive decisions are necessary — they relate to the facilitation of correct action involving appropriate decisions among others. In large measure this is a process of providing for the clear presentment of the issues or choices. At any event, it is easily evident merely from the inspection of the action of the non-executive participants in organization that coördination of action requires repeated organization decisions "on the spot" where the effective action of organization takes place. It is here that the final and most concrete objectives of purposes are found, with the maximum of definiteness. There is no further stage of organization action. The final selection of means takes place at this point.

It should be noted, however, that the types of decisions as well as the conditions change in character as we descend from the major executive to the non-executive positions in organization. At the upper limit decisions relating to ends to be pursued generally require the major attention, those relating to means being secondary, rather general, and especially concerned with personnel, that is, the development and protection of organization itself. At intermediate levels the breaking of broad purposes into more specific ends and the technical and technological problems, including economic problems, of action become prominent. At the low levels decisions characteristically relate to technologically correct conduct, so far as the action is organization action. But it is at these low levels, where ultimate authority resides, that the *personal* decisions determining willingness to contribute become of relatively greatest aggregate importance.

II. The Evidences of Decision

Not the least of the difficulties of appraising the executive functions or the relative merits of executives lies in the fact that there is little direct opportunity to observe the essential operations of decision. It is a perplexing fact that most executive decisions produce no direct evidence of themselves and that knowledge of them can only be derived from the cumulation of indirect evidence. They must largely be inferred from general results in which they are merely one factor, and from symptomatic indications of roundabout character.

Those decisions which are most directly known result in the emission of authoritative communications, that is, orders. Something is or is not to be done. Even in such cases the basic decision may not be evident; for the decision to attempt to achieve a certain result or condition may require several communications to different persons which appear to be complete in themselves but in which the controlling general decision may not be disclosed.

Again, a firm decision may be taken that does not result in any communication whatever for the time being. A decision properly timed must be made in advance of communicating it, either because the action involved must wait anticipated developments or because it cannot be authoritative without educational or persuasive preparation.

Finally, the decision may be not to decide. This is a most frequent decision, and from some points of view probably the most important. For every alert executive continually raises in his own mind questions for determination. As a result of his consideration he may determine that the question is not pertinent. He may determine that it is not now pertinent. He may determine that it is pertinent now, but that there are lacking adequate data upon which to base a final decision. He may determine that it is pertinent for decision now, but that it should or must be decided by someone else on the latter's initiative. He may determine that the question is pertinent, can be decided, will not be decided except by himself, and yet it would be better that it be not decided because his competence is insufficient.

The fine art of executive decision consists in not deciding questions that are not now pertinent, in not deciding prematurely, in not making decision that cannot be made effective, and in not making decisions that others should make. Not to decide questions that are not pertinent at the time is uncommon good sense, though to raise them may be uncommon perspicacity. Not to decide questions prematurely is to refuse commitment of attitude or the development of prejudice. Not to make decisions that cannot be made effective is to refrain from destroying authority. Not to make decisions that others should make is to preserve morale, to develop competence, to fix responsibility, and to preserve authority.

From this it may be seen that decisions fall into two major classes, positive decisions — to do something, to direct action, to cease action, to prevent action; and negative decisions, which are decisions not to decide. Both are inescapable; but the negative decisions are often largely unconscious, relatively non-logical, "instinctive," "good sense." It is because of the rejections that the selection is good. The best of moves may be offset by a false move. This is why time is usually necessary to appraise the executive. There is no current evidence of the all-important negative decisions. The absence of effective moves indicates failure of initiative in decision, but error of action probably often means absence of good negative decisions. The success of action through a period of time denotes excellence of selection and of rejection of possible actions.

III. The Nature of the Environment

Whatever the occasions or the evidences of decision, it is clear that decisions are constantly being made. What is the nature of the environment of decisions, the materials with which they deal, the field to which they relate? It consists of two parts: (*a*) purpose; and (*b*) the physical world, the social world, the external things and forces and circumstances of the moment.

All of these, including purpose, constitute the objective field of decision; but the two parts are of radically different nature and origin. The function of decision is to regulate the relations between these two parts. This regulation is accomplished either by changing the purpose or by changing the remainder of the environment.

(*a*) We may consider purpose first. It may seem strange perhaps that purpose should be included in the objective environment, since purpose of all things seems personal, subjective, internal, the expression of desire. This is true; but *at the moment of a new decision*, an existing purpose, the result of a previous decision under previous conditions, is an objective fact, and it is so treated at that moment in so far as it is a factor in new decision.

This is especially true because organization decisions do not relate to personal purposes, but to organization purposes. The purpose which concerns an organization decision may have been given as a fact to and accepted as such by the person who is responsible for making a new decision. But no matter how arrived at, when decision is in point, the purpose is fact already determined; its making is a matter of history; it may be as objective as another man's emotions may be to an observer.

We must next note, however, that purpose is essential to give any meaning to the rest of the environment.[2] The environment must be looked at from *some* point of view to be intelligible. A mere mass of things, atoms, movements, forces, noises, lights, could produce some response from a sensitive creature or certainly would have some effect on it, or on other things, but the reduction of this mass of everything to something significant requires a basis for discrimination, for picking out this and that as pertinent, relevant, interesting. This basis is that in *this*

---

[2] I am under the impression that in a general way both the form of expression and the concepts stated in the next several paragraphs were derived from or influenced by A. N. Whitehead's *Process and Reality*.

situation something is or is not to be done. The situation aids, obstructs, or is neutral from *this* point of view. The basis for this discrimination is a purpose, an end, an object to be accomplished.

Purpose itself has no meaning, however, except in an environment. It can only be defined in terms of an environment.[3] Even to want to go somewhere, anywhere, supposes some kind of environment. A very general purpose supposes a very general undifferentiated environment; and if the purpose is stated or thought of it must be in terms of that general environment. But when formed, it immediately (if it is not in suspense or dormant, so to speak) serves for reducing that environment to more definite features; and the immediate result is to change purpose into a more specific purpose. Thus when I decide I want to go from A to B my idea of terrain is vague. But as soon as I have decided, the terrain becomes less vague; I immediately see paths, rocks, obstacles that are significant; and this finer discrimination results in detailed and smaller purposes. I not only want to go from A to B, but I want to go this way, that way, etc. This constant refinement of purpose is the effect of repeated decisions, in finer and finer detail, until eventually detailed purpose is contemporaneous accomplishment. But similarly with each new edition of purpose, a new discrimination of the environment is involved, until finally the last obstacle of progressive action represents a breaking up of a general purpose into many concrete purposes, each as it is made almost simultaneously associated with the action. The thing is done as soon as decided; it becomes a matter of history; it constitutes a single step in the process of experience.

Thus back and forth purpose and environment react in successive steps through successive decisions in greater and greater

[3] Care should be taken to keep in mind that environment throughout does not mean merely physical aspects of the environment, but explicitly includes social aspects, although physical rather than other aspects are used for illus-

detail. A series of final decisions, each apparently trivial, is largely accomplished unconsciously and sums up into an effected general purpose and a route of experience.

(*b*) We may now consider the environment of decision exclusive of purpose. It consists of atoms and molecules, agglomerations of things in motion, alive; of men and emotions; of physical laws and social laws; social ideas, norms of action, of forces and resistances. Their number is infinite and they are all always present. They are also always changing. They are meaningless in their variety and changes except as discriminated in the light of purpose. They are viewed as static facts, if the change is not significant from the viewpoint of the purpose, or as both static and dynamic facts.

This discrimination divides the world into two parts; the facts that are immaterial, irrelevant, mere background; and the part that contains the facts that apparently aid or prevent the accomplishment of purpose. As soon as that discrimination takes place, decision is in bud. It is in the state of selecting among alternatives. These alternatives are either to utilize favorable factors, to eliminate or circumvent unfavorable ones, or to change the purpose. Note that if the decision is to deal with the environment, this automatically introduces new but more detailed purposes, the progeny, as it were, of the parent purpose; but if the decision is to change the purpose rather than deal with the environment, the parent is sterile. It is abandoned, and a new purpose is selected, thereby creating a *new* environment in the light of *that* purpose.

This looks like metaphysical speculation if one thinks of it as individual and personal — undemonstrable assumptions, speculative reasoning. But it can be observed in an organiza-

---

tration as simpler. In many organizations, however, the physical aspects are constant and it is the social aspects which are pertinent. This is the case especially when the purpose is a concrete expression of social ideas or attitudes, as, for example, in ritualistic types of action whether religious or political.

tion, at least sufficiently to corroborate it roughly. Thus if the president of a telephone company for good reasons orders [4] two poles carrying a cable removed from the north side of First Street between A and B Streets to the opposite side of First Street, it can, I think, be approximately demonstrated that carrying out that order involves perhaps 10,000 decisions of 100 men located at 15 points, requiring successive analyses of several environments, including social, moral, legal, economic, and physical facts of the environment, and requiring 9000 redefinitions and refinements of purpose, and 1000 changes of purpose. If inquiry be made of those responsible, probably not more than a half-a-dozen decisions will be recalled or deemed worthy of mention — those that seemed at the moment difficult or momentous, or that were subject to question or proved erroneous. The others will be "taken for granted," all a part of the business of knowing one's business. However, a large part of the decisions, purposes, and descriptions and analyses of the various environments will be a matter of record — short-cut, abbreviated, to be sure, but marking the routes of decisions with fair definiteness. Only in the case of individual workmen shall we be almost completely reduced to speculation as to the number and character of the decisions required, because many of them certainly will relate to physiological action.

The purpose of this chapter has been to suggest the climate of concrete decisions as they occur in organizations and to emphasize the radical difference between the process of decision in organizations, when decision is in its important aspects a

---

[4] Partly to illustrate several statements in this essay I may say that it is necessary to imagine extreme conditions to suppose he would issue such an order. Ordinarily what he would do would be to inquire whether it would be feasible to take the action suggested, or what would be involved in doing so, or he would state the problem and ask for its solution, etc. The executive art is nine-tenths inducing those who have authority to use it in taking pertinent action.

social process, and the process of decision in individuals when it is a psychological process socially conditioned. Perhaps the most important inference to be drawn from this description is that within organizations, especially of complex types, there is a technique of decision, an organizational process of thinking, which may not be analogous to that of the individual. It would appear that such techniques differ widely among the various types of organization — for example, religious, political, industrial, commercial, etc. This is perhaps conveyed by the remark often made about the "differences in approach" to similar questions. It may be suspected that more than differences in technological character or even of the ends or purposes are involved.

At any event, it is evidently important to consider the principles of the decisive process as it actually takes place from the organizational viewpoint rather than from that of either psychology or systems of logic. This will be undertaken in the succeeding chapter.

CHAPTER XIV

THE THEORY OF OPPORTUNISM

MANY acts of individuals and a considerable proportion of those of organizations may be regarded as responses to conditions of the environment, involving no process of decision as defined in the preceding chapter. Those acts which are preceded by decisions, whether of individuals or of organization, differ from mere responses in that consciously recognized purposes, ends, or objectives are present as the basis for action in sufficient strength to result in effort. In the case of individuals these ends may arise from physiological requirements or from ideas or states of mind that are in their most significant aspects a consequence of the social history or conditioning of the individual. In the case of organizations, however, all ends of action are arrived at by social processes. In some simple cases organization ends may be considered as no more than a mere translation of ideas uniformly held by the individual participants into the integrating purpose of a coöperative system, but in most cases the ends of organization action are the unique results of the *action* of organization itself. The ends are in part limited by the ideas of the individuals participating, in the sense that their willingness to participate is often affected by the nature of the coöperative objective; but the ends are not determined by such limits. On the contrary they evolve to their precise form, except insofar as they are affected by the means and conditions of coöperative action, on the basis of the "good" of the organization. "Good" may have reference primarily either to the internal equilibrium of the organization as affecting its relations with participants, or to external equilibrium as affecting its relations with the general (including the social) environment. But in any case it always refers to the future, and implies foresight in terms of some standard or norm of desirability.

This aspect of the purpose or ends of organization is the ideal. We shall call it the moral element. It is impossible by definition that formal organizations can act without the moral element. It is indispensable to them.[1] Accordingly, the moral element in organization decisions will be given careful consideration later, especially in Chapter XVII, "The Nature of Executive Responsibility." The present chapter, however, is to be devoted to the antithesis of the moral element, namely, the opportunistic element. This is the element implied by the fact that no action can take place except in the present, under conditions and with the means presently available. Evidently, the opportunistic element in decision is indispensable to the theory of organization.

I

The opportunistic element refers to the objective field within which action must take place. The process of decision so far as it relates to this objective field is essentially one of analysis, even though in practice much of the process will be intuitive or not conscious. The analysis of present circumstances is in part the definition of purpose in immediate terms; but it is also the process of finding what present circumstances are significant with reference to that purpose. What events, what objects, what conditions aid, what prevent, the attainment of purpose?

This analysis will lead to the rejection from present interest or attention of most of the innumerable events, objects, details, circumstances of the situation, since under the conditions they are irrelevant to the purpose. This, of course, is sometimes an easy, sometimes a difficult task. It is easy if it has been done

---

[1] Whereas it is conceivable that an individual can act only in responsive and instinctive ways.

before for similar circumstances, if it yields to an established technique of analysis, if it is a solved scientific problem. It is difficult if it is novel, if there is no technique, or no science. For then the analysis is in effect partly unaided surmise, hypothesis, assumption. This fact, even when the decider is aware of it, does not permit escape from decision, though it may lead to negative decision, that is, to decision not to decide the question for the present. Hence, there is no escape from *some* decision once the process of setting up purpose against environment has begun.

II

The analysis required for decision is in effect a search for the "strategic factors." The notion of the "strategic factor," a term I borrow from Professor John R. Commons,[2] is related to the term "limiting factor" which is common in scientific work. Professor Commons' use of the word is restricted to certain aspects of managerial and bargaining operations in economic systems, but the restriction to this field is unnecessary; the principle involved is the same in whatever circumstances decision is required. The theory of the strategic factor is necessary to an appreciation of the process of decision, and therefore to the understanding of organization and the executive functions as well as, perhaps, individual purposive conduct. As generally as I can state it, this theory is as follows:

If we take any system, or set of conditions, or conglomeration of circumstances existing at a given time, we recognize that it consists of elements, or parts, or factors, which together make up the whole system, set of conditions, or circumstances. Now, if we approach this system or set of circumstances, with a view to the accomplishment of a purpose (and only when we so approach it), the elements or parts become distinguished into

[2] John R. Commons, *Institutional Economics* (New York: The Macmillan Co., 1934), *passim*, but especially chapter IX at pp. 627–633.

two classes: those which if absent or changed would accomplish the desired purpose, provided the others remain unchanged; and these others. The first kind are often called limiting factors, the second, complementary factors. Moreover, when we concentrate our attention upon a *restricted* or subsidiary system or set of circumstances, we often find, on the basis of previous experience or knowledge, that the circumstances fail to satisfy the requirements of purpose because they lack an additional element or elements, that is, elements which are known to exist in the *larger* environment. These are likewise limiting factors.

The limiting (strategic) factor is the one whose control, in the right form, at the right place and time, will establish a new system or set of conditions which meets the purpose. Thus, if we wish to increase the yield of grain in a certain field and on analysis it appears that the soil lacks potash, potash may be said to be the strategic (or limiting) factor. If a tank of water is to be used for cleaning purposes, and is found to contain sediment, the sediment is the strategic (limiting) factor in the use of the water for cleaning. If a machine is not operable because a screw is missing, the screw is the strategic (limiting) factor.[3]

Where the crucial element or part present or absent is a thing or physical element or compound or ingredient it is convenient to call it "limiting" factor; but when personal or organizational action is the crucial element, *as it ultimately is in all purposive effort*, the word "strategic" is preferable. This preference relates to a distinction in the use of the analysis. If its purpose is knowledge for its own sake, that is, if the purpose is immediately scientific, the term "limiting factor" conveys the relatively static situation of the analyst. If the purpose is not

[3] There may be more than one limiting factor, in which they may all be taken as a limiting set, or broken down to single factors for action in some order.

knowledge but decision as to action, "strategic factor" conveys the relatively changing position of the analyst, in which the subjective aspects of decision interact with the objective field in which it is developed.

The fact that a strategic factor is always involved is overlooked because the personal or organization action required often seems trivial; the necessary effort is less than that required to analyze the situation or system. For example, it may require great effort to determine that the land needs potash, but little effort to get the potash. Nevertheless, when the need has been determined, a new situation has arisen because of the fact of knowledge or the assumption that potash is the limiting factor; and instead of potash, the limiting factor *obtaining* potash then becomes the strategic factor; and this will change progressively into *obtaining* the money to *buy* potash, then *finding* John to *go* after potash, then *getting* machines and men to *spread* potash, etc., etc. Thus the determination of the strategic factor is itself the decision which at once reduces purpose to a new level, compelling search for a new strategic factor in the new situation. Says Commons:

> But the limiting and complementary factors are continually changing places. What was the limiting factor becomes complementary, when once it has come under control; then another factor is the limiting one. The limiting factor, in the operation of an automobile, at one time may be the electric spark; at another the gasoline, at another the man at the wheel. This is the meaning of efficiency — the control of the changeable limiting factors at the right time, right place, right amount, and right form in order to enlarge the total output by the expected operation of complementary factors. [4]

If we rephrase this last sentence to accord with our terminology and our broader subject, it will read: "This is the meaning of effective decision — the control of the changeable strategic factors, that is, the exercise of control at the right time, right

[4] *Institutional Economics*, p. 629.

place, right amount, and right form so that purpose is properly redefined and accomplished."

Professor Commons continues:

> But out of the complex happenings, man selects the limiting factors for his purposes. If he can control these, then the other factors work out the effects intended. The "cause" is volitional control of the limiting or strategic factors. . . . The "effects" are the operations of the complementary factors. . . .[5]

With the distinctions in phraseology which Commons makes for his purposes we are not concerned. I think it sound to say that the strategic factor always determines the *action* that is controlling, even in the case of what he calls the limiting factor. It is not the element that is missing but the action that could procure the missing element that is the controlling factor. To determine what element should be changed or is missing is the first step in defining the *action* required. Decision relates to *action*, whether it be in the field of business transactions, political transactions, mechanical operations, chemical combinations, scientific experimentation, or whatever relates to accomplishment of intention.

The strategic factor is, then, the center of the environment of decision. It is the point at which choice applies. To *do* or not to do *this*, that is the question. Often there are tentatively several strategic factors, any one of which meets the immediate situation or satisfies the necessity of immediate purpose. This expands the horizon into the less immediate future, increases the objective field. The final strategic selection will be made on the basis of the estimate of less immediate future consequences.

III

Merely the statement of this theory will show that repeated decisions involving constant determination of new strategic factors are necessary to the accomplishment of broad purposes

[5] *Ibid.,* p. 632.

or any purpose not of immediate attainment. In an individual this requires a sequence of decisions at different times and places. *In an organization it requires a sequence of decisions at different times and also by different executives, and other persons, in different positions.* A broad purpose and a broad decision require fragmentation of purpose into detailed purposes and of principal general decisions into detailed subsidiary decisions. The latter for the most part can only be effectively made in the proper order. It is the series of strategic factors and the actions that directly relate to them that determine the course of events, not the general decisions.

It goes perhaps without further saying that the process of decision is one of successive approximations — constant refinement of purpose, closer and closer discriminations of fact — in which the march of time is essential. Hence those who make general decisions can only envisage conditions in general and vaguely. The approximations with which they deal are symbols covering a multitude of undisclosed details. "This is what we want to do, this is the aim of our effort, this is the direction in which we wish to go; but just what we will do, just how we shall accomplish it, will have to be worked out." I have heard executives make such statements ten thousand times. In other words, purpose will have to be refined to practicable terms, and conditions as they develop in time will have to be accurately ascertained.

IV

The discrimination of strategic factors with accuracy is the aim of technique. Its development is largely technological, depending upon the procurement of the means of magnifying details. Chemical analysis, mechanical analysis, telescopes, microscopes, statistical processes, balance sheets, are the means by which the strategic factors hidden in the superficial are magnified to observable dimensions and are brought into significant focus. Hence, having formulated the general purpose, the general executive often finds that the strategic factor for him is whether processes or tools of magnification or objective facts are sufficient and the men who can use them are available to determine the strategic factors in detail that are essential to useful redefinitions of purpose.

The developments of processes, tools, and men are not equal in all directions. They are not equally good in respect to the various elements of the environmental situation. Every such situation to which the purpose of man applies always involves in some degree physical, chemical, biological, physiological, psychological, economic, political, social, and moral elements. The powers of discrimination are most developed in some such order as that in which I have named these elements; so that there is inevitably an unbalance in the perception of the various elements of the total environment to which *as a whole* every decision relates. Therefore, the precision of decision is greater in the same order.

We have for the physical part of the environment scales, thermometers, barometers, dynamometers, voltmeters, ammeters, pressure gauges, microscopes, spectroscopes, etc., etc. Nothing so precise exists in economics. If the strategic factors of the situation should be physical and economic, the precision of discrimination as to the physical facts will far outbalance that as to the economic facts. In other words, it will be quite objective as to the physical part, relatively subjective as to the economic part.

A similar disparity exists between the economic and the other social factors of the environment. There exists in the social field no such powerful magnifier as the balance sheet which rivets the attention on the significance of the difference between income and outgo, nor any invention of general applicability that approximates in precision money of account that lies back of the balance sheet.[6]

The most useful way of stating the significance, or the effect, of this unbalance is that decisions relating to the physical environment take it as it is *in this existing present*, all history being recognized as irrelevant; whereas in the fields to which technology is less applicable, what has been, how the present was reached, are misread as being a part of the present. The chemist asks only what *are* the elements he now has to work with and what *are* the energies he *now* commands. He does not inquire into the history of the water, how the oxygen and hydrogen were combined, where, when, or by what cause.[7] The past is irrelevant and irrevocable.

But in economics the past is always obtruding on our discrimination of the present. We ask not only what a thing is *now* worth but what it *did* cost, often a fact interesting for deplorable reasons but utterly irrelevant to the present decision that the merchant must make — to sell it for what it is now worth or not sell it at all, whether he shall make a past error of decision the basis for a new error of decision or deal with the present circumstances. When the decision is on the social elements of the environment, almost always what has been is confused with what is. Legislation is almost always directed to conditions now known to have existed formerly, which is often the very best that can be done. Action is then based upon believing the past to be the present, which is unnecessary self-delusion, rather than accepting it as a probable approximation to the present.

Hence, to the unbalance in the discrimination of the facts

[6] The principle concrete tool of social relations is language. Excepting in special departments it is chiefly effective and useful as a means of eliciting responsive action rather than as a means of analysis.

[7] Except of course in the sense that as it may be more convenient, as a means of knowing that a given liquid *is* water, to rely on its history rather than to make a chemical analysis.

of the environment is added the confusion of past with present environments. We decide action of the present or immediate future partly as if it could apply to a past already gone. This condition is in itself an inescapable strategic factor as respects the execution of every relatively general decision. No decision can be rightly taken that does not assume that many of its consequent decisions will be wrongly taken. This is a persistent element of the environment of executive decisions.

The legitimate significance of the past is not in the present objective environment, but in the moral aspect of the formulation of new purpose. For when purpose must be changed or redefined, it must be on the basis of an estimate of future consequences. This is a question of judgment of probabilities of the consequences of action applied to present circumstances. The knowledge of the past can not now affect the facts of the present; but only on the basis of experience can we judge the future significance, in the light of a present purpose, of what we now observe. Purpose is the bridge between the past and the future which functions only as it rests upon the present. There is no future that does not begin after the present, nor any past that did not end before it, nor any purpose which is not purpose in the present.

To summarize, decision in its opportunistic aspect begins with an existing purpose and an objective environment of things physical, biological, social, emotional, moral. The ideal process of decision is to discriminate the strategic factors and to redefine or change purpose on the basis of the estimate of future results of action in the existing situation, in the light of history, experience, knowledge of the past. The discrimination of the environment is inevitably unbalanced as respects its several elements because of differences in available techniques, and because to some extent the past will be misread into the present instead of being used as a part of the basis of estimating the future. The inherent limitations then imposed on the process of decision is itself a strategic factor in making major and general decisions. The probabilities of the results of decision are the probabilities of error. It is comparatively rare that major decisions contemplate specific results, because such decisions usually must be so generally stated as to fit a wide range of possible results. When general decisions have the results contemplated we have not so much a process of detailed decisions as one of applying established techniques. These are much better than decisions, but often lacking, and never final; for the process of decision is never ending. The everchanging present generates ever new purposes in the continuing organization.

Where decisions are personal, the *fact* of decision is specialized to the individual, but the *processes* of decision within the individual are perhaps not specialized, except that decisions are made in some order of time and at particular places. Organization decisions as *accepted facts*, that is, having authority, on the contrary are not specialized to individuals but are *functions* of the organization as a whole; but the *processes* of decision are necessarily specialized. The purposes and action of organization are non-personal. They are coördinated. The efforts of the individual in organization result from decisions which in part are *necessarily* made by others acting non-personally. The concept of organization implies a system of human efforts in which the processes of decision are distributed and specialized. But since decision is a matter of definition of purpose and discrimination of strategic factors, the specialization of the process of decision involves distinctions in the distribution of emphasis upon either purpose or the other environmental aspect of decision. Neither is ever completely absent at any position in organization, but at some points the emphasis is upon definition of purpose, at others upon the discrimination of the environment and the determination of the strategic factors. The emphasis in the executive functions is upon definition of purposes;

among other functions the emphasis is upon discrimination of the environment. Thus, in an industrial organization, workmen, clerks, testers, laboratory assistants, salesmen, technicians, engineers, are characteristically occupied with the strategic factors of the environment external to the organization as a whole. The direct environment of executive decision is primarily the internal environment of the organization itself. The strategic factors of executive decision are chiefly and primarily strategic factors of organization operation. It is the organization, not the executive, which does the work on the external environment. The executive is primarily concerned with decisions which facilitate or hinder other decisions in the effective or efficient operation of the organization.

Finally, it may be said that the opportunistic aspect of decision in general relates to the means and conditions of attaining ends. This is the sector of organization action in which logical and analytical processes and empirical observations, experience, and experiment can be effective. They require and in turn make possible the specialization which is inherent in organization. It is in this sector that the power of coöperation is most apparent.

The moral sector is that of attitudes, values, ideals, hopes, impressed upon the emotions of men through countless channels of physical, biological, and social experiences and distilled into new specific purposes of coöperation. The resistance of the objective environment on the one hand is overcome and the environment modified by these attitudes; and on the other hand, the resistance compels the modification of these purposes and ultimately qualifies the aspirations they represent. The two aspects are synthesized in concrete acts.

PART IV

THE FUNCTIONS OF ORGANIZATIONS IN COOPERATIVE SYSTEMS

CHAPTER XV

THE EXECUTIVE FUNCTIONS

THE coördination of efforts essential to a system of coöperation requires, as we have seen, an organization system of communication. Such a system of communication implies centers or points of interconnection and can only operate as these centers are occupied by persons who are called executives. It might be said, then, that the function of executives is to serve as channels of communication so far as communications must pass through central positions. But since the object of the communication system is coördination of all aspects of organization, it follows that the functions of executives relate to all the work essential to the vitality and endurance of an organization, so far, at least, as it must be accomplished through formal coördination.

It is important to observe, however, that not all work done by persons who occupy executive positions is in connection with the executive functions, the coördination of activities of others. Some of the work of such persons, though *organization* work, is not executive. For example, if the president of a corporation goes out personally to sell products of his company or engages in some of the production work, these are not executive services. If the president of a university gives lectures to a class of students, this is not executive work. If the head of a government department spends time on complaints or disputes about services rendered by the department, this is not necessarily executive work. Executive work is not that *of* the organization, but the specialized work of *maintaining* the organization in operation.

Probably all executives do a considerable amount of non-executive work. Sometimes this work is more valuable than the executive work they do. This intermixture of functions is a matter of convenience and often of economy, because of the scarcity of abilities; or there may be other reasons for it. As a result of the combination of executive with non-executive functions, however, it is difficult in practice merely by comparison of titles or of nominal functions to determine the comparative methods of executive work in different organizations. If we mean by executive functions the specialized work of maintaining systems of coöperative effort, we may best proceed for general purposes to find out what work has to be done, and then, when desirable, to trace out who are doing that work in a particular organization.

This is especially true because executive work is itself often complexly organized. In an organization of moderate size there may be a hundred persons who are engaged part of the time in executive work; and some of them, for example clerks or stenographers, are not executives in any ordinary sense. Nevertheless, the activities of these persons constitute the executive organization. It is to the functions of this organization as a special unit that our attention should be given primarily, the distribution of work between persons or positions being for general purposes quite of secondary importance. This chapter will be devoted to the functions of the executive organization as a whole which exists exclusively for the coördination of the efforts of the entire organization.

The executive functions serve to maintain a system of coöperative effort. They are impersonal. The functions are not, as so frequently stated, to manage a group of persons. I do not think a correct understanding of executive work can be had if this narrower, convenient, but strictly speaking erroneous, conception obtains. It is not even quite correct to say that the executive functions are to manage the system of coöperative efforts. As a whole it is managed by itself, not by the executive organization, which is a part of it. The functions with which we are concerned are like those of the nervous system, including the brain, in relation to the rest of the body. It exists to maintain the bodily system by directing those actions which are necessary more effectively to adjust to the environment, but it can hardly be said to manage the body, a large part of whose functions are independent of it and upon which it in turn depends.

The essential executive functions, as I shall present them, correspond to the elements of organization as already stated in Chapter VII and presented in some detail in Part III. They are, first, to provide the system of communication; second, to promote the securing of essential efforts; and, third, to formulate and define purpose. Since the elements of organization are interrelated and interdependent, the executive functions are so likewise; nevertheless they are subject to considerable specialization and as functions are to a substantial degree separable in practice. We shall deal with them only as found in complex, though not necessarily large, organizations.

I. The Maintenance of Organization Communication

We have noticed in previous chapters that, when a complex of more than one unit is in question, centers of communication and corresponding executives are necessary. The need of a definite system of communication creates the first task of the organizer and is the immediate origin of executive organization. If the purpose of an organization is conceived initially in the mind of one person, he is likely very early to find necessary the selection of lieutenants; and if the organization is spontaneous its very first task is likely to be the selection of a leader. Since communication will be accomplished only through the agency of persons, the selection of persons for executive functions is the concrete method of establishing the *means* of communication, though it must be immediately followed by the creation of positions, that is, a *system* of communication; and, especially in established organizations, the positions will exist to be filled in the event of vacancies.

In other words, communication position and the "locating" of the services of a person are complementary phases of the same thing. The center of communication is the organization service of a person at a place. Persons without positions cannot function as executives, they mean nothing but potentiality. Conversely, positions vacant are as defunct as dead nerve centers. This is why executives, when functioning strictly as executives, are unable to appraise men in the abstract, in an organization vacuum, as it were. Men are neither good nor bad, but only good or bad in this or that position. This is why they not infrequently "change the organization," the arrangement of positions, if men suitable to fill them are not available. In fact, "executive organization" in practice cannot be divorced from "executive personnel"; and "executive personnel" is without important meaning except in conjunction with a specific arrangement of positions.

Therefore, the problem of the establishment and maintenance of the system of communication, that is, the primary task of the executive organization, is perpetually that of obtaining the coalescence of the two phases, executive personnel and executive positions. Each phase in turn is the strategic factor of the executive problem — first one, then the other phase, must be adjusted. This is the central problem of the executive functions. Its solution is not in itself sufficient to accomplish the work of all these functions; but no others can be accomplished without it, and none well unless it is well done.

Although this communication function has two phases, it is usually necessary in practice to deal with one phase at a time, and the problems of each phase are of quite different kinds. The problems of positions are those of location and the geographical, temporal, social, and functional specializations of unit and group organizations. The personnel problems are a special case of general personnel problems — the recruiting of contributors who have appropriate qualifications, and the development of the inducements, incentives, persuasion, and objective authority that can make those qualifications effective executive services in the organization.

I. THE SCHEME OF ORGANIZATION

Let us call the first phase of the function — the definition of organization positions — the "scheme of organization." This is the aspect of organization which receives relatively excessive formal attention because it can apparently be reduced to organization charts, specifications of duties, and descriptions of divisions of labor, etc. It rests upon or represents a coördination chiefly of the work to be done by the organization, that is, its purposes broken up into subsidiary purposes, specializations, tasks, etc., which will be discussed in Section III of this chapter; the kind and quantity of *services* of personnel that can be obtained; the kind and quantity of *persons* that must be included in the coöperative system for this purpose; the inducements that are required; and the places at which and the times when these factors can be combined, which will not be specifically discussed here.[1]

It is evident that these are mutually dependent factors, and that they all involve other executive functions which we shall discuss later. So far as the *scheme* of organization is separately attacked, it is always on the assumption that it is then the strategic factor, the other factors of organization remaining fixed for the time being; but since the underlying purpose of any change in a scheme of organization is to affect these other factors as a whole favorably, any scheme of organization at any

---

[1] See Chapter X, "The Basis and Kinds of Specializations," and Section III of the present chapter.

given time represents necessarily a result of previous successive approximations through a period of time. It has always necessarily to be attacked on the basis of the present situation.

II. PERSONNEL

The scheme of organization is dependent not only upon the general factors of the organization as a whole, but likewise, as we have indicated, on the availability of various kinds of services for the executive positions. This becomes in its turn the strategic factor. In general, the principles of the economy of incentives apply here as well as to other more general personnel problems. The balance of factors and the technical problems of this special class, however, are not only different from those generally to be found in other spheres of organization economy but are highly special in different types of organizations.

The most important single contribution required of the executive, certainly the most universal qualification, is loyalty, domination by the organization personality. This is the first necessity because the lines of communication cannot function at all unless the personal contributions of executives will be present at the required positions, at the times necessary, without default for ordinary personal reasons. This, as a personal qualification, is known in secular organizations as the quality of "responsibility"; in political organizations as "regularity"; in governmental organizations as fealty or loyalty; in religious organizations as "complete submission" to the faith and to the hierarchy of objective religious authority.

The contribution of personal loyalty and submission is least susceptible to tangible inducements. It cannot be bought either by material inducements or by other positive incentives, except all other things be equal. This is as true of industrial organizations, I believe, as of any others. It is rather generally understood that although money or other material inducements must usually be paid to responsible persons, responsibility itself does not arise from such inducements.

However, love of prestige is, in general, a much more important inducement in the case of executives than with the rest of the personnel. Interest in work and pride in organization are other incentives that usually must be present. These facts are much obscured as respects commercial organizations, where material inducements appear to be the effective factors partly because such inducements are more readily offered in such organizations and partly because, since the other incentives are often equal as between such organizations, material inducements are the only available differential factor. It also becomes an important secondary factor to individuals in many cases, because prestige and official responsibilities impose heavy material burdens on them. Hence neither churches nor socialistic states have been able to escape the necessity of direct or indirect material inducements for high dignitaries or officials. But this is probably incidental and superficial in all organizations. It appears to be true that in all of them adequate incentives to executive services are difficult to offer. Those most available in the present age are tangible, materialistic; but on the whole they are both insufficient and often abortive.[2]

Following loyalty, responsibility, and capacity to be dominated by organization personality, come the more specific personal abilities. They are roughly divided into two classes: relatively general abilities, involving general alertness, compre-

[2] After much experience, I am convinced that the most ineffective services in a continuing effort are in one sense those of volunteers, or of semi-volunteers; for example, half-pay workers. What appears to be inexpensive is in fact very expensive, because non-material incentives — such as prestige, toleration of too great personal interest in the work with its accompanying fads and "pet" projects, the yielding to exaggerated conceptions of individual importance — are causes of internal friction and many other undesirable consequences. Yet in many emergency situations, and in a large part of political, charitable, civic, educational, and religious organization work, often indispensable services cannot be obtained by material incentives.

hensiveness of interest, flexibility, faculty of adjustment, poise, courage, etc.; and specialized abilities based on particular aptitudes and acquired techniques. The first kind is relatively difficult to appraise because it depends upon innate characteristics developed through general experience. It is not greatly susceptible of immediate inculcation. The second kind may be less rare because the division of labor, that is, organization itself, fosters it automatically, and because it is susceptible to development (at a cost) by training and education. We deliberately and more and more turn out specialists; but we do not develop general executives well by specific efforts, and we know very little about how to do it.

The higher the positions in the line of authority, the more general the abilities required. The scarcity of such abilities, together with the necessity for keeping the lines of authority as short as feasible, controls the organization of executive work. It leads to the reduction of the number of formally executive positions to the minimum, a measure made possible by creating about the executives in many cases staffs of specialists who supplement them in time, energy, and technical capacities. This is made feasible by elaborate and often delicate arrangements to correct error resulting from the faults of over-specialization and the paucity of line executives.

The operation of such systems of complex executive organization requires the highest development of the executive arts. Its various forms and techniques are most definitely exemplified in the armies and navies of the major powers, the Postal Administrations of several European countries, the Bell Telephone System, some of the great railway systems, and the Catholic Church; and perhaps in the political organization of the British Empire.[3] One of the first limitations of world-wide or even a

---

[3] From a structural point of view the organization of the United States of America is especially noteworthy, but from the viewpoint of the executive functions it is intended to be defective; that is, the system of States Rights or

much more restricted international organization is the necessity for the development of these forms and techniques far beyond their present status.

Thus, jointly with the development of the scheme of organization, the selection, promotion, demotion, and dismissal of men becomes the essence of maintaining the system of communication without which no organization can exist. The selection in part, but especially the promotion, demotion, and dismissal of men, depend upon the exercise of supervision or what is often called "control."

Control relates directly, and in conscious application chiefly, to the work of the organization as a whole rather than to the work of executives as such. But so heavily dependent is the success of coöperation upon the functioning of the executive organization that practically the control is over executives for the most part. If the work of an organization is not successful, if it is inefficient, if it cannot maintain the services of its personnel, the conclusion is that its "management" is wrong; that is, that the scheme of communication or the associated personnel or both, that is, the executive department directly related, are at fault. This is, sometimes at least, not true, but often it is. Moreover, for the correction of such faults the first reliance is upon executive organization. The methods by which control is exercised are, of course, numerous and largely technical to each organization, and need not be further discussed here.

III. INFORMAL EXECUTIVE ORGANIZATIONS

So far we have considered the first executive function only as it relates to the formal communication system. It has been emphasized several times in this treatise that informal organ-

---

dual sovereignty and the separation of legislative, judicial, and executive departments precludes a common center of authoritative communication in American government as a formal organization. It is intended or expected that the requirements will be met by informal organization.

ization is essential to formal organizations, particularly with reference to communication. This is true not only of the organization as a whole, or of its ultimate subordinate units, but also of that special part which we call the executive organization. The communication function of executives includes the maintenance of informal executive organization as an essential means of communication.

Although I have never heard it stated that this is an executive function or that such a thing as an informal executive organization exists, in all the good organizations I have observed the most careful attention is paid to it. In all of them informal organizations operate. This is usually not apparent except to those directly concerned.

The general method of maintaining an informal executive organization is so to operate and to select and promote executives that a general condition of compatibility of personnel is maintained. Perhaps often and certainly occasionally men cannot be promoted or selected, or even must be relieved, because they cannot function, because they "do not fit," where there is no question of formal competence. This question of "fitness" involves such matters as education, experience, age, sex, personal distinctions, prestige, race, nationality, faith, politics, sectional antecedents; and such very specific personal traits as manners, speech, personal appearance, etc. It goes by few if any rules, except those based at least nominally on other, formal, considerations. It represents in its best sense the political aspects of personal relationship in formal organization. I suspect it to be most highly developed in political, labor, church, and university organizations, for the very reason that the intangible types of personal services are relatively more important in them than in most other, especially industrial, organizations. But it is certainly of major importance in all organizations.

This compatibility is promoted by educational requirements (armies, navies, churches, schools); by requirement of certain background (European armies, navies, labor unions, Soviet and Fascist governments, political parties); by conferences and conventions; by specifically social activities; by class distinctions connected with privileges and "authority" (in armies, navies, churches, universities). A certain conformity is required by unwritten understanding that can sometimes be formally enforced, expressed for its negative aspect by the phrase "conduct unbecoming a gentleman and an officer." There are, however, innumerable other processes, many of which are not consciously employed for this purpose.

It must not be understood that the desired degree of compatibility is always the same or is the maximum possible. On the contrary it seems to me to be often the case that excessive compatibility or harmony is deleterious, resulting in "single track minds" and excessively crystallized attitudes and in the destruction of personal responsibility; but I know from experience in operating with new emergency organizations, in which there was no time and little immediate basis for the growth of an informal organization properly coördinated with formal organization that it is almost impossible to secure effective and efficient coöperation without it.

The functions of informal executive organizations are the communication of intangible facts, opinions, suggestions, suspicions, that cannot pass through formal channels without raising issues calling for decisions, without dissipating dignity and objective authority, and without overloading executive positions; also to minimize excessive cliques of political types arising from too great divergence of interests and views; to promote self-discipline of the group; and to make possible the development of important personal influences in the organization. There are probably other functions.

I shall comment on only two functions of informal executive organization. The necessity for avoiding formal issues, that is, for avoiding the issuance of numerous formal orders except

on routine matters and except in emergencies, is important.[4]
I know of major executives who issue an order or judgment set-
tling an important issue rather seldom, although they are functioning all the time. The obvious desire of politicians to avoid
important issues (and to impose them on their opponents) is
based upon a thorough sense of organization. Neither authority
nor coöperative disposition (largely the same things) will stand
much overt division on formal issues in the present stage of
human development. Hence most laws, executive orders, decisions, etc., are in effect formal notice that all is well — there is
agreement, authority is not questioned.

The question of personal influence is very subtle. Probably
most good organizations have somewhere a Colonel House; and
many men not only exercise beneficent influence far beyond
that implied by their formal status, but most of them, at the
time, would lose their influence if they had corresponding
formal status. The reason may be that many men have personal
qualifications of high order that will not operate under the
stress of commensurate official responsibility. By analogy I may
mention the golfers of first class skill who cannot "stand up"
in public tournaments.

To summarize: the first executive function is to develop and
maintain a system of communication. This involves jointly a
scheme of organization and an executive personnel. The processes by which the latter is accomplished include chiefly the
selection of men and the offering of incentives; techniques of
control permitting effectiveness in promoting, demoting, and

[4] When writing these lines I tried to recall an important general decision
made by me on my initiative as a telephone executive within two years. I
could recall none, although on reviewing the record I found several. On the
other hand, I can still recall without any record many major decisions made
by me "out of hand" when I was a Relief Administrator. I probably averaged
at least five a day for eighteen months. In the latter case I worked with a very
noble group but a very poor informal organization under emergency conditions.

dismissing men; and finally the securing of an informal organization in which the essential property is compatibility of personnel. The chief functions of this informal organization are expansion of the means of communication with reduction in the necessity for formal decisions, the minimizing of undesirable influences, and the promotion of desirable influences concordant with the scheme of formal responsibilities.

II. The Securing of Essential Services from Individuals

The second function of the executive organization is to promote the securing of the personal services that constitute the material of organizations.

The work divides into two main divisions: (1) the bringing of persons into coöperative relationship with the organization; (11) the eliciting of the services after such persons have been brought into that relationship.

I

The characteristic fact of the first division is that the organization is acting upon persons who are in every sense outside it. Such action is necessary not merely to secure the personnel of new organizations, or to supply the material for the growth of existing organizations, but also to replace the losses that continually take place by reason of death, resignation, "backsliding," emigration, discharge, excommunication, ostracism. These factors of growth or replacement of contributors require bringing persons by organization effort within range of the consideration of the incentives available in order to induce some of these persons to attach themselves to the organization. Accordingly the task involves two parts: (a) bringing persons within reach of specific effort to secure services, and (b) the application of that effort when they have been brought near enough. Often both parts of the task occupy the efforts of the same persons or parts of an organization; but they are clearly distinct elements and considerable specialization is found with respect to them.

(*a*) Bringing persons within reach of recruiting or proselyting influence is a task which differs in practical emphasis among organizations in respect both to scope and to method. Some religious organizations — especially the Catholic Church, several Protestant Churches, the Mormon Church, for example — have as ideal goals the attachment of all persons to their organizations, and the wide world is the field of proselyting propaganda. During many decades the United States of America invited all who could reach its shores to become American citizens. Other organizations, having limits on the volume of their activities, restrict the field of propaganda. Thus many nations in effect now restrict substantial growth to those who acquire a national status by birth; the American Legion restricts its membership to those who have acquired a status by a certain type of previous service, etc. Others restrict their fields practically on the basis of proportions. Thus universities "in principle" are open to all or to all with educational and character qualifications but may restrict their appeals to geographical, racial, and class proportions, so as to preserve the cosmopolitan character of their bodies, or to preserve predominance of nationals, etc. Industrial and commercial organizations are theoretically limited usually by considerations of social compatibility and additionally by the costs of propaganda. They usually attempt no appeal when the geographic remoteness makes it ineffective.

Although the scope of the field of propaganda is for most organizations not clearly conceived or stated and as a problem only requires active consideration at intervals usually long, the question is nevertheless fundamental. This is best indicated by the methods practically employed in connection with it. In churches the organization of mission work and its territorial scope are the best indications of its importance. In most governments, at present, the accretion of members takes the form of stimulating reproduction by active promotional efforts, as in France and Italy, for example, or by the ease of acquiring citizenship and free land, as until recently in the United States. In many industrial organizations foreign recruiting was once an important aspect of their work, and directly or indirectly the appeal for contributors of capital or credit has been fundamentally international in scope until recent exchange restrictions. In fact, the most universal aspect of industrial organization appeal has been in respect to this type of contributor — for many practical purposes he is not usually regarded as the material of organization, though in the present study he is.

(*b*) The effort to induce specific persons who by the general appeal are brought into contact with an organization actually to become identified with it constitutes the more regular and routine work of securing contributors. This involves in its general aspects the method of persuasion which has already been described, the establishment of inducements and incentives, and direct negotiation. The methods required are indefinitely large in number and of very wide variety.[5] It would not be useful here to add to what has already been said in Chapter XI on the economy of incentives. It is only necessary to emphasize again that fundamentally most persons potentially available are not susceptible at any given time of being induced to give service to any particular organization, large or small.

II

Although the work of recruiting is important in most organizations, and especially so in those which are new or rapidly

[5] I must repeat that although the emphasis is on the employee group of contributors, so far as industrial organizations are concerned, nevertheless "customers" are equally included. The principles broadly discussed here relate to salesmanship as well as employing persons. See page 75.

expanding or which have high "turnover," nevertheless in established and enduring organizations the eliciting of the quantity and quality of efforts from their adherents is usually more important and occupies the greater part of personnel effort. Because of the more tangible character of "membership," being an "employee," etc., recruiting is apt to receive more attention as a field of personnel work than the business of promoting the actual output of efforts and influences, which are the real material of organization.[6] Membership, nominal adherence, is merely the starting point; and the minimum contributions which can be conceived as enabling retention of such connection would generally be insufficient for the survival of active or productive organization. Hence every church, every government, every other important organization, has to intensify or multiply the contributions which its members will make above the level or volume which would occur if no such effort were made. Thus churches must strengthen the faith, secure compliance by public and private acknowledgments of faith or devotion, and secure material contributions from their members. Governments are concerned with increasing the quality of the citizenry — promoting national solidarity, loyalty, patriotism, discipline, and competence. Other organizations are similarly occupied in securing loyalty, reliability, responsibility, enthusiasm, quality of efforts, output. In short, every organization to survive must deliberately attend to the maintenance and growth of its authority to do the things necessary for coördination, effectiveness, and efficiency. This, as we have seen, depends upon its appeal to persons who are already related to the organization.

The methods, the inducements and incentives, by which this is done have already been in general indicated in our discussion

---

[6] As an instance, note the great attention in civil service regulations, and also in political appointments, to obtaining and retaining employment, and the relatively small attention to services.

of incentives and authority. As executive functions they may be distinguished as the maintenance of morale, the maintenance of the scheme of inducements, the maintenance of schemes of deterrents, supervision and control, inspection, education and training.

III. THE FORMULATION OF PURPOSE AND OBJECTIVES

The third executive function is to formulate and define the purposes, objectives, ends, of the organization. It has already been made clear that, strictly speaking, purpose is defined more nearly by the aggregate of action taken than by any formulation in words; but that that aggregate of action is a residuum of the decisions relative to purpose and the environment, resulting in closer and closer approximations to the concrete acts. It has also been emphasized that purpose is something that must be accepted by all the contributors to the system of efforts. Again, it has been stated that purpose must be broken into fragments, specific objectives, not only ordered in time so that detailed purpose and detailed action follow in the series of progressive coöperation, but also ordered contemporaneously into the specializations — geographical, social, and functional — that each unit organization implies. It is more apparent here than with other executive functions that it is an entire executive organization that formulates, redefines, breaks into details, and decides on the innumerable simultaneous and progressive actions that are the stream of syntheses constituting purpose or action. No single executive can under any conditions accomplish this function alone, but only that part of it which relates to his position in the executive organization.

Hence the critical aspect of this function is the assignment of responsibility — the delegation of objective authority. Thus in one sense this function is that of the scheme of positions, the system of communication, already discussed. That is its potential aspect. Its other aspect is the actual decisions and conduct which make the scheme a working system. Accordingly, the general executive states that "this is the purpose, this the objective, this the direction, in general terms, in which we wish to move, before next year." His department heads, or the heads of his main territorial divisions, say to their departments or suborganizations: "This means for us these things now, then others next month, then others later, to be better defined after experience." Their subdepartment or division heads say: "This means for us such and such operations now at these places, such others at those places, something today here, others tomorrow there." Then district or bureau chiefs in turn become more and more specific, their sub-chiefs still more so as to place, group, time, until finally purpose is merely jobs, specific groups, definite men, definite times, accomplished results. But meanwhile, back and forth, up and down, the communications pass, reporting obstacles, difficulties, impossibilities, accomplishments; redefining, modifying purposes level after level.

Thus the organization for the definition of purpose is the organization for the specification of work to do; and the specifications are made in their final stage when and where the work is being done. I suspect that at least nine-tenths of all organization activity is on the responsibility, the authority, and the specifications of those who make the last contributions, who apply personal energies to the final concrete objectives. There is no meaning to personal specialization, personal experience, personal training, personal location, personal ability, eyes and ears, arms and legs, brains and emotions, if this is not so. What must be added to the indispensable authority, responsibility, and capability of each contributor is the indispensable coördination. This requires a pyramiding of the formulation of purpose that becomes more and more general as the number of units of basic organization becomes larger, and more and more remote in future time. Responsibility for abstract, generalizing, prospective, long-run decision is delegated *up* the line, responsibility for definition, action, remains always at the base where the authority for effort resides.

The formulation and definition of purpose is then a widely distributed function, only the more general part of which is executive. In this fact lies the most important inherent difficulty in the operation of coöperative systems — the necessity for indoctrinating those at the lower levels with general purposes, the major decisions, so that they remain cohesive and able to make the ultimate detailed decisions coherent; and the necessity, for those at the higher levels, of constantly understanding the concrete conditions and the specific decisions of the "ultimate" contributors from which and from whom executives are often insulated. Without that up-and-down-the-line coördination of purposeful decisions, general decisions and general purposes are mere intellectual processes in an organization vacuum, insulated from realities by layers of misunderstanding. The function of formulating grand purposes and providing for their redefinition is one which needs sensitive systems of communication, experience in interpretation, imagination, and delegation of responsibility.

Perhaps there are none who could consider even so extremely condensed and general a description of the executive functions as has here been presented without perceiving that these functions are merely elements in an organic whole. It is their combination in a working system that makes an organization.

This combination involves two opposite incitements to action. First, the concrete interaction and mutual adjustment of the executive functions are partly to be determined by the factors of the environment of the organization — the specific coöperative system as a whole and its environment. This involves fundamentally the logical processes of analysis and the discrimination of the strategic factors. We shall consider this aspect in the following chapter. Second, the combination equally depends upon the maintenance of the vitality of action — the will to effort. This is the moral aspect, the element of morale, the ultimate reason for coöperation, to which Chapter XVII will be given.

CHAPTER XVI

THE EXECUTIVE PROCESS

THE executive functions, which have been distinguished for purposes of exposition and which are the basis for much functional specialization in organizations, have no separate concrete existence.[1] They are parts or aspects of a process of organization as a whole. This process in the more complex organizations, and usually even in simple unit organizations, is made the subject of specialized responsibility of executives or leaders. The means utilized are to a considerable extent concrete acts logically determined; but the essential aspect of the process is the sensing of the organization as a whole and the total situation relevant to it. It transcends the capacity of merely intellectual methods, and the techniques of discriminating the factors of the situation. The terms pertinent to it are "feeling," "judgment," "sense," "proportion," "balance," "appropriateness." It is a matter of art rather than science, and is aesthetic rather than logical. For this reason it is recognized rather than described and is known by its effects rather than by analysis. All that I can hope to do is to state why this is so rather than to specify of what the executive process consists.

I shall attempt this by presenting generally the sectors of the total action of organization in which the sense of the whole is

[1] The concrete phenomena are always acts or the effects of acts. Many acts appear so predominantly related to a particular function, however, that it is often convenient to think of function itself as concretely exemplified in an exclusive way. For example, an order appointing a person to a position may be considered exclusively the concrete expression of the function of maintaining the communication system of the organization. It will be evident, however, from the viewpoint of either origin or effect, that the act cannot be divorced from other elements or functions.

the dominating basis for decision. To do so I assume that the reasons for existence, the ultimate purposes, are granted. The question then is whether these reasons can be justified by the results, whether the purposes can be carried out or attained. If so, it will be because the means employed are effective and because the action is efficient. Thus the two considerations to be taken into account from the viewpoint of the whole are the effectiveness and the efficiency of action.

I

It will be unnecessary for our main purpose, which is illustrative, to devote much space to effectiveness. It relates exclusively to the appropriateness of the means selected under the conditions as a whole for the accomplishment of the final objective. This is a matter of technology in a very broad sense of the term, including the technique of schemes of organization, of ritual, of technical systems, as well as the technologies of the applied sciences where they are pertinent. The non-executive view of these detailed technologies seems usually to be that they are technically isolated systems of production or of operation, which if significantly related in a particular coöperative system are so only in their economic aspects, or perhaps in ritualistic operations are related only in symbolic connections. In this view the breaking up of general purpose into detailed tasks involves the selection of a technology appropriate to each task, which may be treated by itself, independently of other technologies of the same coöperative system. What is then required for general effectiveness is only that the detailed technologies shall each be effective.

This is often true in a "practical" sense. In fact the incessant search for the strategic factors requires this emphasis. At a given time, for a given end, under given conditions, which specific technology is to be selected is the variable factor. We select which is the "better" method under the conditions which are granted. However, what must be emphasized here is that treating the total situation as a constant does not eliminate it, and that in fact there is a dependence of each technical process on all others used in the same coöperative system. The breaking up of general purpose into detailed objectives implies this. The precise form of the detailed objective is shaped by the general purpose and the possible process of accomplishing its fragments.

Clear illustrations of this fundamental integration of technologies as essential to the effectiveness of coöperative systems as wholes are easily available in many fields. To take one, the details of innumerable techniques of railroad operation are dominated by the single factor of the gauge of track. Another is the telephone instrument, the standard effectiveness of which, both for transmission and receiving, is the basis for limiting the variations of numerous quite different devices and structures under wide ranges of conditions. In these cases the word "standard" [2] is the expression of one of the concrete methods of insuring technological integration. Where this necessity is not obvious, it nevertheless exists. Disregard of it in principle is no doubt at the root of the incompetence and failure of many organizations. The principle is most significant in its bearing upon the size or the scope of coöperative systems. Much of the large-scale industrial integration of modern times may be ascribed to the necessity of controlling whole chains of technology as the means of effective accomplishment, quite aside from economic considerations. Conversely, the difficulty of avoiding the issue seems often to have meant uneconomic operation,

[2] The word "standard" has both technological and economic implications. Sometimes it has direct social implications also. In the illustrations given it is the purely technological aspect which is in mind; but it is obvious in both cases that both economic (costs) and social (utility) considerations are involved. On the other hand, some standardization is primarily economic. One method is used not because it is necessarily the only one, or better than all others, but solely because economy results from the use of some *one* method.

that is, too large size has diminished flexibility and adaptability and compelled inefficiency.[3]

Thus the executive process, even when narrowed to the aspect of effectiveness of organization and the technologies of organization activity, is one of integration of the whole, of finding the effective balance between the local and the broad considerations, between the general and the specific requirements. As an analytically separable aspect of the executive process this field has been untouched by scientific inquiry, having been confused with economic aspects; but it has been considerably specialized in some organizations in the chief officers of their engineering departments, and so is specifically present in the actual conduct of much executive work.

Control from the view of the effectiveness of the whole organization is never unimportant and is sometimes of critical importance; but it is in connection with efficiency, which in the last analysis embraces effectiveness, that the viewpoint of the whole is necessarily dominant. Under some simple conditions in small organizations this is a matter of common sense — for example, in the government of some small towns or the management of some small businesses. But often this is not the case. The common sense of the whole is not obvious, and in fact often is not effectively present. Control is dominated by a particular aspect — the economic, the political, the religious, the scientific, the technological, with the result that efficiency is not secured and failure ensues or perpetually threatens. No

---

[3] Note the inventiveness and innovations impliedly required in this situation. Technological invention is necessary to the accomplishment of many ends economically which can be accomplished, if economy is not required, by other means. On the other hand some ends which can only be accomplished by a given technological process cannot be economically accomplished without inventions and innovations in organization technique. The distinction seems generally not to be adequately understood. In consequence there is much fervent but indiscriminating discussion of the issues involved, in large- and small-scale production for example — or for that matter in large- and small-scale political or religious organizations.

doubt the development of a crisis due to unbalanced treatment of all the factors is the occasion for corrective action on the part of executives who possess the art of sensing the whole. A formal and orderly conception of the whole is rarely present, perhaps even rarely possible, except to a few men of executive genius, or a few executive organizations the personnel of which is comprehensively sensitive and well integrated. Even the notion which is here in question seems rarely to be stressed either in practical or scientific studies. Any exposition of it must be an oversimplification and only suggestive. Patience is asked for the complexity of the following treatment because of the importance of the subject.[4]

[4] It has repeatedly been made evident to me by inquiring students that this subject is the most difficult so far as the approach to concrete situations is concerned, although intellectually it is grasped easily. Probably the reason is that a sense of a situation as a whole can usually only be acquired by intimate and habitual association with it, and involves many elements which either have not been or are not practically susceptible quickly to verbal expression by those who understand them. For example, I am asked to state to what extent and how economic facts and general economic knowledge govern my decisions in an organization. It is only with difficulty that I comprehend the question. It relates to a kind of world of which I have no experience — an economic world. I recognize economic aspects of my world, but I have to search diligently to find cases which seem exclusively economic. Let the reader take a balance sheet or an income statement — the most unequivocally economic statements I know of — and ask someone who understands those specific statements to explain them. Then observe how little of that explanation is economic except the money values that are assigned, and the arithmetical significance of these values.

All of our thinking about organized efforts tends to be fallacious by reason of what A. N. Whitehead calls "misplaced concreteness." Analysis and abstractions we must and do make in the most everyday conduct of our affairs; but when we mistake the elements for the concrete we destroy the usefulness of the analysis. Executive decisions are preceded by analysis as I have tried to show in Chapter XIV, but decision itself is synthetic. The background out of which strategic factors are analyzed is the whole situation to which the decision relates. This whole situation may be analyzed into physical, biological, social, psychological — and if you will — economic elements or factors, as I have incessantly emphasized; nevertheless the analysis is not the end but the beginning of purposive action.

II

It has already been stated [5] that the meaning of "efficiency" as applied to organization is the maintenance of an equilibrium of organization activities through the satisfaction of the motives of individuals sufficient to induce these activities. This equilibrium will be a resultant of several sets of factors. In principle a large number of specific combinations of these variable sets of factors could produce the same resultant.

I

An organization is a system of coöperative human activities the functions of which are (1) the creation, (2) the transformation, and (3) the exchange of utilities. It is able to accomplish these functions by creating a coöperative system, of which the organization is both a nucleus and a subsidiary system, which has also as components physical systems, personal systems (individuals and collections of individuals), and social systems (other organizations). Accordingly, from the viewpoint of the creation, transformation, and exchange of utilities, the coöperative system embraces four different kinds of economies which may be distinguished as (a) a material economy; (b) a social economy; (c) the individual economies; and (d) the organization economy. It is convenient for many purposes to abstract from these economies those elements which relate to exchange of utilities, as distinguished from the creation and transformation of utilities, under the name economics or political economy; [6] but we shall avoid doing so, so far as the limitations of language and the convenience of money measurements permit.

---

[5] Chapter V, p. 56 ff. and Chapter VII, p. 92 ff.

[6] The thought here is that theoretical economics seems to cut across these four economies, as distinguished from an organization standpoint, including some parts of them and excluding others. In general, economics relates to those aspects that involve conscious exchange or that usually may be valued in terms of money of account.

We shall first discuss the chief considerations as to each of these economies.

(a) The material economy of a coöperative system is the aggregate of the utilities attached by an organization to physical things and forces which are controlled by the action of an organization. Two elements are involved in it: (1) the control; and (2) the assignment of the property of usefulness *by the organization* to these physical things. Both are necessary. Thus if it is believed that a piece of land would have utility if possessed or controlled by an organization, it nevertheless has no utility for the organization unless controlled. Conversely, if a piece of land is so controlled, but ceases to be considered useful to the organization, its utility ceases.

The material economy of a coöperative system will be in continual change, because of changes in the physical factors and changes in the usefulness as determined by the organization economy.[7] These changes will come about by (1) independent variations in the physical factors — for example, the land may be ruined by a flooded river; (2) exchange of the *control* by the organization with individuals or other organizations, either for material or non-material utilities; (3) the depredations of hostile individuals or organizations; and (4) the acquiring of control by the creative act of organization — for example, the shaping of material into a tool. This latter is a form of conversion of non-material (biological and social) utilities into material utilities.

(b) The social economy consists of the organization's relationships (that is, power of exchanging utilities) with other organizations and with individuals *not* connected with the organization in a coöperative way, which relationships have utilities for the organization. It is the aggregate of the potentialities of coöperation with those outside the coöperative system.

---

[7] This does not exclude, but includes, the usefulness that others give to it, *if the organization recognizes this* as giving opportunity for exchange.

The social economy is always changing. These changes result from changes (1) in the *attitudes* of external organizations and persons toward the organization or coöperative system because of *their* economies (affected by value attitudes, norms, institutions, physical conditions, etc.); (2) changes effected by exchanges of material or other utilities.

(*c*) The individual economy has been extensively discussed in Chapter XI. It consists on one side of the power of the individual, regarded here as inherent in or created by the individual, to do work (physical acts, attention, thought); and on the other of the utilities ascribed by him to (1) material satisfactions, (2) other satisfactions which we shall here call social satisfactions.

The economy of the individual is continually changing, because of (1) physiological needs, (2) exchanges made with others, (3) the creation of his own utilities, and (4) other changes in his state of mind, that is, his values or appraisal of utilities, physical and social.

(*d*) The organization economy is the pool of the utilities assigned by *it* to (1) the physical material it controls; (2) the social relations it controls; and (3) the personal activities it coördinates. It is the pool of values as assessed by the *organization* as a social system. It is the aggregate of the judgments or decisions as to the comparative utilities of non-comparable elements. The utility of a man's act is stated in terms of the utility of the work done; the utility of the work done is appraised in terms of the things paid out to him. Thus the utility with which the organization economy is concerned is not personal evaluation, but *organization* evaluation in which the factors are (1) the factors of the physical environment, (2) the factors of the social environment, and (3) the factors of contribution and outgo from and to individuals. The appraisal of an organization is *not* a personal appraisal, nor, except incidentally, a market appraisal, nor the resultant of individual appraisals. It is and must be an appraisal based on its coördinative action — something unique to itself. It appraises physical possessions, social relations, personal contributions, on the basis of what it can do with them. It can create some utilities for itself by its action, it can gain some utilities by exchanges, it can transmute or transfer utilities. Its ability to act depends upon the success of its action in maintaining the pool of utilities it can use.

The physical economy is the pool of physical things and forces controlled by the organization to which it ascribes utility. This pool may go up or down either because of external events or because of organization action; but the sum of the utilities ascribed to it may move similarly or contrariwise, and in disproportionate amounts. What determines the utilities is a set of circumstances not the same as those controlling the physical things themselves. The two sets of circumstances have in common some elements — the physical things. Other elements are diverse.

Similarly, the social economy is a pool of social relationships of the organization. Being immeasurable, they are difficult to state generally. They fluctuate, partly by reason of organization action, partly because of external events. They have utility for the organization, but the utilities change because of another set of circumstances.

Similarly, the individual economies or the aggregate of them change constantly partly by reason of organization action, partly because of external factors. But the utilities either of contributions from or expenditures to the individual economies will be dependent upon different sets of circumstances. It is hardly conceivable that the utility of a service should be the same thing to an individual and to the organization that uses it.

Therefore it is possible to analyze the status of a coöperative system from the point of view of any one of these economies. It can be stated what its physical possessions are, and in some sense (depending upon the criterion used), their economic value. It can be stated what the social *position* or assets of an organization are; and occasionally some kind of appraisal of the economic value is possible. It can be stated what the individual economies are in various sets of statistical enumeration — hours of labor, purchases made, wages paid, etc. It is often useful, and in many organizations necessary, to make such analyses or statements in terms of economics; and *parts only* of all of them are usually combined in balance sheets for commercial and most other organizations. *But the only statement of the organization economy is one that is in terms of success or failure; and the only analysis of that economy is the analysis of the decisions as to action of the organization. There is no unit of measurement for the economy of organization utility.*[8]

II

The equilibrium of the organization economy requires that it shall command and exchange sufficient of the utilities of various kinds so that it is able in turn to command and exchange the personal services of which it is constituted. It does this by securing through the application of these services the appropriate supplies of utilities which when distributed to the contributors ensure the continuance of appropriate contributions of utilities from them. Inasmuch as each of these contributors

---

[8] Compare, in this connection Pareto's distinction between the utility *of* a society and the utility *for* a society (*Sociologie Générale*, paragraphs 2128 ff.), also Talcott Parsons (*The Structure of Social Action*, pp. 241–249). I judge that what Pareto was talking about and what I am attempting to develop are equivalent in principle; but I am not certain. Using his phraseology I am saying that the aggregate of the utilities of the organization connection of each "member" of an organization is one economy and may be called the utility *for* an organization; but that there must be a utility *of* the organization which is based upon entirely different factors but includes the *individual* utilities. This utility *of* the organization is necessarily the social evaluation by the system of its own action and *cannot* be the sum of individual appraisals. In my phrase the utility *of* the organization is the organization economy, that is, I stress its incessantly dynamic character.

requires a surplus in *his* exchange, that is, a net inducement, the organization can survive only as it secures by exchange, transformation, and creation a surplus of utilities in its own economy. If its operations result in a deficit, it is less and less able to command the organization activities of which it consists. The organization must pay out material utilities and social utilities. It cannot pay out more than it has. To have enough it must secure them either by exchange or by creating them.

For illustration, take first a religious organization. It could not, in most cases, have command of a surplus of material utilities, yet it must have such utilities in order to pay them out to those who require them — principally clergymen and lay assistants of various kinds who devote most of their efforts to the church. Its supply of these utilities must therefore come from communicants (contributors), who may contribute little effort beyond attention, attendance at services, etc. For these material utilities it exchanges what we have called social utilities, which are partly a result of its ritual and community creations. This is in part a transformation of material utilities to social utilities. In order to do this it may have to expend both material utilities and social utilities in proselyting, which will result in additional contributors who increase either the surplus of physical or of social utilities. To do this it will pay material utilities to some (those who require them for direct or indirect missionary effort) and social utilities to others (those who possess "zeal" for the missionary cause). Thus in the organization economy the factors are interacting and interdependent.

For a second illustration, take a government. Even when not a creator or direct securer of physical utilities, it requires great quantities of them. It also requires social utilities in the form of support and acquiescence of organizations and individuals.

It will secure its physical utilities by taxes on individuals and organizations, but must also secure social contributions under the form of patriotism, willingness to be taxed, etc.

Take a third illustration, an industrial organization. It must produce physical utilities, for which purpose it is adapted, and must also distribute social utilities. If it can produce surpluses of physical utilities they can be used to some degree to secure social utilities for distribution, but some of the latter at least it must also create. If there is a scarcity of both, it may expend some of either to change a state of mind, reducing the necessity for the drain on its supplies of one or the other or both.

III

It will aid in appraising the objective bases of these generalizations to give an illustration in terms much more concrete, but unrealistically simple. Let us assume that we find five men, A, B, C, D, and E, who have spontaneously created an organization for the purpose of gathering firewood. They begin with no leader. For convenience we value their aggregate efforts at $20 per day or $4 per man. Working independently A can produce about $3.75 per day, B about $3.40, C about $3, D about $2.70, and E about $2.25. The efforts which each contributes to the system are correspondingly varied, being $1\frac{1}{4}$ x for A, $1\frac{1}{8}$ x for B, x for C, $\frac{7}{8}$ x for D, and $\frac{3}{4}$ x for E, when x equals the average. Initially the inducement to coöperate consists of equal shares in the coöperative product, that is, $4 per day per man. It is evident that so far as increased material is an inducement, each man will profit by coöperation, although the amount and the proportions of the profit will differ. But it is not merely physical effort that is contributed by each man, nor merely material inducements that are offered. A, being a capable individualist, dislikes the restrictions on personal freedom involved — social inducements are negative — so that he is barely induced to coöperate. C, on the other hand, is much pleased by working in a group, and would be willing to do so even if there were no net material inducement. Thus at the very outset we find physical work on the environment through the expenditure of physiological energy, motivated by physical material as an inducement, partly offset by social disadvantage in one case, and substantially enhanced by social incentives in another.

A, B, C, D, and E, under the conditions postulated, produce $20 worth of firewood, and take equal quantities of the product, or $4 worth each. From the beginning, changes both on the social and on the physical side take place. On the physical side, the difficulties of obtaining firewood increase, so that more energy, or less product, or more effective coöperation is required. On the social side, the satisfactions from association increase for some, the dissatisfactions of coördination (regimentation) increase for others. Moreover, there takes place a social dissatisfaction as to some, and a satisfaction as to others, *because of the equality* of the distribution of the product. Thus A, who puts forth more effort than B, thinks he should have a larger share. He does this because he thinks in terms of cause and effect as a result of personal experience. So do his fellows, except when this seems to affect the satisfaction of *their* motives adversely.

A therefore decides to put forth less effort or secure more product. If he does the first, the result may be slight; and C, who derives social satisfaction from the organization endeavors to compensate for the loss by improved coöperation, that is, by a social contribution. But if A decides to have more compensation without change in efforts, this may be only possible by reducing the shares of the others. Some are willing because they like working together; others not, because their satisfaction comes from the material payment. They accept the conditions, however, because they still will have more than they can get by working alone.

But they have a feeling that the result is unjust, and without intention they begin to decrease their contributions of effort by malingering. This social reaction again threatens the total production, whereupon C, to save the whole system, tries to create an offsetting enthusiasm or morale, that is, to secure sufficient material to meet the requirements of material payments by increasing the social payments.

Note that each step by each participant relates to the strategic factor as he sees it, although his rationalizations about it are likely to be on a cause-and-effect basis, that is, on assumption of an absolute equivalence of contribution and production.

It soon appears to C that the system will break down. It is impossible to maintain the material production under the increasing difficulties of the environment and to provide the material compensation now demanded. He concludes that the strategic factor is A, and that F, although F can contribute less energy than A, should be substituted for A for two reasons: initially F will demand less of the material than A so that C can then continue to satisfy the requirements of B, C, D, and E; and subsequently F's eagerness to join the group will lead him to reinforce C's efforts to make the system socially satisfactory, on which basis the production of material satisfactions can be adequately maintained, and the social satisfactions increased. C accomplishes the ejection of A and the enlistment of F.

This succeeds so well that production actually increases, and working together is so satisfactory that others wish to join the group. It is decided that the addition of others under the conditions will not be satisfactory. Then C concludes that since he has been the factor which has kept the organization together he should have a larger share of the material product. He persuades the others that this is just — that is, they regard him as the strategic factor in the system that gives them material and social satisfactions. B, D, E, and F begin to take a great deal of pride in their organization and in C as their leader. But ultimately the difficulties of the environment result in a substantially lower production. C justifies keeping up the material payment to himself as the strategic factor in the system, so that the material shares of the others go down. They go down so far that they are less than each man could obtain by working individually. They nevertheless remain contributors to the organization because of their social attachment; but the margin is small and they find it increasingly difficult to accept C's orders. Then B dies. C secures G to replace him. But G is not well satisfied by the social aspects, and only comes in because he does very poorly by himself. He is willing to accept low material inducements, but, lacking in energy, he does not contribute as much as he gets, and directly and indirectly he creates an unsatisfactory social situation. Since the social satisfactions to the others thereby diminish and the material product is less, they threaten to quit.

At this point C, who has become the leader or executive of the organization, concludes that the difficulties of the physical environment, the physiological limitations of the men available, the demands of men for an amount of product which will exhaust the productive capacity of the organization, as a whole make necessary a new purpose if the organization is to be maintained. He concludes that the cutting of cordwood would be a purpose that could be effective. He succeeds in winning E, F, and G to this view; D drops out; and C enlists H to replace him. But since time must elapse before actual cordwood can be distributed as an inducement to his men, C induces I to supply material inducements in the form of maintenance (food) to C, E, F, G, and H, pending usable production, by agreeing to give I a share of the production when ready. His situation then is: C contributes effort plus managerial and social services to maintain the system; E, F, G, and H contribute manual labor jointly, and I contributes material. C, E, F, G, and H derive material immediately (contributed by I), and social satisfactions from working together, and the prospect of more material later. I is induced solely by the prospect of material gains later. And so on indefinitely.

We may now make the following observations:

1. It is not correct to impute to any one of the men a *definite* product. The increase (or decrease) of material product results from the combination or coördination of efforts. It may well be that if any one of the five should decline to contribute there would be no effectiveness in the coöperation of the remainder, or that the decrease of effectiveness would be more, or less, than proportional to the contributions of the individual withdrawing. The initial distribution of positive inducements is an equal share in the product. It is obvious that the *general* incentives, however, are different. A dislikes the social aspect, C likes it very much.

2. Since C contributes a positively favorable influence on the system, and since the results can only be secured by coöperation, C may be more essential than any other although he contributes only average energy. Hence, the *social* contribution of one person is a factor in maintaining the system of coöperation, which elicits *physical* energy from participants, which is converted into *material* at desired places.

3. The statement that C, or any other person, is more essential to the system than any other can only be made on the assumption that all other essential elements in the coöperation remain the same. Except for this assumption there can be no significant statement regarding the contribution of any person relative to the general or total results. This is to say that no specific statement can be made significantly except it be in terms of *differential effect*. It can be stated or estimated what the effect of the withdrawal of C from the system is; or the effect of the substitution of the services of a new man, F, for C will be.

Hence, the notion of cause and effect in an absolute sense is not pertinent. The only measurable variations in the effect of single factors is with respect to them when they are treated as strategic. Strategic factors are those which are recognized as controllable alternatives. It can be stated what the net effects of taking C out of the system will be as compared with leaving him, or of substituting F for him. All of the results, however, are results of the coöperative system as a whole. We can approximately measure the effects of *changes in the system*, not of absolute contributions of any one factor; these effects, of course, to be determined from the point of view of purpose.

4. At one stage of the history many individuals desired to join this organization — and were rejected. This is an instance in which the organization had created for itself a social utility. It made no direct use of it by enlisting those who desired to join; but its possession at once made the connection more satisfactory to its members, who thereby derived a satisfaction from this social asset. Under many circumstances such a general utility would greatly strengthen the organization economy and react on all the other economies. It will be noted that only in the most indirect ways would it be possible to translate this social asset into economic terms, or to secure it by any direct economic process.

Thus in every organization there is a quadruple economy: (1) physical energies and materials contributed by members and derived by its work upon the environment, and expended on the environment and given to its members; (2) the individual economy; (3) the social utilities related to the social environment; and (4) a complex and comprehensive economy of the organization under which both material services and social services are contributed by members and material things are secured from the environment, and material is given to the environment and material and social satisfactions to the members. The only measure of this economy is the survival of the organization. If it grows it is clearly efficient, if it is contracting it is doubtfully efficient, and it may in the end prove to have been during the period of contraction inefficient.

The nature of this economy must be strongly emphasized because fixed notions in current use so often conceal it. For example, it is said that a commercial organization cannot survive unless its income exceeds its outgo, a statement that begs the point. It is only true if no one will contribute the deficit in commercial goods for non-commercial reasons. But this not infrequently occurs. Family pride, philanthropic motives, etc., often induce economic contributions for non-commercial motives that enable an organization that is economic in character to survive. And the fact is plain that organizations in large numbers that are unsuccessful economically nevertheless continue to exist, whatever may be the motives. They can only exist, however, if the economic and *other* satisfactions which they produce or secure as a whole can pay for the economic and other services which they consume as a whole.

Again it is often evidently the opinion that religious organizations, being non-materialistic in purpose, can disregard or are exempt from consideration of materialistic economy, yet nothing is more obvious than that they never are. They merely are not necessarily direct producers of material things, but they are always consumers of physical energies and materials. Material profit is not their reason for existence, but they do not thereby escape the tyranny of the balance sheet.

Underlying this quadruple economy of all organizations is the essential fact that it is *impossible* to balance output and input in detail. This is another way of saying that in the nature of coöperative systems they are, or what they produce or what they consume is, more or less than or different from the sum of their constituent parts or contributions.

Coöperation is an expression of human will and purpose in a physical environment. It is *never* a creator of, and only to a limited degree an operator on, physical material. It is a creator and convertor of utilities. When certain chemical elements are combined there may remain the atoms with which the process began, minus or plus energy given off or received. But if the resulting compound is hard whereas its constituent elements were soft the human purpose involved in the act of combining finds something in the effect that was not in the origin.

However, as we have repeated, most possible coöperation is not undertaken or is not successful. To be successful it must create something, and this must not be so dissipated in the detailed processes of the coöperation that it cannot satisfy human motives. Since the details cannot be summed up into a whole, and the results of coöperation cannot be known except by the event, the final efficiency of organization is dependent upon two quite different factors: (*a*) the efficiency of detail; and (*b*) the creative economy of the whole.

(*a*) The initial process is to procure every contribution of every kind with as little counter distribution as possible. Each incoming contribution goes into a pool, as it were, and each outgoing distribution goes out of a pool, but the two cannot be identified. They cannot be identified because it is utilities, not the things to which utilities are ascribed, which are paid in and paid out; and the utilities are changed in the process. That is the reason for coöperation. In the plainest possible English this is to say that prices can never be and never are based on costs. They are based on values at both ends of the coöperative process. This is true even in the purely economic aspects when measured in money, although in this field contrary illusions are general and often convenient and useful under stabilized conditions. But when non-money values which are always present are concerned, no one even claims anything else. Nor does anyone for this reason disregard those values in practice. Any merchant or politician knows that smiles have values, and that sometimes the presence or absence of smiles may be the strategic factor between success or failure; but no one can measure their effects. Anyone knows that good will, whether of customers or of employees, or of investors, is value, but no one knows how to price it;[9] and it is a commonplace that it cannot be secured by money alone, and frequently not at all by money.

This means that efficiency of organization results from two controls: the control of output and income in detail at the point of exchange, at the periphery of organization; and coördination, which is internal and the productive factor in organization. Exchange is the distributive factor; coördination is the creative factor.

We are now giving attention to the distributive factor. If we for the moment limit ourselves to industrial organizations, we may say that efficiency of distribution involves the following separate economies: the customer economy, the labor economy, the credit economy, the supply economy, the technological economy. In all of them the rule must be that you give, so far as possible, what is less valuable to you but more valuable to the receiver; and you receive what is more valuable to you and less valuable to the giver. This is common sense, good business sense, good social sense, good technology, and is the enduring basis of amicable and constructive relations of any kind. This does *not* mean that you give as little as you can from the *receiver's* point of view. In terms of money, you give a man dollars for his services which are worth more to you than the dollars. No sane man would admit anything else. If you give services for dollars it must be that the dollars are worth more to you than the services. Unfortunately for simplicity, neither side of the transaction can be confined to or measured completely in dollars, even in commercial enterprises; and in noncommercial enterprises the exchange is extremely intangible.

What conceals this simple fact of experience so often is that subsequent evaluations may change, though this is then beside

[9] Of course under some conditions some *parts* of good will of various kinds are valued commercially.

the point. I may pay a man $10 today with pleasure, and find tomorrow that I need $10 very badly, but cannot use the services I paid for. I am then perhaps disposed to think I made a bad exchange. I read the past into the present. This leads to the false view that what exchange *should* be is as little as possible of what the *receiver* wants, regardless of its value to me. This philosophy of giving as little as possible and getting as much as possible in the *other man's values* is the root of bad customer relations, bad labor relations, bad credit relations, bad supply relations, bad technology. The possible margins of co-operative success are too limited to survive the destruction of incentives which this philosophy implies.

This is the cause of much failure of organization. Valuable incentives are not offered; or they cannot be afforded, because the corresponding contributions are less valuable.

The application of this theory is extremely varied and complex. I shall give one illustration from the field of employee relations. Efficiency means the giving of money up to the point when it becomes valuable to the employer and of little value to the employee, and the giving of additional incentives that cost little to the employer but are valued much by the employee; and the rejection of those who give as little as they can to the employer. It confirms the saying that a good employer pays good men well; and good men pay a good employer well. But in neither case is the word "good" the appraisal of oneself by oneself, as a matter of sentiment, good intention. The proper criterion is efficiency — that is, personal satisfaction.

Crude and unsatisfactory as is this theory of efficiency when stated in terms of ordinary economic relationships, which obscure so many aspects of the exchange of values, it is at least suggestive of the substance of the idea. But in the fields of political, governmental, fraternal, and religious organizations there is no current language known to me that covers the idea. Nevertheless, attentive observation and reason both confirm the statement that the process is essentially the same. In one way or another in all these organizations either great loyalty and deep faith, which are most essential to them, or other services to the organization, are and must be the material of their vitality. Those who give little of the things required can receive little of the things desired. Said D. L. Moody, "The reward of service is more service," which expresses the economy of organization efficiency at its highest level.

(b) The creative side of organization is coördination. The securing of the appropriate combination of the elements of the organization to produce utilities is the basis for the endurance of coöperative systems. It goes by various roughly approximate names — "all around management," "executive perspective," "practical sense of the whole," etc. No matter what efficiency is obtained in the distributive factor, it at least in most cases probably could not attain an aggregate greater than the aggregate of satisfactions individually obtainable without coöperation. To survive, coöperation must itself create a surplus. The necessity for conservatism in distribution arises from the probability that the surplus from coöperation, small perhaps in most successful organizations, will not be sufficient to permit dissipation by waste, and the organization will be destroyed by that fact. Under most circumstances, therefore, the quality of coördination is the crucial factor in the survival of organization.

The control of distribution may become, and often does, a matter of highly developed technique. Creative efficiency on the other hand, although it may involve the invention of techniques as a result, is essentially non-technical in character. What is required is the sense of things as a whole, the persistent subordination of parts to the total, the discrimination from the broadest standpoint of the strategic factors from among all types of factors — other executive functions, technology, persuasion, incentives, communication, distributive efficiency. Since there can be no common measure for the translation of the physical, biological, economic, social, personal, and spiritual utilities involved, the determination of the strategic factors of creative coöperation is a matter of sense, of feeling of proportions, of the significant relationship of heterogeneous details to a whole.

This general executive process is not intellectual in its important aspect; it is aesthetic and moral. Thus its exercise involves the sense of fitness, of the appropriate, and that capacity which is known as responsibility — the final expression for the achievement of coöperation. To this we shall devote the following chapter.

CHAPTER XVII

THE NATURE OF EXECUTIVE RESPONSIBILITY

IN many instances it has been unavoidable in this study to refer to the dependance of action in formal organizations upon personal choice, motives, value attitudes, appraisals of utility, norms of conduct, ideals. In Chapter II all these elements were aggregated with others in the conception of "personal psychology" and taken as granted without inquiry as to their sources. In Chapter XI on the Economy of Incentives these elements were presented in summary in relation to inducements and incentives and to persuasion as the means of securing organization activities. In Chapter XII on the Theory of Authority the same elements were implicit in the discussion of the subjective aspects of authority. In Chapters XIII and XIV concerning the processes of decision the reference to what was in one place called the "moral sector" was to these same elements. In Chapter XVI the conception of "utility" in the relations of persons to organizations implied these same aspects of personality.

Nevertheless, the effort has heretofore been so far as possible to avoid the consideration of the moral aspects of coöperation in order that we might first have a common understanding of the principles of the structure and of the processes of organization. There has been in this approach necessarily some distortion. Close study of the structure of organization or of its dynamic processes may induce an overemphasis upon some one or several of the more technical aspects of coöperation. Usually, however, the obscurity of the structural features and the elusiveness of the operative elements drive one to take refuge in "leadership" as the factor of chief significance in human coöperation. The limitations imposed by the physical environment and the biological constitution of human beings, the uncertainties of the outcome of coöperation, the difficulties of common understanding of purpose, the delicacy of the systems of communication essential to organization, the dispersive tendencies of individuals, the necessity of individual assent to establish the authority for coördination, the great role of persuasion in securing adherence to organization and submission to its requirements, the complexity and instability of motives, the never-ending burden of decision — all these elements of organization, in which the moral factor finds its concrete expression, spell the necessity of leadership, the power of individuals to inspire coöperative personal decision by creating faith: faith in common understanding, faith in the probability of success, faith in the ultimate satisfaction of personal motives, faith in the integrity of objective authority, faith in the superiority of common purpose as a personal aim of those who partake in it.

Nevertheless, to suppose that leadership, that the moral elements, are the only important or significant general factor in organization is as erroneous as to suppose that structure and process of coöperation without leadership are sufficient. Either view is out of accord with reason and experience. Purposeful coöperation is possible only within certain limits of a structural character, and it arises from forces derived from *all* who contribute to it. The work of coöperation is not a work of leadership, but of organization as a whole. But these structures do not remain in existence, they usually do not come into being, the vitality is lacking, there is no enduring coöperation, without the creation of faith, the catalyst by which the living system of human efforts is enabled to continue its incessant interchanges of energies and satisfactions. Coöperation, not leadership, is the creative process; but leadership is the indispensable fulminator of its forces.

Leadership has two aspects. One is local, individual, particular, ephemeral. It is the aspect of individual superiority — in physique, in skill, in technology, in perception, in knowledge, in memory, in imagination. This is the immediate aspect, highly variable through time and in place; subject to specific development by conditioning, training, education; significant chiefly in conjunction with specific conditions; relative; rather easily determinable; comparatively objective; essential to *positive* action; commanding admiration, emulation. This is the technical aspect of leadership. Important as it is, it has by implication been included at length in the preceding chapters.

Now we shall confine our thoughts to the second aspect of leadership — the more general; the more constant; the least subject to specific development; the more absolute; the subjective; that which reflects the attitudes and ideals of society and its general institutions. It is the aspect of individual superiority in determination, persistence, endurance, courage; that which determines the *quality* of action; which often is most inferred from what is *not* done, from abstention; which commands respect, reverence. It is the aspect of leadership we commonly imply in the word "responsibility," the quality which gives dependability and determination to human conduct, and foresight and ideality to purpose.

In this chapter we are to consider the moral factor in organization, focused in its aspects of leadership and executive responsibility. With the exception of one important respect we shall avoid any inquiry into the general and ultimate sources of individual morality or psychology, whether physiological, or arising from the physical environment or from the social influences, although we cannot avoid some consideration of the nature of the internal processes of individuals in immediate situations. The one exception is the reaction of specific formal organizations upon the psychology or morality of individuals who have close and lasting connections with them. The *fact* of such reactions is a major principle of the processes of organization, and hence of the executive functions and of leadership and executive responsibility.

The elements and processes of leadership are observed and abstracted with great difficulty. In the present attempt to elucidate the subject it is first necessary to consider what we mean by moral character of persons and the nature of personal responsibility. Thus we must briefly indulge in some speculative description of internal processes, which are only to be surmised — with the aid of subjective experience — from external phenomena, though the latter are matters of common experience. We shall then note certain characteristic differences in the morals, responsibility, and moral status of individuals. This will lead to stating some significant differences between the moral positions of individuals as affected by the executive functions. Finally, we shall consider the executive function of "moral creativeness" as the highest expression of responsibility.

I

I shall describe the concept implicit in "moral factor," "moral element," "morals," for our purposes, by the following definition:

Morals are personal forces or propensities of a general and stable character in individuals which tend to inhibit, control, or modify inconsistent immediate specific desires, impulses, or interests, and to intensify those which are consistent with such propensities. This tendency to inhibit, control, or modify inconsistent and to reinforce consistent immediate desires, impulses, or interests is a matter of sentiment, feeling, emotion, internal compulsion, rather than one of rational processes or deliberation, although in many instances such tendencies are subject to rationalization and occasionally to logical processes. When the tendency is strong and stable there exists a condition of responsibility.

Morals arise from forces external to the individual as a person. Some of them are believed by many to be directly of supernatural origin; some of them derive from the social environment, including general, political, religious, and economic environments; some of them arise from experience of the physical environment, and from biological properties and phylogenetic history; some from technological practice or habit. Many moral forces are inculcated in the individual by education and training; and many of them accrue through absorption, as it were, from the environment — by limitation or emulation, and perhaps also in the negative form of absence from concrete experience.[1]

It is convenient to conceive of these innate forces or general propensities as a private code of conduct consisting of positive and negative prescriptions. In this way these forces are more easily susceptible of verbalization, although by definition morals cannot be a code in an ordinary sense, but are an active resultant of accumulated influences on persons, evident only from action in concrete conditions. That is, they are to be inferred from conduct under actual conditions, and to some extent from the verbal reflections of sentiments.

What has just been said about the origin of morals suggests the convenience of postulating several sets of general propensities or codes in the same person, arising from different sources of influence and related to several quite diverse types of activities. It implies that all persons must have such private codes. This conforms to the commonly accepted view that all sane men are "moral" beings. The present thought may be expressed by saying that the conduct of every man is in part governed by several private moral codes. What these are determines his moral status, which may be simple or complex, high or low, comprehensive or narrow.

[1] For example, one hesitates to do things of some kinds which are not done by others, or have never been done before, even when there is no apparent reason that they should not be done.

Moral status and responsibility are not identical. Responsibility, as I define it for present purposes, is the power of a particular private code of morals to control the conduct of the individual in the presence of strong contrary desires or impulses. For instance, two men may have substantially identical codes as respects a given field of activity, but the code will be dominant as respects the conduct of one man under adverse immediate conditions, while it will not be dominant as respects the other under the same or similar conditions. With reference to that code, the first man is said to be responsible, or to possess responsibility, or to have the capacity of responsibility; the second man not.

Since all men possess several, if not many, private codes, it is possible that a man may be responsible with respect to some of them and not so with respect to others. I observe cases in which this appears to be true, considering only major or important codes. For example, persons may be very responsible as respects national or religious obligations generally (that is, what *they* feel to be obligations), and be quite irresponsible as respects ordinary business obligations (what *they* also feel to be obligations). But except as to minor or inconsequential codes, it appears usually true that men who are responsible in one major respect are so also in other respects; that is, they possess a general capacity under adverse conditions for conduct consistent with their stable sentiments and beliefs. The important point here is that persons of high moral status may be weakly controlled by their moral codes, and are then relatively irresponsible; and vice versa.

There are many persons who are responsible provided the issues by which they are confronted are simple conformance or non-conformance with particular codes. But if there exist several or many private codes governing the conduct of an individual, specific acts or concrete situations are likely to involve conflicts between codes; that is, a desire or impulse may be entirely consistent with one code but inconsistent with another. In fact, one code may intensify a desire or impulse, or justify it, when the reverse is true of another code. This is a frequent situation in conduct regarded by the individual as purely private, for which illustration will be given later.

When there are occasions under which conflicts of codes may arise it may be that one of the codes involved is a superior or dominant code. In this case there is usually no serious personal difficulty, and the actor is usually not aware of conflict. The dominant code is the one which governs as a matter of course; and the action may involve inconsistency only from the point of view of an observer. In such cases the personal problem at most is one of sincerity or of the possibility of apparent violation of consistency.

When, however, codes have substantially equal validity or power in the subject affected, conflict of codes is a serious personal issue. The results of such a conflict may be of three kinds: (1) either there is paralysis of action, accompanied by emotional tension, and ending in a sense of frustration, blockade, uncertainty, or in loss of decisiveness and lack of confidence; or (2) there is conformance to one code and violation of the other, resulting in a sense of guilt, discomfort, dissatisfaction, or a loss of self-respect, or (3) there is found some substitute action which satisfies immediate desire or impulse or interest, or the dictates of one code, and yet conforms to all other codes. When the second situation of non-conformance to one code is the resolution and it is repeated often, it will have the effect of destroying that code, unless it is very powerful and is kept alive by continuing external influences. When the resolution of the conflict is accomplished by substitution of a new action for that originally conceived, all the codes are strengthened by the experience; but such a solution frequently requires imaginative and constructive ability. The way has to be "worked out" to meet all the requirements.

II

Some private codes of morals may be regarded as common to many persons, others are special or particular to individuals or relatively small numbers of persons. Only where the code is very common is it likely to be recognized as "moral," that is, as a public code; and in the United States generally only that code or the codes which derive from or are inculcated by the Christian churches may be considered *the* moral code or codes. But there are other common codes of great importance which are not generally so recognized: for example, those relating to or governing what is called patriotic conduct — the sense of obligations or duties of the citizen. There are others relating to commercial conduct which are comprehended in the word "integrity." There are others that relate to manners, social conduct, etc. In many respects these codes coincide; for example, "Thou shalt not steal" is Hebrew morals, Christian morals, governmental morals, commercial morals, and good social conduct. But in other respects these codes do not coincide and may even conflict. To illustrate, gambling is prohibited in governmental morals, but not in Christian morals, I believe, except it be by indirect interpretation; nor is it prohibited by the standards of social conduct generally observed.

Codes commonly regarded as important or dominant are those most professed publicly. The mere fact that they are publicly professed unquestionably has an effect upon conduct generally, although the conduct affected is not necessarily in harmony with such public codes. Moreover, it does not follow because such codes have important effects that they are dominant or the most important codes in a majority of individuals or even in any single individual. For example, occasionally a person may be observed who subscribes to the publicly professed Christian codes and the patriotic codes, and whose conduct is undoubtedly modified by that fact, but who nevertheless is governed, under many circumstances, primarily by a code derived from the organization to which he is most attached. In case of conflict that code will be dominant. Doing things the "right" way is a dominant *moral* code in the specialized work of many fine mechanics, musicians, artists, accountants, engineers, for example. No other code on earth dominates their conduct in case of conflict; and the domination will be so complete that they will not be aware of the conflict until perhaps after the event. Even then they will recognize or admit nothing but an apparent inconsistency, perhaps embarrassing and difficult to justify. To regard such domination as merely an incidence to technical habits is to miss the point. In these cases it is not a matter of better or worse, of superior or inferior processes — a judgment rationally arrived at. It is a matter of *right* or *wrong* in a moral sense, of deep feeling, of innate conviction, not arguable; emotional, not intellectual, in character.

Current opinion puts into the realm of important moral codes those most publicly professed and believed most dominant socially, and rejects all others, assigning to them a variety of names — for example, attitude, influences, psychological characteristics, technological standards, politics — in this way concealing the fact that these others are of the same nature even if of different origin or effect. Hence, in a vague way, we are led to think of responsibility as existing only when there is a strong conformance to the public codes; and, if non-conformance to such codes is observed, to believe that this is evidence of lack of responsibility. Or, if codes not recognized by the *observer* as socially important, but his own private codes instead, are the criterion, he denies the quality of responsibility when he sees non-conformance of others to *his* codes. In this way judgment of desirability or broad notions of ethics govern the popular appraisal of responsibility. An appraisal of moral status is confused with capacity of responsibility.

In illustration: I know men whose morals as a whole I cannot help believe to be lower ethically than my own. But these men command my attention and sometimes my admiration because they adhere to their codes rigidly in the face of great difficulties; whereas I observe that many others who have a "higher" morality do not adhere to their codes when it would apparently not be difficult to do so. Men of the first class have a higher sense of responsibility than those having, as I view them, the higher ethical standards. *The point is that responsibility is the property of an individual by which whatever morality exists in him becomes effective in conduct.*

Let us apply these definitions and observations in an illustration that may be recognized as typical of common experience. Mr. A, a citizen of Massachusetts, a member of the Baptist Church, having a father and mother living, and a wife and two children, is an expert machinist employed at a pump station of an important water system. For simplicity's sake, we omit further description. We impute to him several moral codes: Christian ethics, the patriotic code of the citizen, a code of family obligations, a code as an expert machinist, a code derived from the organization engaged in the operation of the water system. He is not aware of these codes. These intellectual abstractions are a part of his "system," ingrained in him by causes, forces, experiences, which he has either forgotten or on the whole never recognized. Just what they are, in fact, can at best only be approximately inferred by his actions, preferably under stress. He has no idea as to the order of importance of these codes, although, if pressed, what he might say probably would indicate that his religious code is first in importance, either because he has some intellectual comprehension of it, or because it is socially dominant. I shall hazard the guess, however, that their order of importance is as follows: his code as to the support and protection of his own children, his code of obligations to the water system, his code as a skilled artisan, his code with reference to his parents, his religious code, and his code as a citizen. For his children he will kill, steal, cheat the government, rob the church, leave the water plant at a critical time, botch a job by hurrying. If his children are not directly at stake, he will sacrifice money, health, time, comfort, convenience, jury duty, church obligations, in order to keep the water plant running; except for his children and the water plant, he cannot be induced to do a botch mechanical job — wouldn't know how; to take care of his parents, he will lie, steal, or do anything else contrary to his code as a citizen or his religious code; if his government legally orders him to violate his religious code, he will go to jail first. He is, however, a very responsible man. It not only takes extraordinary pressure to make him violate any of his codes, but when faced with such pressure he makes great effort to find some solution that is compatible with all of them; and because he makes that effort and is capable he has in the past succeeded. Since he is a very responsible man, knowing his codes you can be fairly sure of what he will do under a rather wide range of conditions.

Now if we introduce a single disturbing factor, the use of alcoholic beverages, we have a considerable change. Our "case" becomes rather irresponsible. The use of alcohol does not violate any of his codes. Because of it, however, he neglects the children, he botches his work, he has been discharged from the water system as undependable, his parents are on public support, he steals for liquor, etc., etc. He is irresponsible; but for the present his codes remain still the same. He will even fight about them if challenged, though intoxicated. He is as moral now as before. He sincerely believes all his conduct has become reprehensible and is sick with genuine remorse when sober; but he is irresponsible, nevertheless.

It may seem to some reader an exaggeration to call devotion to a water system a moral code. Many persons appear unaware of the force of such codes derived from organization associations. But organizations depend greatly upon such moral codes.

I recall a telephone operator on duty at a lonely place from which she could see in the distance the house in which her mother lay bedridden. Her life was spent in taking care of her mother and in maintaining that home for her. To do so, she chose employment in that particular position, against other inclinations. Yet she stayed at her switchboard while she watched the house burn down.[2] No code, public or organizational, that has any general validity under such circumstances governed her conduct, and she certainly violated some such codes, as well as some of her own. Nevertheless, she showed extraordinary "moral courage," we would say, in conforming to a code of her organization — the *moral* necessity of uninterrupted service. This was high responsibility as respects that code.

These illustrations suggest the usefulness of considering the relation of sanctions to codes and to responsibility. Some codes, being the accumulated effect of custom, general opinion, and similar "states of mind" of society, and of *informal* organizations of large and small size, have usually no specific sanctions associated with them which support their moral power. Other codes arise from experience and contact with *formal* organizations. These often have specific sanctions related to some details of conduct pertinent to them. For example, the code of citizenship is somewhat reinforced by penalties for violations or failure to conform. The codes related to industrial organizations are partly reinforced by possibilities of discharge, etc. It may be said that these sanctions help to establish codes, but not responsibility. Thus where conformance is secured by fear of penalties, what is operating is not the moral factor in the sense of the term as used here, but merely negative inducements or incentives. In practice, it is often, perhaps usually, impossible to distinguish the reasons for compliance; but it is quite well understood that good citizenship, for example, is not obtainable

[2] The mother was rescued.

by such specific inducements. Only the deep convictions that operate regardless of either specific penalties or specific rewards are the stuff of high responsibility.

The private code of morals which derives from a definite formal organization is one aspect of what we have previously referred to as the "organization personality." [3] It is also an aspect of the "zone of indifference." [4] Those who have a strong attachment to an organization, however it comes about, are likely to have a code or codes derived from it if their connection has existed long; but whether they appear responsible with respect to such codes depends upon the general capacity for responsibility and upon their place in the spectrum of personal codes.

Hence, the assent of an individual to an order or requirement of an organization, that is, the question of whether he will grant authority to it, is very complex. It depends upon the effect of the order or requirement as a positive or negative incentive, modified by the sanctions, if any, involved in denying authority to it; upon whether or not the individual has a code of morals derived from the organization; upon whether there is conflict of his codes in respect to the specific requirements; upon how important the organization code is as compared with others; upon his sense of responsibility; and so on. If the sense of responsibility is generally weak, conflict of codes is not important but specific incentives and sanctions are. If the sense of responsibility is strong, conflict of codes will result in denial of authority if the organization code is the less important, and specific incentives in that event will usually be unimportant influences.

Persons differ not only as to the quality and relative importance of their moral codes, or as to their sense of responsibility toward them, or with respect to the effect of incentives; but

[3] See page 88.
[4] See page 169.

also because of wide variations in the *number* of codes which govern their conduct. There are many causes of such variations in number. For one example, persons who live in one place and work in another, or those who live in different places at different seasons, are likely to have more codes than those who are more fixed. But probably the principal cause of variation in number of codes is difference in the number of organizations to which persons are attached. Most persons living and working on farms are likely to have relatively few organization connections; but many town and city dwellers have several important connections and a number of others of minor importance, and some men have many such connections.

Differences in the number of moral codes of individuals are of great significance. Conflicts of code will increase, as a matter of probability, with increase in number of codes, and perhaps in something like geometric ratio. To take a comparatively trivial matter for illustration, conflicts as respects appointments, meetings, etc., alone introduce active decisions for responsible men as to relative obligations; and these conflicts increase more rapidly than the number of such obligations. They are occasionally quite serious and by no means a negligible strain, as many can testify.

It is probable that some persons, though possessing quite complex moralities, are seldom plagued with conflicts because they are inactive. This is probably true of retired persons, for example. Conflicts appear to be a product of moral complexity and physical and social activity.

The dilemmas which result from numerous conflicts imply in general at least one of the following consequences: either general moral deterioration, beginning in frustration and indecisiveness; or diminution of the general sense of responsibility, manifest in the tendency to let decisions hinge on chance, external and irrelevant determinants, incidental pressures; or a deliberate withdrawal to a less active condition, thereby reducing the occasions of conflict; or the development of an ability to avoid conflicts, known as "keeping out of trouble," "avoiding temptation," "avoidance of responsibility"; or the development of the ability to construct alternative measures that satisfy immediate desires or requirements without violating any codes. When the last alternative is taken it undoubtedly increases the general sense of responsibility and perhaps usually the moral status of the individual; but it requires resourcefulness, energy, imagination, general ability.

In short, neither men of weak responsibility nor those of limited capability can endure or carry the burden of many simultaneous obligations of different types. If they are "overloaded," either ability, responsibility, or morality, or all three, will be destroyed. Conversely, a condition of complex morality, great activity, and high responsibility cannot continue without commensurate ability. I do not hesitate to affirm that those whom I believe to be the better and more able executives regard it as a major malefaction to induce or push men of fine character and great sense of responsibility into active positions greatly exceeding their technical capacities. Unless the process can be reversed in time, the result is destruction. In the doubtful cases, which are quite frequent, the risk of such results, I think, is commonly regarded by such executives as among the most important hazards of their decisions.

III

Executive positions (*a*) imply a complex morality, and (*b*) require a high capacity of responsibility, (*c*) under conditions of activity, necessitating (*d*) commensurate general and specific technical abilities as a *moral* factor. These are implicit in the previous discussion; in addition there is required (*e*) the faculty of *creating* morals for others. It is pertinent now to restate what has already been said, and to amplify and apply it in relation to formal organizations and to the discharge of the executive functions.

(*a*) Every executive possesses, independently of the position he occupies, personal moral codes. When the individual is placed in an executive position there are immediately incumbent upon him, officially at least, several *additional* codes that are codes of his organization. Codes of the organization are themselves accruals largely of intangible forces, influences, habitual practice, which must be accepted as a whole. These codes are quite different among organizations, being affected by their status — supreme, as in the case of governments or churches — or subsidiary, subordinate, dependent; and by their purposes — educational, industrial, commercial political party, fraternal, governmental, religious, etc.; and by their technologies.

It will be sufficient for present purposes of illustration to take a hypothetical industrial organization, and to suppose the case of an executive head of an important department. The *organization* codes to which he should conform are: (1) the government code as applying to his company, that is, the laws, charter provisions, etc.; (2) obedience to the general purpose and general methods, including the established systems of objective authority; (3) the general purpose of his department; (4) the general moral (ethical) standards of his subordinates; (5) the technical situation as a whole; (6) the code of the informal executive organization, that is, that official conduct shall be that of a gentleman as *its members* understand it, and that personal conduct shall be so likewise; (7) the code that is suggested in the phrase "the good of the organization as a whole"; (8) the code of the informal organization of the department; (9) the technical requirements of the department as a whole. There will often be others, but these will serve for example.

It will be quite evident from this brief discussion without consideration of specific organizations that the executive, by virtue of his position, adopts a more complex morality than he would otherwise have. This complexity is not peculiar, however, to executives. Both executives and professional men differ as a class from non-executive or non-professional persons as a class in that the conditions of their positions impose upon them numerous additional codes. These are chiefly non-personal in their significance; most official or professional activities can be carried out with no involvement of strictly private codes. Therefore, the complexity of the individual's moral situation is not perhaps increased in proportion to the additions arising from organization and professional functions. But inevitably, at times, some action or requirement does involve the whole gamut. Then we say that a man cannot divorce his official or professional conduct from his private morals. When such issues occur, the alternatives presented are either to violate one's personal morality or to fail in an official or professional obligation. Resignation or withdrawal is often a solution which circumstances "legitimately" permit. Then the result is maintenance of personal integrity. When, however, resignation or withdrawal is itself highly immoral, as is sometimes the case, there is potential tragedy. The penalty for lack of ability to avoid or find substitute action in such cases is severe.

That which is unique to the executive functions, however, is that they also impose the necessity of *creating* moral codes. Thus, to the moral problem of individuals generally, organization adds in the case of the executive substantial increase of moral complexity, and of tests of responsibility, and the function of creating moral conditions. The latter is a distinguishing characteristic of executive work, to be discussed later.

(*b*) The capacity of responsibility is that of being firmly governed by moral codes — against inconsistent immediate impulses, desires, or interests, and in the direction of desires or interests that are consonant with such codes. Our common word for one aspect of this capacity is "dependability," by which we mean that, knowing a man's codes — that is, being aware of his "character" — we can reasonably foresee what he is likely to do or not to do, usually under a variety of circumstances.

Almost uniformly, in all types of organizations, persons of executive capacity are assigned initially to executive positions of low rank. The fact of sense of responsibility is there demonstrated. The conditions of these lower-rank positions are those of relatively limited moral complexity and possibly somewhat lower states of activity. The chief difference between the lower and the higher ranks is not in the capacity of responsibility but in the condition of moral complexity. In other words, the higher positions impose more responsibilities, as is often correctly said, but do not require greater *sense* of responsibility in important degree.

(*c*) Generally the conditions of executive work are those of great activity. This is not obvious, because the word "activity" too much suggests physical action. But it is clear that the higher the position the more exposed the incumbent to action imposed from numerous directions, calling for the activity of decision. The increase of this activity is in practice not proportional to the level of position because it is deliberately controlled. This is a necessity which was referred to in Chapter XIII, "The Environment of Decision," [5] where some of the methods by which breakdown is avoided are stated.

(*d*) The capacity of responsibility is in executive ranks rather a constant, and the tendency of activity to increase with scope of position is often controllable. The increase in complexity of moral conditions, however, is not controllable by the person affected, so that despite control of activities the burden increases from conflicts of morals as the scope of the executive position broadens. For example, since a preliminary proposal usually raises a conflict of codes, and since proposals for con-

[5] Page 190.

crete decision in non-routine matters increase with position, an executive position is exposed to more and more moral conflicts the higher it is, and the process of decision becomes morally and often technically more and more complex.

Where there is high sense of responsibility, these conflicts can only be resolved by one of two methods: either to analyze further the pertinent environment with a view to a more accurate determination of the strategic factor of the situation, which may lead to the discovery of that "correct" action which violates no codes; or to adopt a new detailed purpose consistent with general objectives, that is, the more general purposes. Both methods are tests of general ability, the first of ability in discrimination, analysis; the second of imagination, invention, innovation. Either process in an important aspect is an expression of that phase of responsibility which is known as "determination."

The moral complications of the executive functions, then, can only be endured by those possessing a commensurate ability. While, on one hand, the requisite ability without an adequate complex of moralities or without a high sense of responsibility leads to the hopeless confusion of inconsistent expediencies so often described as "incompetence," on the other hand, the requisite morality and sense of responsibility without commensurate abilities leads to fatal indecision or emotional and impulsive decisions, with personal breakdown and ultimate destruction of the sense of responsibility. The important distinctions of rank lie in the fact that the higher the grade the more complex the *moralities* involved, and the more necessary higher abilities to discharge the responsibilities, that is, to resolve the moral conflicts implicit in the positions.

It is apparent that executives frequently fail. This failure may be ascribed in most cases, I believe, to inadequate abilities as a first cause, usually resulting in the destruction of responsibility. But in many cases it may be inferred that the conditions impose a moral complexity and a moral conflict presumably not soluble. Some actions which may within reason appear to be dictated by the good of the organization as a whole will obviously be counter to nearly all other codes, personal or official.

For example, suppose a combination of circumstances such that an appearance of malfeasance will lie against a particular executive, which, if known, would seriously injure the prestige of his organization. Suppose it impossible to refute that appearance, although, in fact, the charge is not true. Suppose that the only available alternative is for the executive to falsify books or records in such a way as to direct an accusation against a fellow executive, this not to be attended with the same damage to the organization. The only code supporting such nefarious action is one which derives from a sense of the good of the organization as a whole — obviously a powerful influence, especially in military and religious organizations. The action proposed would violate several other codes, both "official" and personal.

Such clear-cut cases are rare in industrial organizations but undoubtedly have occurred not infrequently in political, governmental, and religious organizations. They occasionally occur also in family organizations; an extreme illustration is suicide for benefit of family through life-insurance proceeds. These are cases where the code of the organization as a whole is completely dominant and there is very high sense of responsibility, such that the dominant end justifies any means, that is, the violation of all other conflicting codes.[6]

Rare though such cases may be, in practice they will range from these extremes through to those where "every consideration" leads to supporting a particular action — an opposite extreme probably also rare. Between these limits are the great

[6] I have no doubt that in some cases where there is a false or "framed" victim, he is a voluntary sacrifice, that is, he is even more dominated by "the good of the organization."

majority in which action first contemplated is consonant with some codes, violates others. Most frequently the conflict is between organization codes and not between organization and personal codes, but there are many cases of the latter type, nevertheless. The consequences of failure, where no organization action interposes, are either the destruction of the sense of responsibility or the destruction of codes, leading to a simpler moral status. The best solution in such case would often be resignation, demotion, or discharge, which would reduce activity, moral complexity, and the requirements of ability.

It seems probable that moral deterioration and loss of personal responsibility is more frequent among executives, especially in political organizations, than among other persons. The very complexity of the moral situation and the "overloading" that is inescapable under many conditions make this credible. This is, I think, confirmed by current observation. Either moral bewilderment or loss of ability — for example, from ill health — can and does produce "collapse of character." It seems to me inevitable that the struggle to maintain coöperation among men should as surely destroy some men morally as battle destroys some physically. When considering cases of failure where there were enough facts available to warrant a judgment, it has seemed clear to me that in most of them the cause was promotion beyond capacity as respects ability, not initial lack of responsibility, or even inferior morality. The cases may most frequently be observed in the political field, where, as compared with educational or industrial fields, selection is made, *and is almost necessarily made*, to a relatively high degree on the basis of loyalty as the prime qualification with minimum regard to ability. Its inevitable result is "double-crossing," etc. — not really due to personal perfidy, though its effect may be the same, but to inability to find "honest" solutions. Reason and history suggest that this condition is pronounced in political organizations, especially party organizations.

(c) The distinguishing mark of the executive responsibility is that it requires not merely conformance to a complex code of morals but also the creation of moral codes for others. The most generally recognized aspect of this function is called securing, creating, inspiring of "morale" in an organization. This is the process of inculcating points of view, fundamental attitudes, loyalties, to the organization or coöperative system, and to the system of objective authority, that will result in subordinating individual interest and the minor dictates of personal codes to the good of the coöperative whole. This includes (also important) the establishment of the morality of standards of workmanship.

The function of moral creativeness, though not ordinarily described in this way, is of long history. Some aspects of it, such as those related to organization enthusiasm, are well appreciated; and what has already been said in this study concerning the economy of incentives, and especially concerning the necessity of the method of persuasion in the recruiting of organization forces, makes it unnecessary to elaborate the matter at greater length here. There is enough experience of the subject to make it clear that failure with respect to moral creativeness arises from inadequate attention, lack of persistence in the face of the inertia of human reluctance, and lack of sincerity of purpose.

But there is another aspect of moral creativeness that is little understood, except in the field of jurisprudence. This is the inventing of a *moral* basis for the solution of moral conflicts — variously called "handling the exceptional case," "the appellate function," "the judicial function." This function is exercised in the cases that seem "right" from one point of view, "wrong" from another. The solution of such cases lies either in substituting a new action which avoids the conflict, or in providing a moral justification for exception or compromise. We are accustomed to call the first solution "executive," the second "judicial." They are both executive functions in the broad sense used in this essay. Were it not for the separation of powers in American government, we should better recognize that the judicial process is a highly specialized executive process.

There is no escape from the judicial process in the exercise of executive functions. Conflicts of codes in organization are inevitable. Probably most of them are solved by substitute action, largely a matter of technological decision. But often the requirements of technology (in the narrow sense), of organization codes, and of personal codes, press in conflicting directions. Not to do something that is technologically "necessary" because it conflicts with an organization code (as expressed for example in an economic interest) does great violence to the moral codes arising from technological fitness. Its manifest result is discouragement, lack of interest, disgust. To do something that is technologically "sound" but is economic heresy similarly destroys the general sense of economic appropriateness. It implies disregard of the economy of the organization, and tends to its destruction. To do something that is required obviously for the good of organization but which conflicts with deep personal codes — such as the sense of what is honest — destroys personal probity; but not to do it destroys organization cohesiveness and efficiency. The codes governing individual relationships to organized effort are of wide variation, so that either action or failure to act in these cases does violence to individual moralities, though the alternatives will affect different persons in different ways.

The judicial process, from the executive point of view, is one of morally justifying a change or redefinition or new particularizing of purpose so that the sense of conformance to moral codes is secured. One final effect is the elaboration and refinement of morals — of codes of conduct. This is most easily seen in the judicial process as exemplified in the law cases. That it can degenerate into mere subtlety to avoid rather than to discharge obligations is apparent in all executive experience. The invention of the constructions and fictions necessary to secure the preservation of morale is a severe test of both responsibility and ability, for to be sound they must be "just" in the view of the executive, that is, really consonant with the morality of the whole; as well as acceptable, that is, really consonant with the morality of the part, of the individual.

IV

The creative aspect of executive responsibility is the highest exemplification of responsibility. As to the great proportion of organization decisions required of the executive, the conflict of morals is within organization codes, and personal codes are not directly involved. The "organization personality" alone is concerned. The conflict may be treated with relative objectivity, as a "problem." In fact, probably most executive decisions appear in the guise of technical decisions, and their moral aspects are not consciously appreciated. An executive may make many important decisions without reference to any sense of personal interest or of morality. But where creative morality is concerned, the sense of personal responsibility — of sincerity and honesty, in other words — is acutely emphasized. Probably few persons are able to do such work objectively. Indeed, few can do it long except on the basis of personal conviction — not conviction that they are obligated as officials to do it, but conviction that what they do for the good of organization they *personally* believe to be right.

The creative function as a whole is the essence of leadership. It is the highest test of executive responsibility because it requires for successful accomplishment that element of "conviction" that means identification of personal codes and organization codes in the view of the leader. This is the coalescence that carries "conviction" to the personnel of organization, to that informal organization underlying all formal organization that senses nothing more quickly than insincerity. Without it, all organization is dying, because it is the indispensable element in creating that desire for adherence — for which no incentive is a substitute — on the part of those whose efforts willingly contributed constitute organization.

V

The most general strategic factor in human coöperation is executive capacity. In the nature of the physical world and of the social world as well, opportunity and ideals outrun the immediate motives and interest and the practical abilities that are required of leaders. The accumulation of capital, the invention of processes, the innovations of human relationships that effective and efficient coöperation need as a preliminary necessity, call for special abilities in the technologies of materials, physical forces, economic systems, and organization arts. Though indispensable, these abilities will not be put forth, will not even be developed, without that sense of responsibility which makes the sacrifices involved a matter of course, and which elicits the initial faith in coöperation. These abilities and capacities are sufficient to bring into life many organizations of low quality and of inferior or anti-social purposes, and to maintain their vitality for a time. The short interest, the immediate purpose, the impulses of the moment, may be as well served by new combinations as by old, and the appeal to individual self-existence is often gratified best by change if only immediate and material needs are at stake. Organizations endure, however, in proportion to the breadth of the morality by which they are governed. This is only to say that foresight, long purposes, high ideals, are the basis for the persistence of coöperation.

Thus the endurance of organization depends upon the quality of leadership; and that quality derives from the breadth of the morality upon which it rests. High responsibility there must be even in the lowest, the most immoral, organizations; but if the morality to which the responsibility relates is low, the organizations are short-lived. A low morality will not sustain leadership long, its influence quickly vanishes, it cannot produce its own succession.

Leadership, of course, often is wrong, and often fails. Perhaps frequently the leader believes his personal morality and that of his organization are identical when they are not. Perhaps he is ignorant of the codes in the organization that are necessary by reason of the environment, which he fails to see objectively. Perhaps he mistakes a purely personal motive for an organization purpose. In these cases, the facts destroy his responsibility, his leadership fails, he no longer can create, he is trapped between the incompatibility of purpose and environment, insincerity rots his influence. But until that happens — as perhaps it inevitably does in time to all leaders, since established organizations often seem to outgrow their leaders — until that happens, the creation of organization morality is the spirit that overcomes the centrifugal forces of individual interests or motives. Without leadership in this supreme sense the inherent difficulties often cannot be overcome even for short periods. Leadership does not annul the laws of nature, nor is it a substitute for the elements essential to coöperative effort; but it is the indispensable social essence that gives common meaning to common purpose, that creates the incentive that makes other incentives effective, that infuses the subjective aspect of countless decisions with consistency in a changing environment, that inspires the personal conviction that produces the vital cohesiveness without which coöperation is impossible.

Executive responsibility, then, is that capacity of leaders by which, reflecting attitudes, ideals, hopes, derived largely from without themselves, they are compelled to bind the wills of men to the accomplishment of purposes beyond their immediate ends, beyond their times. Even when these purposes are lowly and the time is short, the transitory efforts of men become a part of that organization of living forces that transcends man unaided by man; but when these purposes are high and the wills of many men of many generations are bound together they live boundlessly.

For the morality that underlies enduring coöperation is multi-dimensional. It comes from and may expand to all the world; it is rooted deeply in the past, it faces toward the endless future. As it expands, it must become more complex, its conflicts must be more numerous and deeper, its call for abilities must be higher, its failures of ideal attainment must be perhaps more tragic; but the quality of leadership, the persistence of its influence, the durability of its related organizations, the power of the coördination it incites, all express the height of moral aspirations, the breadth of moral foundations.

So among those who coöperate the things that are seen are moved by the things unseen. Out of the void comes the spirit that shapes the ends of men.

CHAPTER XVIII

CONCLUSION

I

IN closing this study I shall first state what at the present time seem to me to be the more important general conclusions which may be drawn from it; and then offer certain more personal observations on its significance as a whole. The conclusions to which I would especially invite attention follow:

1. Physical and biological factors are basic in coöperation; if these factors permit, then social factors are essential to secure it. Coöperation, thus, may be called the process of synthesizing in action three quite different orders of factors.

2. From the point of view of organization, which is the chief instrument in economic development, all capital, whether of improvements, or machines, tools, and edifices, is always a part of the physical environment. The direct significance of capital is that it reduces the limitations imposed by the natural environment on coöperation. Its indirect result is the expansion of the incentives to coöperation.

3. All complex formal organizations grow from and consist of unit organizations, the inherent properties of which are the determining factors in the character of the complex.

4. The properties of unit formal organizations are determined by physical, biological, and social factors. The understanding of those factors and of the processes essential to conformation to them is the central method of the study of formal organizations.

5. The major structure of any society of substantial size is its complex of formal organizations, rather than its institutions,

customs, etc., which are abstractions chiefly constructed on observed uniformities in the concrete acts, including the verbalizations, of such organizations as well as of individuals.

6. Informal organizations are found within all formal organizations, the latter being essential to order and consistency, the former to vitality. These are mutually reactive phases of coöperation, and they are mutually dependent.

7. Disturbances of the equilibrium of coöperative systems have come from false ideologies, particularly on the part of those who are leaders or executives in formal organizations. The effect of these false notions is to vitiate the sense of experience when consciously dealing with problems of the theory of organization, and to reinforce personal predilections, prejudices, and interests, as destructive factors, in the guidance of organization practice.

8. In this way arise four principal errors: an oversimplification of the economy of organization life; a disregard of the fact and of the necessity of informal organization; an inversion of emphasis upon the objective and the subjective aspects of authority; and a confusion of morality with responsibility.

9. The essential process of adaptation in organizations is decision, whereby the physical, biological, personal, and social factors of the situation are selected for specific combination by volitional action.

10. Error of decision must be large because of the unbalance due to the difference in the precision of perception as respects the physical, the biological, and the social environments. This is a general factor limiting successful coöperation.

11. Since any coöperative system contains physical, personal, and social factors, at least three secondary abstract systems of utilities, related to these factors respectively, are pertinent. To these must be added a primary system of utilities related to the whole organization. Each of these secondary systems comprises the phenomena or factors of the respective classes, together

with the utilities attached to them by the organization. The aggregate of these utilities in each system varies with the phenomena or factors and the utilities assigned to each factor. The primary system comprises the aggregate of these utilities and the phenomena and factors involved as a whole. These systems I have called economies. The respective economies are heterogeneous as between themselves, and widely variable as between the corresponding economies in other coöperative systems. They do not admit of quantitative comparison. These conceptions are on the whole new, and not now understood or adopted. They are theoretical and their use is limited at present to the analysis and description of coöperative systems. They are, however, intuitively taken into account in specific situations by those skilled in the executive arts and by others.

12. All scientific knowledge is expressed in languages and symbolic systems. These are socially developed with meanings that are socially determined; and all "finally" accepted observations of phenomena are coöperatively arrived at. Therefore, all sciences in the widest sense comprehend both social factors and others of different orders, depending upon their subject matter. Disregarding the social factors of science in the sense just stated, we find two kinds of abstract systems of knowledge other than those stated under 11, next above, as follows: (a) systems which relate exclusively, or substantially so, to one or the other order of factors (physical, biological, social), and (b) those which "cut across" or comprehend two or more orders of factors.

(a) Examples of systems of the first class are the systems of physical science, containing many sub-systems, including everyday or commercial classifications of materials; biological systems; and purely theoretical social systems.

(b) Examples of systems of the second class are: biochemical, architectural, engineering, and other technological systems;

systems of psychology; economic systems; social, political, and ethical systems.

Abstract systems of the first class are basically scientific and are also practical. They do not attempt to explain coöperative phenomena. They involve few disadvantages except those of "misplaced concreteness" and an unbalanced approach to problems of coöperation. Abstract systems of the second class are often primarily practical and are also the subjects of scientific study. Some of these systems, especially those called "social," involve effects that often render them useless and even harmful through misstatement and false explanation of coöperative phenomena. In general they are developed without comprehension of the nature of coöperative systems, and accordingly their character and the limits of their usefulness are often misconceived.

13. An increasing degree of coöperation implies an increasing moral complexity. It is impossible for men to endure a high degree of moral complexity without commensurate technological proficiency.

14. The strategic factor in coöperation generally is leadership, which is the name for relatively high personal capacity for both technological attainments and moral complexity, combined with propensity for consistency in conformance to moral factors of the individual.

15. The strategic factor in the dynamic expression of leadership is moral creativeness, which precedes, but is in turn dependent upon, technological proficiency and the development of techniques in relation to it.

16. The strategic factor in social integration is the development and selection of leaders. The process is usually unbalanced by excessive emphasis either upon technological proficiency or upon moral status. In some ages moralities may have been cultivated in excess of the technological capacity to support them. In the present age the emphasis is upon technological profi-

ciency which is not adequately guided by the necessities of the coöperative system as a whole.

II

I estimate that in the United States not less than 5,000,000 individuals are engaged in the work of executives, of whom 100,000 occupy major executive positions. Concerning certain technical aspects of the various fields in which they work there is literature and instruction; but concerning the instrumentality with which they work — organization — and the techniques appropriate to it, there is little. More important is the lack of an accepted conceptual scheme with which to exchange their thought.

Important consequences of this state of affairs are unbalance and false emphases upon matters concerning which there is already much knowledge and appropriate language — for example, in the technologies like accounting and financial practice, in certain aspects of personnel work and measures — and concomitant disregard of equally important matters which heretofore have not been much discussed. Back of failure in personnel effort is often incompleteness of understanding of what I have called the "economy of incentives." Much abortive management arises from almost total disregard, in *thinking*, of the subjective aspects of authority. Despite its importance, *informal* organization in formal organizations is ignored as far as possible. The limits of the size of formal groups, although major considerations in the elaboration of organizations, are disregarded often for comparatively trivial reasons.[1] The moral fac-

[1] For example, as Director of the Emergency Relief organization in New Jersey I was in effect required *by law* to have not less than twenty-one immediate subordinates. Actually, I required twenty-five or twenty-six. Five should have been the maximum for this work and perhaps three would have been more effective and more efficient. There were some good reasons for the requirement; but I believed it impossible to convince enough legislators that it was such bad organization that the requirement should be changed.

tors upon which the vitality of organization depends are treated mostly as subjects for glowing generalities in inspirational addresses and there is woeful lack of appreciation of the interrelationships between personal character and ability.

Would a thoroughly scientific approach to the problems of coöperative systems and organization provide a useful tool for the executive arts? It is my belief that it ultimately would, and that the development of such a science is important in further progress in these arts and hence in coöperation generally. This belief is based upon reflection concerning the failure observed in many concrete instances to take into account all the elements of the situation as a whole. This failure is promoted by a specialization in *thinking* that arises in part from the specialization of the sciences. The action which is the essence of organization, or the coördination of action which is the function of the executive, relates to the synthesis of physical, biological, and social factors. The problems of mutual adjustment are outside these specific fields.

Neither the consideration of present experience nor that of the pertinent aspects of history permits escape from the suspicion that much sheer lack of good sense in human relations is to be explained by the history of the sciences. There is no science of organization or of coöperative systems; and the development of the sciences called social has clearly lagged far behind those called physical and mathematical. One reason for this appears to be a false emphasis upon intellectual and mental processes both as factors in human relations and as matters of study.

However, it is well to be quite clear as to the significance of a science in its relation to the arts. It is the function of the arts to accomplish concrete ends, effect results, produce situations, that would not come about without the deliberate effort to secure them. These arts must be mastered and applied by those who deal in the concrete and for the future. The function of the sciences, on the other hand, is to explain the phenomena, the events, the situations, of the past. Their aim is not to produce specific events, effects, or situations but explanations which we call knowledge. It has not been the aim of science to be a system of technology; and it could not be such a system. There is required in order to manipulate the concrete a vast amount of knowledge of a temporary, local, specific character, of no general value or interest, that it is not the function of a science to have or to present and only to explain to the extent that it is generally significant.

In the common-sense, everyday, practical knowledge necessary to the practice of the arts, there is much that is not susceptible of verbal statement — it is a matter of know-how. It may be called behavioral knowledge. It is necessary to doing things in concrete situations. It is nowhere more indispensable than in the executive arts. It is acquired by persistent habitual experience and is often called intuitive.

Nevertheless, the power of the arts and the arts themselves are capable of expansion when there is available scientific knowledge — explanations, concepts. Thus in the hands of those who apply themselves to the control of future events a developed science, even though it will be later superseded, *in conjunction with* local, temporary, specific, and behavioral knowledge and intuitional talents, is an additional means of great importance when properly used. This has been the case in recent years (and chiefly in recent years only) in the technological and medical fields. It has also been true in less degree in technical fields in which economic and political sciences have been used.

The present extent and success of coöperation is proof that the executive arts are already highly developed, but the restriction of coöperation in innumerable directions of which we are so unpleasantly aware shows that they are not sufficiently developed. The deficiency appears to be chiefly in lack of proportion. The executive arts are highly developed in the fields called technological; they are well developed in the technical commercial fields; they are least developed in the techniques of human interactions and organization. Relatively, this was not always so. The solidarity of small peoples, the long history of the Roman Republic and Empire, are examples of organization and control of human interrelations showing that the development of these arts in relation to the technological and economic arts was high.

Whether the present essay is a contribution to the science hoped for remains to be determined by others. What has been presented is a hypothetical scheme which at present explains roughly to me what I have observed in many years of practical work with organizations of various kinds and what I have constructed from the experience of others, supplemented, of course, by a little knowledge of the social sciences. It is not the work of a scientist or a scholar, but rather of an interested student of affairs.

For this reason perhaps its chief value, if presently it has any, will merely lie in its expression of one view of experience. By it I have at least submitted my mental processes in this field to inspection. If it has any further value it will lie in the suggestion it may give to more competent inquiry, which I hope can be undertaken. The test of it will come from its application to social phenomena as a whole, as they present themselves to others — many others.

Most persons of affairs will find much difficulty in applying that test, because the form of statement which seems to me necessary in work of this kind is so very different from that which they habitually employ. The administration of affairs proceeds on the basis of limited fictions, working hypotheses, practical assumptions, and highly symbolic expressions, which are local, special, or technical within a particular organization. Conventional attitudes must be modified to some extent at least to test a scheme such as this; and many for this reason may think the treatment unrealistic and impatiently throw it aside.

I hope that the social scientist, on the other hand, may attempt a preliminary testing of it against the background of present knowledge. More concretely, I hope for a social anthropology, a sociology, a social psychology, an institutional economics, a treatise on management, etc., written with the concepts of a coöperative system and an organization which have been presented as a part of the working scheme. For what this kind of thinking requires at present is not so much the testing of details as the ascertainment of whether or not there is correspondence between it and general experience and social knowledge as a whole.

But we should not deceive ourselves by thinking that either a science of coöperation and organization or the further development of the executive arts will alone promote a greater integration of social forces, or even maintain the present status. The ethical ideal upon which coöperation depends requires the general diffusion of a willingness to subordinate immediate personal interest for both ultimate personal interest and the general good, together with a capacity of individual responsibility. The senses of what will be for the ultimate personal interest and of what will be for the general good both must come from outside the individual. They are social, ethical, and religious values. For their general diffusion they depend upon both intelligence and inspiration. Intelligence is necessary to the appreciation of the interdependence of peoples in a crowded world on their combined technological competence — an intelligence that perhaps will be derived from experience in coöperation rather than from anything suggestive of formal education. Inspiration is necessary to inculcate the sense of unity, and to create common ideals. Emotional rather than intellectual acceptance is required. No one who reads, or who observes the events of our times, but will recognize, it seems to me, the supreme importance of belief in ideals as indispensable to coöperation.

Men are now dismayed by the evidences of world disorganization, as if it represented a radical change from world integration; but their very discouragement is evidence of their belief in the need of greater integration which must precede its realization. Until that faith is universal and until the techniques of coöperation have been developed for much wider ranges than has as yet been possible, conflict may itself be the chief process toward ultimate integration. The possibilities of world coöperation might not be learned until half the world is organized against the other half. That would represent perhaps a greater integration than has yet occurred, but would make more evident than ever before the disorganization that remains.

However, the present questioning and discouragement do not come, it seems clear to me, merely from economic disturbances and international conflict. Much more do they arise from a deep conflict of beliefs concerning coöperation itself. There are two beliefs that are far apart, both struggling not only against each other but also against unrecognized limitations. One of them centers upon the freedom of the individual and makes him the center of the social universe. At the present time, on the whole, it is critical and pessimistic. It lays its emphasis upon failure of coöperation, upon wars and conflicts, confusion and disorganization, waste, hunger, disease and death, and yet it preaches uncritically an extreme liberty, an ideal individualism, a self-determination, that in their unrestricted dogmatism would prevent all formal coöperation beyond that imposed by the most obvious immediate opportunities and necessities.

The second extreme faith is adulatory and optimistic. It places its emphasis upon the order, the predictability, the consistency, the effectiveness, of untold myriads of concrete acts that are coöperatively determined, in systems so extensively interrelated that the effects have been enormously to expand the world's population and to advance measurably the material and cultural state of many millions. Those who speak from this point of view are likely to advocate uncritically a vast regimentation, an endless subordination, a completeness of coördination, that in *their* unrestricted dogmatism would stifle all development of individuals beyond that found inescapable.

And so we find ourselves again with the very problem with which we began; for the issue between these faiths, I think, is unconsciously centered upon the old question of free will and determinism, or on sentiments from which this question takes its origin. Those who carry the banners of individualism are crying for the right of the individual to choose; and those who trumpet so loudly for the state and society proclaim the folly of individual choice and seek to prevent it. Thus what once was the center of philosophic and theological speculation, and more recently of the controversy of philosophically-minded scientists now becomes the battleground of nations fighting for social dogmas.

This issue I found, not in the philosophies or the theologies or the scientific papers or the polemics of Marxism, but in the behavior of men in coöperation, in the social limitations of organizations, in the essential burdens of the executive. I found it not as an abstract question unrelated to the daily lives of men, but as one evident in the collapse of actual coöperation and in the moral disintegration of living men and women. Scarcely a man, I think, who has felt the annihilation of his personality in some organized system, has not also felt that that same system belonged to him because of his own free will he chose to make it so. Many an executive, I believe, has seemed to himself at times to be merely the channel of imponderable universal forces, of all his associates the least free; and yet he has also believed that when men do not choose, do not will, do not regard themselves as responsible and are not so regarded by others, the very stuff of coöperation dissolves.

This study, without the intent of the writer or perhaps the expectation of the reader, had at its heart this deep paradox and conflict of feelings in the lives of men. Free and unfree, controlling and controlled, choosing and being chosen, inducing and unable to resist inducement, the source of authority and unable to deny it, independent and dependent, nourishing their personalities, and yet depersonalized; forming purposes and being forced to change them, searching for limitations in order to make decisions, seeking the particular but concerned with the whole, finding leaders and denying their leadership, hoping to dominate the earth and being dominated by the unseen — this is the story of man in society told in these pages.

Such a story calls finally for a declaration of faith. I believe in the power of the coöperation of men of free will to make men free to coöperate; that only as they choose to work together can they achieve the fullness of personal development; that only as each accepts a responsibility for choice can they enter into that communion of men from which arise the higher purposes of individual and of coöperative behavior alike. I believe that the expansion of coöperation and the development of the individual are mutually dependent realities, and that a due proportion or balance between them is a necessary condition of human welfare. Because it is subjective with respect both to a society as a whole and to the individual, what this proportion is I believe science cannot say. It is a question for philosophy and religion.

Anyone who sees all this, naturally rushes to the conclusion of which I was speaking, that no mortal legislates in anything, but that in human affairs chance is almost everything. And this may be said of the arts of the sailor, and the pilot, and the physician, and the general, and may seem to be well said; and yet there is another thing which may be said with equal truth of all of them.

What is it?

That God governs all things, and that chance and opportunity cooperate with Him in the government of human affairs. There is, however, a third and less extreme view, that art should be there also; for I should say that in a storm there must surely be a great advantage in having the aid of the pilot's art. You would agree? — PLATO, *Laws*

APPENDIX

MIND IN EVERYDAY AFFAIRS

A Cyrus Fogg Brackett Lecture before the Engineering Faculty
and Students of Princeton University, March 10, 1936 [1]

THE subject of this lecture may be considered either with reference to
its "scientific" or its "practical" aspects. If the first, we should be concerned at least with neurology and psychology, and perhaps logic, epis-
temology, and metaphysics on one side, and the social sciences on the
other. It would require many lectures to give even a rough idea of the
knowledge and the speculations of these fields of study, and a life-time
at least to master more than a few of them. Important and useful as
these studies are, they are either so incomplete or the various systems
and conclusions so speculative as yet, that they are as a whole difficult
to apply to more than a few aspects of personal experience in everyday
affairs. Yet it is with the everyday phenomena with which we must be
concerned in living and working, and it is as necessary to learn about
them independently of the scientific questions involved as it is to learn
how to use water for drinking, swimming, or sailing without special
reference either to the physical or chemical properties of H_2O.

What I shall attempt to do is to present a personal attitude or understanding concerning the mental aspects of human beings in the work of
everyday affairs — the understanding that would underlie in part the
advice that I might give to young men concerning their careers, or that
would explain my attitude or conduct with reference to many business
and public problems. I have been led to this subject because in my
experience in a number of positions in different kinds of work with
people of many classes and vocations, I have been impressed with two
difficulties especially, both observed in others and experienced personally.

One of these difficulties is that of adjustment to a new kind of work
or a new position. I recall that several times when my position was
changed, even though I had in advance all the essential knowledge required, it took many months to function adequately and acceptably. A
different point of view seemed to call for a rather complete mental
readjustment.

The other difficulty is related to the first. It is that of attaining a
mutual understanding between persons or groups. Often, where there

[1] Copyright, 1936, by Chester I. Barnard.

is extreme difficulty of this character, it is obviously not due to difference in knowledge of facts. Indeed, when there is merely difference in knowledge of facts, it is often comparatively easy to secure mutual understanding.

Of several explanations of these difficulties, each an answer only in part, two have seemed to me of special importance: the difference in mental processes, often reflected and expressed by such phrases as difference in "mental attitude," in "point of view," in "way the mind works"; and the wide divergence of opinion, often not realized, as to what constitutes a proper intellectual basis for opinion or deliberate action, that is, what is good evidence, proof, or justification. In other words, a difference in mental processes quite independent of knowledge or experience is at the root of these very important practical difficulties in many cases.

I have found it convenient and significant for practical purposes to consider that these mental processes consist of two groups which I shall call "non-logical" and "logical." These are not scientific classifications, but I shall ask you to keep them in your minds for the present, as I shall use them throughout this lecture. In ordinary experience the two classes of intellectual operations are not clearly separated but meld into each other. By "logical processes" I mean conscious thinking which could be expressed in words, or other symbols, that is, reasoning. By "non-logical processes" I mean those not capable of being expressed in words or as reasoning, which are only made known by a judgment, decision or action. This may be because the processes are unconscious, or because they are so complex and so rapid, often approaching the instantaneous, that they could not be analyzed by the person within whose brain they take place. The sources of these non-logical processes lie in physiological conditions or factors, or in the physical and social environment, mostly impressed upon us unconsciously or without conscious effort on our part. They also consist of the mass of facts, patterns, concepts, techniques, abstractions, and generally what we call formal knowledge or beliefs, which are impressed upon our minds more or less by conscious effort and study. This second source of non-logical mental processes greatly increases with directed experience, study and education.

A most significant difference in men and in the various types of work that men do lies, in my opinion, in the degree to which actual thinking, that is, reasoning, is used or is required. For example, rigorous logical reasoning is apparently a major characteristic of the work of the mathematician and the exact scientist, and of the lawyer or the accountant in important aspects of his work. On the other hand, reasoning is little evident in some kinds of "high-pressure" trading, in a great deal of salesmanship, in many political activities, in much of the work of business men or executives.

The significance of this is obscured by the general belief that reasoning indicates a higher order of intellect than do the non-logical processes underlying quick judgments. In order that you may understand my point of view and get the practical bearing of this lecture, it is necessary that I should first overcome the bias in favor of the thinking processes, and to develop an appreciation of the non-logical processes.

The chief causes of the overstressing of logical processes in contrast to the non-logical appear to be two: misconception concerning the nature of logical reasoning, and a deep desire or need to argue and to justify by rationalization; that is, to make action and opinion appear plausible when the real motives are concealed or are unconscious. These causes are of so much significance in regard to the behaviour of people that a short discussion of them may be of general interest.

The most interesting and astounding contradiction in life is to me the constant insistence by nearly all people upon "logic," "logical reasoning," "sound reasoning" on the one hand, and on the other their inability to display it, and their unwillingness to accept it when displayed by others. Where the higher intellects, especially those engaged in the more exact sciences, are involved, this contradiction is of course on a higher plane and more subtle than among ordinary folk who are not trained reasoners; but the difference seems one of degree. The correctness of reasoning is the issue in violent differences of opinion in every subject.

The simultaneous insistence upon and refusal to accept "sound reasoning" is justified on the one hand by the cumulative results of reasoning in undoubted progress of science (and other things, many of them very ordinary), and on the other by the undoubted and repeated errors of reasoning in all fields of work. Many of these errors are discovered only after substantial periods of time. Many of them are seen quickly. The validity of much reasoning is not accepted in practice, though not formally denied. It is my belief that if an inventory of the reasonings of competent intellects could be made it would be found that an extremely high percentage was in error. This is the implied verdict of both scientific and practical men in their insistence that inferences from reasoning as a general rule should not be accepted without experimental test in the scientific case, and without the test of experience in the case of ordinary affairs. Most reasoning readily received is accepted because it confirms what we already understand or believe, or because it is the expression of an authority which we would accept without such reasoning. It then instructs us.

It might be expected that reasoning would be unreliable from an examination of the logical process. Leaving aside inductive reasoning by which we obtain a general rule from observing concrete instances or cases or objects, and which is less rigorous and more open to inspiration than strict logic, we may consider three aspects of the process. The last one, the drawing of the conclusion or inference from the premises, is the least unreliable in trained minds; but it is easy to be fallacious and not always easy to detect the fallacies, of which there are a number of classes. The second aspect has to do with words, the statement of the premises. The great difficulty here is to avoid or detect the use of words in different senses in the same reasoning. In ordinary affairs this is a common source of error. It is avoided in scientific, engineering, accounting and legal work, for example, only by painstaking care in precise and unambiguous definition and by standardization of terms. The first aspect is that of stating either observed facts or accepted axioms and postulates, or established theorems, laws, dicta, generalizations. This is the most vulnerable stage, because in practice the symbols or words, if correct, are themselves usually the topmost layer in an immense pyramid of "knowledge," the errors or assumptions of which are not obvious. The errors involved in their summarized statement or in their application to the point are also often not self evident. This means in practice that the validity of reasoning cannot usually be determined by someone who has none of this background. "Set a thief to catch a thief" applies here. It takes an expert to refute an expert. Every class of persons is therefore accustomed in important matters to seek expert advice on the reasoning of experts.

We are, therefore, justified in our distrust of reasoning; but we are also justified in our acclaim of it because we know from experience that it is a useful screen against the errors of non-logical mental processes, or that it is an intermediate stage between idea or hypothesis and test and experience. Its cumulative value to civilization is enormous. Moreover, logical expression is the method required to transmit knowledge. In fact, it seems not too much to say that reasoning is a social rather than an individual function, always involving the mind of both the speaker or writer and that of the listeners or readers.

The need for expressing reasons is one of the most deep-seated of human necessities. To talk is largely to reason, and to reason is to talk. The fact that much reasoning and much talking is loose, incorrect and bad does not gainsay this view. The evidence of it is daily available at every hand, and we are so accustomed to discounting for it that we only occasionally give much attention to it, although many of our jokes and jibes are at its expense. ("Oh, Yeah!") Small children rationalize freely. Persons in the hypnotic state are said to do so about all their actions, although in fact these are at the behest of the control. Primitive people do it. Pareto's *Sociologie Générale* is a long demonstration that the institutions of society from ancient to modern times are based upon non-logical motives and that they are accompanied by an incessant din of reasons. Much of the error of historians, economists and of all of us in daily affairs arises from imputing logical reason to men who could not or cannot base their actions on reason.

Thus, the real usefulness of genuine logical reasoning, the training in it that goes with education, and the pseudo-logic of rationalization are all causes of the false emphasis on the importance of reasoning. The harm, however, lies in the consequent deprecation of non-logical mental processes more than in the misuse of reason. I shall, therefore, say a few words concerning the intuitions, frequently scorned, and the quick mental processes.

Non-logical mental processes run all the way from the unreasoning determination not to put the hand in the fire twice, to the handling of a mass of experience or a complex of abstractions in a flash. We could not do any work without this kind of mental process. Some of it is so unexplainable that we call it "intuition." A great deal of it passes under the name of "good judgment." Some of it is called "inspiration" and occasionally it is the "stroke of genius." But most of it is called "sense," "good sense" or "common sense," "judgment" or the "bright idea."

Despite the constant use of non-logical processes in daily life, they are so unconscious and so much a matter of course that a few concrete illustrations may not be amiss. Take first judgment of distance in golf or for ball throwing. It is a matter of observation that some persons are fast and accurate judges of distance, that frequently the capacity for such judgment increases with practice, and that sometimes the measurement of distance by conscious comparison destroys the capacity for quick judgment. Similarly, innumerable judgments and decisions in practical affairs often represent a very complex but accurate mental process.

A second type of case might be the ability of a high school boy to solve a quadratic equation. Involved in this is a large part of the arithmetic and algebra learned through years from the time when his mother taught him to count, an intellectual process beyond many primitive people, to his last lesson in algebra. The discrimination and selection required to effect the solution would indicate the use or mental control of most of this acquired knowledge. Unless it could be marshaled and applied quickly, the problem could hardly be solved. Yet not only will the boy be unaware of what his brain actually does, but he will be unable to recall many of the broad steps that actually must have been taken. He could not write the text books which are registered in his mind.

There are many accountants and business men who can ordinarily take a comparative balance sheet of considerable complexity and within minutes or even seconds get a significant set of facts from it. These facts do not leap from the paper and strike the eye. They lie between the figures in the part filled by the mind out of years of experience and technical knowledge. That is what makes out of a set of figures something to which then reason can usefully be applied.

These non-logical processes are essential even in the most rigorous scientific work. This is well stated in Professor Wolf's article on "Scientific Method" in the *Encyclopaedia Britannica* which I now quote, emphasizing the words which connote non-logical processes:

"In every inductive investigation, common sense, accumulated experience and knowledge, some *originality*, and a *spirit of adventure* are indispensable. Nothing, not even a study of scientific method, can serve as a substitute for these things.

"One can only indicate briefly how investigators are commonly guided in *discriminating* between what is likely to be relevant and what is likely to be irrelevant. The most important *clue* is that afforded by previous knowledge. Antecedents and circumstances, the effects of which are already known, and are known to be different from the phenomenon under investigation, are generally dismissed as irrelevant, unless there is some *prima facie* ground for *suspecting* that they may be *influencing* it to *some extent* by way of modification or resistance. In this way the knowledge of what is relevant, like every other part of human knowledge, can only be improved or confirmed by more knowledge. Another *clue* is almost *too vague* for precise description, yet its *influence* is very real. It just consists of a *vague feeling*, or *intuition*, that certain things are relevant and others are not. This *feeling* 'in our marrow' is probably an outcome of previous experience that has *not yet emerged into articulate thought*. Its very vagueness shields it from critical scrutiny." [2]

To be sure, as we all know, the non-logical processes, like the logical processes, are frequently wrong. It should go without saying that both kinds together are much better than either alone if the conditions permit;

[2] 1930 Edition. Italics ours.

but when this is not possible, good sense would suggest that if there are various processes available for doing work, one should be selected that is best adapted to it. It seems that this does not occur with sufficient frequency and that it takes a good deal of judgment and experience to do it well.

Perhaps the idea of "selecting" a mental process for application will be novel to those accustomed to believe that all brain work worth considering is "thinking" or "reasoning." If so, it will be desirable to show what are the conditions to which minds must be applied. For this purpose I shall confine my remarks to three aspects of the question:

I. Three Purposes of Mental Effort.
II. The Speed Factor.
III. The Nature of the Material to Which the Mind Is Applied.

I. *Three Purposes of Mental Effort*

Brief consideration is sufficient to show that the purpose or object of mental effort must substantially affect the processes used. Let us take three types of purpose of mental effort: (*a*) To ascertain the truth, (*b*) to determine upon a course of action, (*c*) to persuade.

(*a*) The search for truth is a matter of ascertaining a fact or formulating a generalization acceptable to others because both the premises and the reasoning can withstand examination under techniques effective within the field and the tests of experiment or experience. These rules and tests differ widely, for example, between physics, trials at law, engineering studies, accounting, in each of which the truth is sought, and in each of which a specific "system" really defines what shall be considered truth. As compared with the mental processes applicable to other purposes, susceptibility to test by experiment or examination is the essential difference and affects the "point of view." It must be logical because it must be expressed in words to be available to meet these tests.

(*b*) When truth is the object of the mental process, the past or the present is chiefly in view and the conclusion is subject to review and test, whereas decisions as to a course of action look to the future. Moreover, the actual result of such a decision is a unique event, into which many unforeseen or unforeseeable factors may enter, and it is frequently not possible conclusively to know whether or not the result sought has been attained and to what extent it is due to the decision. This, despite the prevalent habit of rationalizing decisions, obviously requires a speculative type of thinking and a diminution of the element of rationality.

Rigorous reasoning when applied to this type of problem of decision is, strictly speaking, not possible and the effort to do it indicates a lack of proper balance of mental processes. This is probably why it is difficult to make correct decisions without responsibility. The right "frame of mind" is not easily possible when a question is treated as merely an intellectual problem. Too many intangibles must be left out so to treat it.

(c) I suppose that most people would say that others are, or at least should be, convinced only by sound reasoning, and few are willing to admit they themselves can be convinced by anything else. It is, of course, true that to a considerable extent conviction, in so far as it can be effected by direct effort, requires rationalization. Reasons must be given, but they must appeal to those attitudes, predilections, prejudices, emotions, the mental background, which govern actions. This implies a task of great difficulty. It requires discerning the mental state and processes of the person to be convinced, adopting his mentality, "sensing" what is valid from his point of view and meeting it by apparently rational expression, which in fact may be utterly fallacious. A little reflection will indicate that this is a great intellectual feat, that it involves extraordinary mental processes different from those required when other purposes are involved. The talent for doing it is outstanding in salesmen, teachers, statesmen, clergymen, possessing, of course, other necessary qualifications. Because the immediate results are often apparently shortlived and because the quality of the reasoning as expressed is frequently poor (though it may be perfectly adapted to the purpose), or because its object may not appeal to us, this business of persuasion is often erroneously considered one of low-grade intellect.

II. *The Speed Factor*

A second condition affecting the adaptation of mental processes is that of the time available for their operation. In general, the time available for effort to ascertain or formulate the truth when this is the primary purpose is ample. Haste is then hardly an acceptable excuse for poor reasoning or for the acceptance of a conclusion from non-logical processes without the application of reason when possible as a check. In contrast, it is evident that in many circumstances mental efforts must be accomplished with such rapidity that the word "thinking" does not apply. This is well illustrated by a case relating to purposive physical action quoted by Koffka.[3] " 'During the war he (von Allesch) was on patrol

[3] *Principles of Gestalt Psychology* (New York: Harcourt, Brace & Co., 1935), pp. 626, 627.

in the Alps. He had to make a descent from a rocky crag by means of a chimney whose upper mouth gaped about ten metres under and far to the side of his position. Having climbed down on a rope he found himself hanging in the air and several metres to the left of the chimney, with no more rope for a further descent which would have landed him on a ledge by which he hoped to reach the chimney. He determined to reach the opening by swinging on the rope. In doing this, the rope slipped from his feet, and his hands were not able to support his weight. . . . The next moment he realized that he had taken hold of the rope with his teeth. . . . In the next moment his feet waving in the air had caught hold of a projecting piece of the slab, (etc.)' The important point in the process is, that this action, not belonging to the technique of mountain climbing, never previously considered, and, of course, never previously practised, the only one which could save me, arose spontaneously without any conscious deliberation. . . . Here was a real problem which we might put as a question to test a subject's intelligence: What would you do under those conditions? And the solution was *not* produced by an act of thought, but at a time when the rational part of the organism had concluded that no solution was possible."

Between the extremes of rigorous thinking and fast mental action not called thinking, there is a wide range and many degrees. In active parliamentary debate, in much newspaper work, in the line of battle, in other emergency conditions, in some forms of trading, to give only a few illustrations, rapid mental processes are obviously essential. The limited capacity of many highly intellectual people to function acceptably under severe conditions as to speed indicates an uncommon order of mentality. It is sometimes wrongly considered by ponderous reasoners as evidence of a poor order of intellect.

III. *The Nature of the Material to Which the Mind Is Applied*

The nature of the subject matter to which the mind is applied determines the kind of mental process which can or cannot be used. It seems to me this is apparent from a consideration of the various kinds of material. Without attempting a classification that is technical, precise or exhaustive, we may consider the material that we have to work with, of three classes:

1. Material that consists of precise information.

This consists of observations from which a conclusion may be drawn by scientific method, and propositions or facts previously established or widely accepted as true, to which formal logic can be applied. A great deal of such material is now involved in ordinary affairs, as is evident in legal work and in the great extension of cost accounting and statistical methods, and in other highly technical processes in business. Much of the progress of recent years in many businesses has been achieved by developing methods of measurement that furnish material of this type. Of course, statute laws, the provisions of contracts, legal decisions and definite formulations of policy are also material of this kind.

2. Material of hybrid character.

This consists of data of poor quality or limited extent, propositions recognized as of doubtful validity or of tentative character, and qualitative facts which cannot be expressed numerically, requiring such adjectives as good or poor, bright or dim, orange or yellow, fine or coarse, stable or unstable, etc. A large part of the mental work in business and government is certainly applied to material of this character. As its quality decreases, reasoning applied to it becomes more and more hypothetical and is quite speculative. The form of logical inference may be preserved but the premises become more and more mere verbal expressions without definable content and the reasoning mere rationalization, judgments and intuitions in the verbal form of thinking.

3. Material of a speculative type.

This consists of impressions and probabilities not susceptible of mathematical expression and purely contingent uncertainties, including the possibility or the probability of the existence of unknown factors and their possible effect. This type of material is an important and vital part of what the mind must be applied to in ordinary affairs, so much so that much of the skill required in the management of business and public affairs consists in avoiding so far as possible positions of uncertainty; but, in the nature of things, only a relative success can be attained. No matter how expressed, the processes involved in reaching a judgment here are subjective and non-logical.

The main point is that it is impossible effectively to apply the logical reasoning process to material that is so insecure that it cannot bear the weight of ponderous logic. We know, however, that the mind must deal with just this kind of material in a very large part of personal and general affairs. The much ridiculed "woman's intuition" is the only mental process that can apply to it. If you have a choice of having that appendix out today and missing an important engagement tomorrow, say, to be married, or of having it out next week and going on with the ceremony, you will settle the choice by non-logical processes. You must settle it and reasoning will not do it. If you live, you are likely to describe the excellent reasoning by which you made the perfect choice, but there will be little truth in it.

It may be pertinent and useful to comment on several consequences of these considerations.

One is that the inculcation of the notion that reason can and should always guide what we do often produces a deplorable state of mind evidenced by hesitation, fear and lack of initiative. Men become afraid to trust their judgment, yet they see that they cannot apply reason. I have seen more than one partly incapacitated for useful work due to this cause and I believe there are many such cases, although there are usually other factors also involved.

The ability to work effectively by non-logical processes often produces the appearance of "courage." Properly viewed, however, it takes no more courage to decide a question on the basis of judgment than it does to decide it on the basis of a logic that may be fallacious or of make-believe reasoning when that is all that is possible. The decision by either method may be wrong, but seems to me more likely to be wrong if based upon fallacious reasoning. In an emotional sense, it may take more courage to guess than to calculate, if something important is at stake, but if there is no basis for calculation, it is more intelligent to guess than to manufacture data for false calculation.

In the case of the business man, executive, politician, salesman or mechanic, the normal situation is that a conclusion must be reached, a decision must be made, by a date, frequently at once, on the spot. Whether the data are adequate in quantity and quality, whether there are elements of quality not numerically measurable, whether there are mathematically measurable probabilities or uncertainties, whether knowledge is inadequate, and whether all possible factors may be known, or not, a conclusion must nevertheless be reached. Of course, a decision to do or say nothing is a positive decision in most affairs. Moreover, upon the correctness of that decision in many cases, or of a series of such decisions, personal reputation, personal fortunes, the welfare of others, and many social consequences depend, so that the conditions of decision usually include a state of tension due to personal responsibility.

These considerations affect the approach of the non-scientific man. He is capable of, uses and appreciates the need of logical reasoning and scientific method, although his technique is often limited; but he knows that usually this mental process can be employed effectively as to only a part, and frequently a small part, of the subject concerning which decision must be made. The correctness of such decisions must, therefore, depend upon the effectiveness of the mental processes of the type that can handle contingencies, uncertainties and unknowables.

To the casual observer decisions made in this way appear to be merely guesses, or what we sometimes call "hunches." Some of the decisions or conclusions reached in the course of ordinary affairs must be guesses in the sense that no more intellect needs to be used than would be the case if reliance were placed in the toss of a coin. Many simple questions of the "yes" or "no" type would be answered correctly in half the cases by this method. But most questions are not of this simple type. The alternatives and degrees of possible decision are numerous and could not readily be selected by chance.

Yet, although the difference between mere guessing and judgment cannot be evident in the individual case, good or bad judgment is evident in a series of cases by the results. If we did not too commonly ascribe good judgment to mere knowledge and professional technique, we would appreciate more than we do how great is the difference in the quality of non-logical minds. A friend once expressed the point when he said of a third person of extensive knowledge and experience in his business that "he knew more about it and could do less with it than any one else he had met." We know from ordinary experience and observations that among men of apparently equal training, education and knowledge there is a wide difference in "good judgment," ability to be "far seeing," in "perspective."

If, then, we put aside the bias we normally have against the non-logical processes, open our minds to their great extent and usefulness, and examine what determines the kind of process that is useful, we find that purpose, speed and the nature of the material are all involved. It is then easy to see that a great variety of mental processes is required, ranging from the very rapid intuitional, frequently even called "feeling," to the formal logical processes of scientific reasoning. All these processes appear to be required in any kind of work; the differences are in the relative emphasis upon the various parts of the scale of processes. In scientific work, no matter how much the intuitional may be required, logical formal reasoning of high excellence is essential. Thought and knowledge cannot be transmitted or examined unless it is expressed. In the world of affairs, on the other hand, where correctness of decision or persuasion is often the purpose, the intuitional processes should be supplemented by the more conscious reasoning processes where feasible; but the practical necessities in many activities require chiefly the non-logical processes.

These considerations, I think, produce a feeling of distrust on the part of the scientifically minded for speculative philosophy, which employs formal reasoning without experimental test, and for the non-logical intellectuality of the men of professional and practical affairs. This distrust is justified as related to scientific fields. It is unintelligent as applied to many other fields, excepting those phases, usually special aspects, to which formal reasoning is adapted.

Conversely, the man of affairs, despite his constant use of the words "logical," "sound reasoning," "reasonable," etc., in his rationalizations, even more distrusts the formal reasoning processes for the fields in which he works. This distrust likewise is well founded. It seems to me undoubtedly true that unbalancing of judgment in many cases comes from a distortion of problems because some factors are susceptible advantageously to reasoning processes while the other factors are not. This is most easily observed in matters involving engineering studies or statistical work. The appearance of completeness and precision, secured by laying aside the factors not susceptible of mathematical treatment or of orderly presentation, is deceptive, especially when accompanied by words, blueprints and statistics in profusion. Then, again, the love of rationalization predisposes many men to select for attention those aspects of questions which readily lend themselves to verbal display. This subtle tendency is most manifest in those public speakers or writers whose honest opinions gradually come to be based upon what they find easy to say or write or even what they think their audiences like to hear or read.

But the most important basis for distrust of logic on the part of many experienced persons is, I suspect, a fear that too much reasoning inhibits the intuitional processes which they regard as generally indispensable and as the more reliable in many circumstances. Habitual analysis, in other words, may teach more about a thing, but may at the same time destroy the sense of the thing as a whole. It is not without significance to me that several of the "brainiest" and most effective and capable men I have known have been almost inarticulate. Not what they could say but what they could do showed the power of their minds. Many glib talkers and writers, not being capable of understanding such men, read into their silence either inferior intellects or sinister purposes. It is an error of judgment well to avoid in your own careers.

Fictions

This discussion would be lacking without some reference to fictions, misunderstanding concerning which is at the root of some false opinions concerning reasoning. A fiction, as the word is used here, is an assertion that a fundamental statement is true when it is recognized that its truth cannot be demonstrated either by theoretical reasoning or by experimental evidence. Fictions are called by different names: axioms, self-evident truths, postulates, sanctions, presumptions, assumptions, facts "as a matter of course," etc. There are many examples in mathematics, logic, and the physical sciences. Others in the social fields are the "presumption" that all men know the law, the "will" of the people, the "personality" of a corporation, the "infallibility" (i.e., the non-debatability) of an organization order, the correctness of a ballot count (in the absence of certain challenges within a time limit). Little fictions are common in many fields of daily life.

Some of these fictions have never been proven not to be true. Others are known not to be true; in fact, they may exist in conjunction with other fictions that are logically inconsistent. For example, under our law, *all* men are presumed innocent until proved guilty, but since *some* men are found guilty, this denies the justification of the presumption. The mere fact that a man is accused makes a presumption of innocence a contradiction in terms. Yet we all feel that this presumption should be treated as truth within some limitations.

The important difference between these various fictions seems to me to lie between the probability of their truth on the one hand, and their usefulness on the other. Let me quote from Dantzig's delightful popular philosophy of mathematics: "This affirmation of the power of the mind which knows itself capable of conceiving *the indefinite repetition of an act, when this act is at all possible, may be pure fiction, but it is a convenient and therefore a necessary fiction.*" [4] The variation in the scope, usefulness and probability of truth of fictions is very wide. That is, there is considerable difference in their dignity. In most of the ordinary fields of life, the extent of their application is limited both in area and time. We say, "for this purpose" or "for the present" or "under these conditions," "thus and so is 'true' or 'may be accepted as a fact' or is a 'working principle.'" One result of this is that a man, more often than he realizes, will affirm something as if it were a law of nature in one connec-

[4] Tobias Dantzig, *Number, the Language of Science* (The Macmillan Co., 1930), p. 247. Italics in the original.

tion, and deny it in another. It may thereupon often be assumed either that he is ignorant (does not know what he is talking about), or that he is unable to reason (he is unsound), or that he lies. All are unfortunately correct indictments too frequently. Nevertheless, often there is no foundation for such aspersions. It is because a man knows what he is talking about, or because he is sound, or because he tells the truth, that the apparent discrepancy often arises.

This means that the difference between the fictions of ordinary affairs and the great fictions of science, the fundamental axioms, is not so much in their lack of logical basis as in their scope and purpose. The frequent apparent inconsistencies of position in the practical world seem to me unavoidable, if the world is to remain practical.

I like to illustrate this view in the application of mathematics to the fields of human affairs. I should suppose that 2 plus 2 make 4 in abstract numbers is not to be considered a fiction except in a most extreme sense. But the moment numbers are applied to things difficulty begins. It doesn't work to add units of butter and units of buttercups. Like can numerically be added only to like. It is easy to say that of course there must be discrimination, definition and identification before arithmetic can be used. But our faith in arithmetic is deep and our powers of definition and identification are weak, so that we are all the time adding unlike things and only finding it out when "the answer does not make sense." In fact, that is the way we find out that many things we thought were alike are not, or are different in more respects than we suspected. To say that one should be careful in definitions and identifications is excellent advice but it is often not possible to apply it.

I have found this especially true as respects the activities of human beings, so that instead of assuming that mathematics is perfect and that the fault lies in its application, I assume that it is defective. I proceed on the belief that in this field it is rarely possible to define attributes and characteristics of human beings with sufficient accuracy and significance so that arithmetic can be used except in an approximate and preliminary way. Two and two do not make four. The reasons for this little private fiction, which is basic in my present point of view, I shall make look more reasonable by two illustrations.

Take apples and the satisfaction of eating them. The apples are all the same (we would say) and we hardly know how to express what we want except in terms of *an* apple. Yet in a series of six apples to be eaten, I hardly need to tell you that the first is one thing and the sixth quite another. Two and two will not make four, unless you can introduce a large dose of something called time. This is a familiar type of illustration of the diminishing of utility in economics.

I think I hear you say that it is nonsense to talk of numerical addition as a fiction in this connection; that in one case I am talking about a number of physical objects and in the other about taste, satisfaction and subjective things, qualities that cannot or have not been measured and that the two things cannot be identified. Precisely. But if you are working in the world of people, you will find very often no way practically to avoid such false identifications. You will find that by a non-logical but highly intelligent mental process, you perform the translation from the world of objects to the world of mind. Indeed you must do so, if you are going to sell apples successfully or if you are going to buy advantageously. Since you and everybody else will continue to mix up apples and the satisfactions that apples give, it is well to remember, as I do, that two apples plus two apples do not make four apples unless you are not going to eat them — but then that is what apples are for — to eat.

Take a second illustration from organization: Six men and a boss are set to dig a ditch. They may do as much work as seven men individually or they may do more or they may do less. Probably in most cases it is expected that they will do more, otherwise there would be no gain by organization — because six men and a boss working together as a group are what we mean by organization. But, in fact, such an organization not infrequently does less. Perhaps the boss is a poor one, perhaps the men cannot work well together, perhaps the organization is too big for the space in which it works.

For many years the illusions of applied arithmetic especially puzzled me in connection with organization. It seemed to me that the manifest efficiency of many organizations might be explained by the something called direction, management, which was added to the sum of individual efforts. But from this point of view the remuneration of management did not seem to support the theory — it was not enough when successful and too much when a failure. Then the answer seemed to be specialization, but this also is what organization implies. So finally, I adopted an attitude of mind which said, "Whatever the causes, my experience and that of others tell me that some organizations accomplish more than the sum of the possible individual accomplishments, some less and some occasionally about the same. So be careful not to be logically arithmetical about organization." Yet this only partly met the conditions. What I later learned and now think is correct to say is, "The whole is sometimes merely more or less than the sum of its parts. It is more often something

else than the sum of its parts, wherever human beings are involved." [5]
There is analogy to this conception in Ford's statement to the effect that
modern production methods are not merely a case of efficiency; they produce what could be had in no other way.

You will miss the point if you think I am forcing it. Our logical
methods and our endless analysis of things has often blinded us to an
appreciation of structure and organization. Yet our physical and social
worlds are full of structures, organizations and organisms. It seems slowly
to be recognized even in pure physics, which is partly responsible for our
blindness in this respect, that organization is a new entity. You cannot
get organization by adding up the parts. They are only one aspect of it.
To understand the society you live in, you must *feel* organization —
which is exactly what you do with your non-logical minds — about your
nation, the state, your university, your church, your community, your
family.

The Last Complication — Reaction

And now one last complication that explains some strange things in
the mental processes of men — and what minds have to do.

The most important difference between scientific and other work is not
in the composition of the mental processes required but in the reaction
or absence of reaction of these processes on the subject to which they are
applied. Pure physical science has for its object the ascertainment of
truth about the physical universe but it has neither for its purpose nor
its effect a change in that universe. The application of its researches
through engineering, commercial chemistry, etc., may be conceived to
effect to an appreciable degree the distribution of matter and its organization on the fragment of the physical universe called "earth"; but the
causal or statistical laws are not affected by discovering them.

It is not so of the world of affairs. The expression of opinion, the
description of a condition, the writing of a law or the determination of
an action in the world of men changes that world. It necessarily changes
both the position of the actor and of those whom action affects. Viewing
the mass of mankind, these changes may be very slow and stable; but
if restricted groups are under consideration, very great changes in mental
attitudes and in action come from the minds of men or their concrete
expressions. The result is a constant readjustment of political, economic
and social conditions, both to action and to expressions of opinion. Failure
or inability to take this into account is probably very often the reason that

[5] Paraphrased from Koffka, *Gestalt Psychology*.

the consequences of acts or of a series of acts conforming to a policy have produced in the end results the reverse of those sought to be accomplished or avoided. Major examples are the conquest of Greece and Macedonia by the Roman Republic against its own wishes and policy; the British political control of India which both the East India Company and the British Government sought to avoid for many years; the change of position in the Reformation from one directed toward reform of administrative, fiscal and political conditions in the Church to a conflict of dogma.

In many of the more restricted problems of government and business, the principle is more definitely present and more easily seen. For example, in a political or commercial organization a strong difference of opinion concerning some matter of policy seizes the personnel or citizens, so that friction ensues. Suppose that the difference of opinion is the result of incomplete knowledge or understanding. An authoritative explanatory statement would theoretically be sufficient to compose the difference and allay the friction; but, by the time that the need for it is evident, other circumstances such as emotional forces and personal animosities have arisen. Parties have formed. The correcting statement then may be insufficient and in fact may crystallize the opposing elements because it seems to favor the position of one side or the other. It is necessary to direct the boat upstream to reach the opposite point. The mere discussion of the matter may ipso facto change the situation to a new one calling for a different, new and uncertain treatment.

Such situations are common in ordinary affairs. Examples are frequent in labor relations. Another is the prohibition amendment which in innumerable instances increased rather than allayed the pre-existing demand for alcoholic beverages. Much, if not all, of advertising and a great deal of salesmanship is a positive recognition of this principle, the purpose being to change the mental attitude in advance to meet a desired or contemplated production and distribution program.

It is this factor in practical affairs that so often explains the propensity to silence about, or apparent avoidance of, issues in many circumstances both by politicians and executives. It is also the factor that makes persuasion so vital a necessity in society. But for illustrations it is unnecessary to search beyond purely personal and intimate relations.

This reaction between mind and the social field is the cause of a special type of mental difficulty in that it produces great moral or ethical strains. This is a matter of personal experience with most people, I am sure, but it seems not to be generally recognized as the critical aspect of much effort in affairs. A long time ago a friend of mine, an expert in publicity, said that the truth could not ordinarily be conveyed by stating it exactly. This is certainly true. Not only do words mean different things to different people or under different circumstances; but there is a tendency unintentionally to discount or to read into statements what is not intended. It is consequently necessary to say things in a form which is not correct from the standpoint of the speaker or writer, but which will be interpreted by the listener or reader in a sense which will be true. To do this often becomes a matter of habit. Hence, the speaker must often be dishonest in statement from his own point of view in order to achieve honesty of result, although he ceases to be aware of it. It is a fatal dilemma for many people, who are unable to withstand either the moral or intellectual strain.

It should be noted that the moral strain is quite different from that which we ordinarily have in mind in personal morality. That is a question of resisting a personal temptation to violate a code of personal morals. The emotional difficulty is often great, but there is less frequently an intellectual problem of great difficulty. What is involved in statements to others in business and public affairs, however, is an intellectual difficulty. In this case, the end is the *only* justification of the means. We talk to convey a meaning to a person or a group. If we fail, it is poor talk. Yet the practice of short-cutting explanations, of using false analogies, of suppressing confusing qualifications, which are practical necessities, tend to destroy sincerity by creating a habit of misstatement from the speaker's point of view. In the intellectual difficulty of working in two personalities at once, I think I see the moral deterioration and finally the intellectual collapse of more than a few men.

* * * * * * * *

If I could have succeeded as I would wish, all that I have said would seem commonplace. But unfortunately it may appear quite abstract and unrealistic. For this reason I venture to state very briefly my estimate of the variations between a few of the common vocations as regards the major emphasis in the composition of the minds required. It should be remembered that in most instances there is a considerable specialization of work and that no general statement would fit the vocation closely. Moreover, I am expressing my present opinion in several cases perhaps without adequate experience or opportunity for close observation, merely for illustration.

1. The Scientist:
His work requires the mastery of the technique of rigorous logical

reasoning, especially in the mathematician. Nevertheless, all the able and the great scientists seem to possess non-logical, highly intuitional mental processes.

2. The Trial Lawyer:
The non-logical type of mind. Logical reasoning entirely subordinate within limits. Rationalization and persuasion and very rapid mental processes required.

3. The Appellate Lawyer:
The logical processes predominantly necessary.

4. The Counsel:
Balanced mental processes, with emphasis upon the non-logical rather than the logical.

5. The Politician:
Predominantly non-logical processes required.

6. The Statesman:
Balanced mental processes, but emphasis on the intuitional.

7. The Accountant:
Primarily logical processes, with non-logical processes at the minimum except in the administrative field.

8. The Engineer:
Initially the logical processes predominate in the strictly technical field; but in the major engineering positions, the intuitional processes may need to predominate, because commercial and economic coördination become very important, and exposition and persuasion are frequently controlling requirements.

9. The Salesman:
Non-logical processes necessary, so much so that the logical processes are often deleterious. In this case, as in that of the politician, there is frequently a necessity for artistic rationalization which should not be mistaken for genuine reasoning.

10. The Junior Executive:
Non-logical processes chiefly necessary, except in the highly technical fields.

11. The Major Executive:
Logical reasoning processes increasingly necessary but are disadvantageous if not in subordination to highly developed intuitional processes

From my standpoint the consideration of this subject arises out of practical experience and its usefulness lies in the aid that can be derived from it in the improvement of personal development and conduct, especially as respects the promotion of mutual understanding, and in a better appreciation of some of the problems of our social world. A few words on the significance of the subject in these respects will serve to conclude this lecture.

It seems to me that merely to recognize the importance of the non-logical mental processes, to see how essential they are and to understand their effectiveness for many conditions and purposes, should destroy a harmful kind of intellectual snobbishness. The subtle effect of the educational process, which is necessarily logical in its form, I think obviously leads to a false sense of intellectual superiority which closes the mind of many to the powers and the merits of others, either of inferior formal education or of education in other fields. This produces a kind of conceit. It leads to a serious misjudgment of the importance of personal experience and of deliberately acquiring it. The five-ton mind thinks itself superior to the one-ton mind even for one-ton jobs. It is an expensive error. Many men have a hard time discovering that mental skill is often a superior substitute for mental toil, though they see this perfectly as to physical work.

It seems to me clear that, whatever else may be desirable, it is certainly well to develop the efficiency of the non-logical processes. How can this be done? No direct method seems applicable. The task seems to be one of "conditioning" the mind and to let nature do what it then can. The conditioning will consist of stocking the mind properly and in exercising the non-logical faculties. The mind will be stocked by experience and by study. Experience means doing things, action, the taking of responsibility. It is the process by which an immense amount of material is unconsciously acquired for the mind to use, and intelligence can aid in selecting the field for action, the line of experience, that is promising. Study supplements that process by introducing facts, concepts, patterns that would fail of perception through undirected experience. Action or experience at the same time gives the opportunity for practice. There seems to be no substitute for using the mind, applying it, working it, to develop its power.

I hope nothing that I have said will be construed as minimizing the importance of the reasoning processes by themselves. There are too many people who depend upon quick judgments and hasty conclusions as a substitute for measurements, calculations and reason when they are possible. Giant dams, railroads, telephone switchboards, good legislation, contracts are not successfully constructed or written this way. Nor should non-logical processes, even when they are the only kind really possible, be confused with snap judgment. Most men whose judgment I respect take plenty of time on major problems and make time if possible. They do not decide until it is necessary to do so. They "think it over" carefully but not necessarily logically. What I have tried to emphasize is the insufficiency of logical processes for many purposes and conditions and the desirability of their development in intelligent coördination with the non-logical, the intuitional, even the inspirational processes, which manifest mental energy and enthusiasm. This is by no means easy. To rely upon "feeling," to give weight to first impressions, to reject logical conclusions and meticulous analysis in favor of an embracing sense of the whole, involves an inconsistency of attitudes. It means developing the artistic principle in the use of the mind, attaining proportion between speed and caution, between broad outlines and fineness of detail, between solidity and flexibility. As in other arts, the perfection of subsidiary techniques and their effective combination both require constant practice.

And finally, the proper use of the mind seems to me to require a moral attitude. "Intellectual honesty" too often means a puritanical and disinterested acceptance of conclusions under a mere code of reasoning. Its broader and higher sense may often require subjection of all processes to honesty in purpose; and, when there are involved instruction, persuasion or leadership, which I think call for the highest manifestations of the mind in all fields, the test of character is the final test of intellect as well as of morals.

One can hardly contemplate the passing scene of civilized society without a sense that the need of balanced minds is real and that a superlative task is how socially to make mind more effective. That the increasing complexity of society and the elaboration of technique and organization now necessary will more and more require capacity for rigorous reasoning seems evident; but it is a super-structure necessitating a better use of the non-logical mind to support it. "Brains" without "minds" seem a futile unbalance. The inconsistencies of method and purpose and the misunderstandings between large groups which increasing specialization engenders need the corrective of the feeling mind that senses the end result, the net balance, the interest of the all and of the spirit that perceiving the concrete parts encompasses also the intangibles of the whole.

INDEX

INDEX